T0265841

MASSACRE AT ORADOUR-SUR-GLANE

Massacre at Oradour-sur-Glane

Nazi Gold and the Murder of an Entire French Town by SS Division Das Reich

Vincent dePaul Lupiano

Essex, Connecticut

An imprint of Globe Pequot, the trade division of The Rowman & Littlefield
Publishing Group, Inc.
4501 Forbes Blvd., Ste. 200
Lanham, MD 20706
www.rowman.com

Distributed by NATIONAL BOOK NETWORK

British Library Cataloguing in Publication Information available

Library of Congress Cataloging-in-Publication Data available
ISBN 978-1-4930-7374-0 (hardcover)
ISBN 978-1-4930-7375-7 (e-book)

Printed in India

For

Eugene Brissie

His patience abounds

And my thanks are plentiful

Quid non mortalia pectora cogis, auri sacra fumes!

"To what cannot you compel the hearts of men, O cursed lust for gold!"

—VIRGIL'S *AENEID*

No one forgets the truth; they just get better at lying.

—RICHARD YATES

Nothing gets in the way of the truth like a good lie.

—UNKNOWN

Contents

Part I **1**

1: Das Reich (The Realm) 3
Rob Peter, Pay Paul

2: The Gold 31

3: Hubris 45

4: Leipzig, Germany—Summer, 1933 47

5: On the Road to Tulle 59

6: The Hangings at Tulle 69

7: The Ambush 91

8: Confrontation 103

9: Court-Martial 127

10: Bordeaux Trial 151

11: Dresden and Oradour—What Was the Difference? 157

Part II **165**

12: Fox Face 167

13: Golden Goose 181

14: Zone Franche 195

15: The Fox 215

16: Thonon-les-Bains 231

Bibliography 237

A Word about SS Ranks 239

Glossary 241

2nd SS Panzer Division—Tanks and Armor 243

Index 245

PART I

Das Reich (The Realm)

Rob Peter, Pay Paul

IN STORIES OF WAR, THERE IS WHAT WE SEE AND WHAT IS HIDDEN. There is a contest between truth and lies. And inside this war, truth and lies commingle, shrouded by the gatekeeper of mystery and never revealed.

Until good faith intervenes and shines the gold light of truth.

***

The trek of 2.SS Panzer Division *Das Reich* from the Eastern Front to Southern France began on 6 April 1944 at a large map spread on a wooden conference table in Adolf Hitler's *Führerhauptquartier* (Führer Headquarters) in the Gorlitz Forest in East Prussia.

The buildings consisted of concrete and brick hutments with steel shutters to protect the windows and accommodations for Hitler, his staff, and security personnel, a mess hall, a communications center, a garage, and a heating plant. In addition, there were solid, timbered buildings, including a *Teehaus*, which Hitler favored as a place of relaxation. The sky was cerulean and crisp, the air fragrant mire and pine.

The complex straddled the hardtop road from Rastenburg to Angerburg and shiny rails and newly hewed timbers that ran broadly parallel. Work on the soggy site was almost continuous from when first sod was cut in 1940 to Hitler's final departure in November 1944. As vast and rustic as it was, personnel had little to do; boredom was rampant. The most serious menace was squadrons of pervasive mosquitoes that seemed to have wingspans more deadly than the day's menacing bombers. Most of the staff—especially Hitler's secretaries—remained indoors to avoid hostilities with the stinging hordes. Military personnel, the guards, and support staff who had to work outside wore mosquito netting around their heads.

On 6 April, in the main conference room of the *Führerhauptquartier*, four men stood around a massive map of southern France discussing a desperate situation—the Allies' looming invasion of Europe and how to shore up the battle lines along the Normandy coast. A discussion of "how to rob Peter to pay Paul." What further German units would Hitler dare detach from the Eastern Front and weaken that flank to reinforce the tenuous Normandy coast against the coming Allied invasion? This was the essential item on today's agenda among these men.

The future of the once formidable and lauded, 2.SS Panzer Division Das Reich was at the heart of the discussion. Formidable indeed: Das Reich produced the most Knight's Cross recipients during the war.

A transcript of this conference exists today, and although it is mangled, enough fragments have survived to present a compelling picture of the task at hand.

The four men around the map table—some more sordid than others—included Adolf Hitler, the dictator or Führer of Nazi Germany from 1933 until his suicide in 1945.

Leaning over the map next to Hitler, the smarmy Hans Otto Georg Hermann Fegelein, thirty-nine, at this moment an *SS-Gruppenführer und Generalleutnant der Waffen-SS* (Major General and Lieutenant General of the Waffen-SS), a man with no formal training in military tactics, a former equestrian and once Olympic hopeful.

The politically motivated marriage of the suave Fegelein—ruthless, ambitious, cynical, and opportunistic—to Gretl Braun, sister of Hitler's future wife Eva Braun, took place on 3 June 1944 at *Schloss Mirabell* (Mirabel Palace) in Salzburg, Austria, placing Fegelein decisively in Hitler's most esteemed firmament. The Fegeleins' reception after their wedding occurred at the Eagle's Nest in *Obersalzburg*—it endured for two days, going from the Eagle's Nest to Martin Bormann's residence a few hundred feet from Hitler's home.

Traudl Junge, one of Hitler's favored, comely secretaries, said of Hermann Fegelein:

> He had a very large nose and wore the Knight's Cross with Oakleaves and Swords. No wonder he was used to women flocking around him. In addition, he had a refreshing, sometimes very dry wit, and never minced words, you felt he was a naturally frank and honest person. That helped him forge a remarkable career quickly and unexpectedly. No sooner had he appeared than he was sitting with us at a table in the Berghof. He went to Bormann's nocturnal parties, drank to the health of all the important people there, and all the women were at his feet. Those who were not his friends were his enemies until he was firmly in the saddle. He was clever but ruthless and had some very attractive qualities such as honesty with which he admitted that at heart he was a terrible coward and had won his decorations doing heroic deeds out of fear.

Journalist William L. Shirer wrote that Fegelein was "cynical and disreputable"; Albert Speer didn't think much of him either; he said Fegelein was "one of the most disgusting people in Hitler's circle." And historian Michael D. Miller said that Hermann Fegelein was "an opportunist who ingratiated himself with Himmler," and "who granted him the best assignments—mostly related to cavalry—and rapid promotion through the ranks." Henning Pieper, studied the period extensively, noting that "Fegelein's lack of formal training as an officer led to deficiencies in the way the SS Cavalry Brigade was prepared for active service."

In his masterful book, *The Bunker*, concerning Hitler's final days below the Reich Chancellery, James P. O'Donnell wrote that those close to Fegelein had nicknamed him "Flegelein," a *Flegel* in German is a euphemism meaning "lout" or "brat," someone who lacks manners and behaves improperly. Almost to the man, Hitler's inner circle thought Fegelein to be unctuous, a man who never met a woman he did not like—including Hitler's future bride, Gretl's sister, Eva.

Despite this, Fegelein had numerous awards bestowed up him: On 30 July 1944, he received the eighty-third award of the Swords to the Knight's Cross of the Iron Cross with Oakleaves; the General Assault Badge; the Infantry Assault Badge; the Close Combat Clasp; the *Verwundetenabzeichen* (Wound Badge) in Silver (for at least two wounds, or one serious); the German Cross in Gold; and the extremely rare—Wound Badge of 20 July 1944 presented to him by Hitler because he was present in Hitler's conference room at the Wolf's Lair when a bomb exploded next to Hitler's legs in a failed assassination attempt. Twenty-four were awarded. Hitler excluded himself.

Hermann Fegelein grew up in Ansbach, Austria, where he was born on 30 October 1906. At the time, his father, Hans, owned a reputable equestrian riding school in Munich, where Hermann became a proficient rider. Because of this and his participation in and enthusiasm for equestrian events, Hermann aspired to be an Olympian and strove for a Gold Olympic Medal—a quest never fulfilled. However, he won many prestigious riding school awards: top-most among them was the *Braunes Band von Deutschland* (Brown Ribbon of Germany) and the *Deutsches Spring un*

Dressurderby in an international tournament in 1937, among others. At the same time, he studied at Munich University for two terms and then joined the Reiter Regiment Cavalry. In 1927 he became an officer cadet at the Bavarian State Police school in Munich; it did not last long. Two years after enrollment, Hermann Fegelein was caught stealing exams and was, according to the Munich police, expelled. Hermann's story was that he "resigned" for "family reasons" and to "better serve the Nazi party and the burgeoning SS."

At this time, Hans Fegelein formed the *Reitinstitut Fegelein*. The year was 1926, and Hermann had been pulled from destitution by working for his father as an instructor. In 1935 his charm, expertise, and good looks led him to become the leader of the *SS-Reitersturm* for all German events at the Berlin Olympic games. This fortuitous appointment brought attention to the alluring Hermann: He was immediately promoted to *SS-Sturmbannführer* (Major) in January 1936, a leap in rank few others in the SS had achieved or would even aspire to; Hermann knew the right people.

But then Hermann's rising star started to dull.

He wanted to be on Germany's Olympic equestrian team. But the competition was intense, and he could not overcome the formidable Cavalry School from Hanover.

Nevertheless, he came to the attention of *Reichsführer-SS* Heinrich Himmler, from this point forward, a most perilous person in the Third Reich. It would be because of this relationship with the nefarious Himmler that Fegelein was saved from punishment for past and future transgressions.

In April 1941, Fegelein's Waffen-SS unit was caught robbing money and sending it home to Germany. For this, he was court-martialed. However, once again the court-martial was annulled by Himmler.

Soon, because of his boyish face, obsequious attitude, and connection to Himmler, he earned a nickname: Golden Boy.

Under Fegelein's command, during an operation in the Byelorussian SSR in 1941, over seventeen thousand civilians were killed during the Pripyat swamps action.

Fegelein's unit killed dozens of partisans in March–April 1940, all unarmed. Toward the end of April the unit slaughtered 250 Polish men in nearby villages, an action that Fegelein described as "clean and decent." Why this action was "clean and decent" has never been adequately explained (Himmler again?). In this and other wrong-headed wanderings, he was spared punishment again by the powerful Himmler, who took a liking to him. And it would not be long before he was appointed Himmler's liaison to Adolf Hitler.

Good connections came to Hermann's rescue again—this time in a more serious charge than the others: Fegelein was accused of an improper sexual relationship with a Polish woman. The woman became pregnant by him, and he ordered her to have an abortion. Reinhard Heydrich, head of the Reich Security Main office, tried several times to investigate the matter and bring charges against Fegelein. Again, Himmler quashed the attempt. Heydrich, an appalling figure, thought ill of Fegelein—the pot calling the kettle black.

On 27 April 1944, days before WWII ended, the Reich Chancellery radio announced "that *Reichsführer-SS* Heinrich Himmler"—loyal and true Heinrich—"had allegedly met Swedish Red Cross diplomat, Count Folke Bernadotte four times to negotiate a surrender in the west."

Hitler assumed that, as Himmler's liaison officer, Hermann Fegelein had taken part in Himmler's cloak-and-dagger negotiations or at least had intimate knowledge of them. The two were in cahoots!

This was not the end of the melodrama:

Another crushing blow descended with ferocity on Hitler's head on 28 April when Hitler's Deputy Press Secretary,

Hauptschriftführer (chief clerk) Heinz Lorenze, handed the Führer a press release from Reuters news confirming that Himmler, indeed, had been negotiating with the Allies through Count Bernadotte. Adding insult to injury, Himmler was also jockeying for the top spot in the Third Reich—Führer *and* Reich Chancellor.

According to the Fuhrer, this was beyond treasonous—a kick in the groin he took personally. Witnesses said he was apoplectic.

Hitler wanted Fegelein standing before him *immediately*—a quick search did not produce Hermann in or around the decimated Chancellery Garden nor the plush Reich Chancellery.

Then, on 26 April, Hermann telephoned Eva Braun from his private apartment in Berlin, saying: "Eva, if you can't persuade the Führer, you must leave Berlin immediately without him. Don't be stupid—it's a matter of life and death now!"

"Where are you, Hermann? Come here at once; the Führer is asking for you; he wants to speak to you." Then the connection was cut off.

Hitler, his rage ascending with the velocity of a misguided rocket, immediately ordered *Reichssicherheitsdienst* (RSD) deputy commander *SS-Obersturmbannführer* (Lieutenant Colonel) Peter Högl, an experienced take-no-prisoners police detective to scour the Reich Chancellery building, the battle-pocked garden, and the entire city of Berlin if he had to, for the elusive Hermann. It was immediately apparent that Fegelein had abandoned Adolf Hitler abruptly at this most crucial moment at the *Führerbunker* to save his neck after deciding that this was not an auspicious time to "join the suicide bunch where the inmates are running the asylum."

Later, it would be revealed that Fegelein tried to entice Eva to leave Berlin with him. Surrounded by Russian forces, Berlin was a battlefield under a relentless cannonade of Russian rockets and rifle fire. Eva decided to go down with the ship, rats or no rats on board, instead of leaving the city with the oily Herman and his suitcase of plunder.

Högl and three of his troopers, at considerable risk to their lives because the ongoing battle was becoming more severe by the minute, took on the task of finding Hermann Fegelein, albeit hesitantly because they were sure some of them would not be coming back intact from the evening's loathsome hunt.

The first place they went to was Fegelein's lux apartment at *Bleibtreustrasse* 10–11 in Berlin, Charlottenburg, off the fashionable *Kurfürstendamm*—a combination of New York City's Madison and Fifth Avenues.

And, no surprise, there was Fegelein, flat on his unmade bed, inebriated, incoherent, sans his decorated bespoke uniform, instead wearing a natty civilian business suit and a hand-painted Italian tie, preparing for a sprint to Sweden or Switzerland. Next to him was a careworn leather suitcase throbbing with cash—German, French, Swiss, et al.—and jewelry, some of which belonged unequivocally to Eva Braun and were gifted to her by Hitler. Högl also found conclusive evidence of Himmler's treasonous peace negotiations with the Allies.

Fegelein, weaving and bobbing was so intoxicated that he could barely pull his shoulders back. Högl ordered him off the bed and into his uniform; he needed the powerful shoulders of Högl's SS men.

While Hermann was exchanging his disguise, Högl and his troopers heard a clatter in the kitchen: A tall, gorgeous, freckle-faced redhead in a glittering red evening gown was escaping through the kitchen window without her pumps. The woman and her pretty feet vanished forever; several bunker survivors knew who she was but never gave up her name—she would later be known as the "Lady in Red," a principal player in a vignette that only adds to the tale of this hard-to-comprehend evening.

Högl did not have to be the salt and pepper detective that he was to put two and two together: The former equestrian with Olympic aspirations, the horse lover, was seriously AWOL and was trying to fly the coup with money, jewels, false passports, foreign currency, and a wonderfully handsome redhead wearing a sparkling red evening gown but without her glittery pumps on.

What could go wrong?

Högl, an *SS-Obersturmbannführer* (Lieutenant Colonel) and subordinate by several ranks to Hermann, an *SS-Gruppenführer* (Major General), at Hitler's explicit direction, arrested Hermann there in his bedroom and shanghaied him and his inestimable suitcase stuffed with pillage to the *Führerbunker*, where things were escalating into a Charlie Chaplin movie.

Anger among Hitler's circle was now scorching the bunker's cream-colored walls. All were indignant, affronted that Fegelein would do this to their Führer. Högl and his men manhandled Hermann like a sack of yesterday's laundry down to the street, heave-hoed him into their jeep, and shot straightaway to the most famous address in Germany, *Wilhelmstraße 77*, and then down and down to the *Führerbunker*.

Between Fegelein's eloquent apartment and the insane asylum that the bunker was devolving into, one of Högl's men was seriously slammed by a wayward Russian bullet and almost bled out in the pursuit and capture of a scoundrel.

Fegelein was locked in a makeshift cell, where he sat sniffling, groaning, and vomiting.

Then, Hitler caught a BBC broadcast from Reuters detailing Himmler's "backdoor surrender" with the western Allies through contact with Count Bernadotte. Hitler was now in a frenzy over this evident perfidious behavior, and Fegelein faced excellent prospects of being put against a wall and shot.

Because Hitler perceived a connection between Fegelein's disappearance and Himmler's betrayal, Hitler ordered *SS-Gruppenführer* (Major General) Heinrich Müller, chief of the *GeheimeStatsPolizei*, a.k.a. the Gestapo, to interrogate Fegelein and find out what he knew of Himmler's plans to give up Germany to the Allies and take over as Führer. Not that it mattered that much. Because, at this point, everyone knew the war was lost, and it didn't matter what Himmler was doing. But Hitler was taking it personally.

The notorious Müller was just the ticket for the job: extremely solemn. He had attended the January 1942 Wannsee Conference ordered by *Reichmarshall* Hermann Göring and was pivotal in instigating the genocide of all Jews in German-occupied Europe—a.k.a. the "Final Solution" to the Jewish Question. He was commonly called "Gestapo Müller" to distinguish him from an SS general named Heinrich Müller. Gestapo Muller was in and out of the *Führerbunker* in Berlin and was seen there on 1 May 1945. Never captured, Müller is the most senior officer of the Nazi regime to have not been confirmed dead. A mysterious cloud lingers above his name.

Müller quickly arranged a drumhead court-martial but quickly realized he was going nowhere fast. (Drumhead courts-martial started in 1876 and were conducted in the field, sometimes during a battle, to process urgent charges of offenses committed in action. The term *drumhead* came from using a drumhead as an improvised writing table. It often connotes summary justice.)

Fegelein, still blitzed, insisted he reported *only* to Heinrich Himmler, *not* Adolf Hitler—a most tendentious excuse—and that he was not obliged as a general in the SS to take orders from anyone except Himmler, to whom he reported directly.

He then unbuttoned his fly and urinated at the boots of the commission members preparing the court-martial.

This was not a good move on Hermann's part.

It did not endear him.

Müller had had enough.

Figuring he did not need Hitler's permission, Müller ripped off Fegelein's epaulets and the melton rank gorgets on his lapels and all of his decorations and threw them at the shiny yellow pool of

Fegelein's earlier untimely indignation—Fegelein was now a *soldat*, a private, in the span of four seconds.

Now, Hitler had decided what to do with the wayward SS general, Hermann.

In the words of Otto Günsche (Hitler's main SS adjutant), "Hitler ordered Fegelein to be spared and transferred to *Kampfgruppe Mohnke*, a battle group fighting the Russians around the bunker to prove his loyalty in combat and that would end the matter." Hitler now had stumbled upon a soft spot in his heart for the Braun sisters, Eva and Gretl.

Enter Eva Braun to defend her brother-in-law, Hermann (with whom some said she had a brief romantic tour). With abundant tears and sobbing, Eva pleaded profusely with Hitler to pardon dear Hermann, reminding Hitler that Gretl was pregnant with Fegelein's child (to be named Barbara, who would commit suicide in 1976 using E606, a toxic substance used in weedkillers and insecticides).

Hitler would not listen and changed his mind; he ordered Fegelein to be court-martialed and let the results fall wherever.

But Mohnke presented a fact that stopped the court-martial cold.

With Fegelein sitting on a stool and vomiting, Mohnke told his fellow officers that in German legal proceedings, a law stated that "no soldier can be court-martialed when he is drunk."

And Fegelein was certainly soused.

Traudl Junge—an eyewitness to the bunker operatic landscape—stated that "Eva Braun pleaded with Hitler to spare her brother-in-law's life and tried to justify Fegelein's actions"—but *nein*! said the Führer.

Fegelein was dragged up two flights of stairs to the battle-scarred garden of the Reich Chancellery on 28 April, and, with Russian shells creasing the air around them, Hermann Fegelein was "shot like a dog" in the back of the head.

Rochus Misch, an *Oberscharführer* (Sergeant) in the 1.SS Panzer Division *Leibstandarte SS Adolf Hitler* (LSSAH), witnessed the whole subterranean drama. After recovering from an earlier wound he received in Poland, he joined the *Führerbegleitkommando* (*Führer* Escort Command, or *FBK*) as a batman, courier, telephone operator, and all-around aide; Misch was the last survivor of the *Führerbunker*. He disputed aspects of the above account. According to Misch, "Hitler did not order Fegelein's execution, only his demotion," which Mohnke had already affected. Misch also claimed to know the identity of Fegelein's killer(s) but never revealed the name(s). He died in September 2013 and had appeared many times in documentaries.

Journalist and author of *The Bunker*, Harvard-educated writer for *Newsweek* magazine, James P. O'Donnell, interviewed dozens of bunker survivors in the 1970s and provided a compelling account of Fegelein's court-martial.

SS-Brigadeführer Wilhelm Mohnke resided over the drumhead court-martial ordered by Hitler and formed a tribunal consisting of three general officers: Wilhelm Burgdorf—who would subsequently commit suicide in the *Führerbunker* on 2 May—*General der Infanterie* Hans Krebs, *SS-Gruppenführer* Johann "Jonny" Rattenhuber, and himself.

Fegelein, still lit up like a blowtorch, repeatedly refused to accept the court's authority; he did not have to answer to Hitler. He shouted, *"I am an SS general and only report to my good friend Reichsführer-SS, my friend,"* and yelling, *"Fickt euch Selbst"*—"Go fuck yourselves!" Fegelein was so drunk that he was crying and vomiting, according to Misch; he could not stand and urinated copiously again on the floor.

Mohnke was undecided at this crucial moment. On the one hand, he had orders from Hitler, and on the other, there were questions of legality.

Both civilian and military law stated that a "defendant had to be of sound mind and understand the charges against them."

In Mohnke's mind, he was "certain Fegelein was 'guilty of flagrant desertion.' It was the opinion of the judges that 'he was in no condition to stand trial.'" So, it seems, Mohnke threw up his hands, shut down the proceedings, and turned the defendant over to General Rattenhuber's security squad.

Neither Mohnke nor Misch ever laid eyes on Fegelein again. Last they knew, he was marched out into the courtyard and shot in the back of the head by one of the *Sicherheitsdienst des Reichsführers-SS* boys. Ironic, too, because the *Sicherheitsdienst* was under the command of Fegelein's former benefactor, Heinrich Himmler.

To this day, no one knows what happened to Hans Otto Georg Hermann Fegelein's remains, his stuffed suitcase, his bespoke suit, and that attractive barefoot redhead bailing out the kitchen window like a rabbit.

Günsche and Bormann argued that Fegelein would desert again, *especially* as a *soldat*.

Hitler then ordered Fegelein to be demoted and court-martialed by a court led by Mohnke.

At this point, the accounts differ again. Confusion adds to the battle smoke. The years that have passed since then obfuscate what occurred.

After the war, Stalin ordered the Russian NKVD to compose a dossier for his eyes only regarding Hitler's death. *The Hitler Book: The Secret Dossier Prepared for Stalin from the Interrogations of Otto Guensche and Heinze Linge, Hitler's Closest Personal Aides* stated that "Fegelein was court-martialed on the evening of 28 April by a court headed by Mohnke, SS-*Obersturmbannführer* Alfred Krause, and SS-*Sturmbannführer* Herbert Kaschula. The tribunal sentenced Fegelein to death." Some accounts state that one man shot Fegelein; others say he was put up against a wall and shot by a formal execution squad according to German regulations. The names in the dossier differ from those of O'Donnell. We believe accuracy comes down on O'Donnell only because of his extensive interviews of bunker eyewitnesses almost immediately after the war concluded.

So, on 6 April, in a conference room at the *Führerhauptquartier*, Hermann Fegelein, many months away from being shot for treason, future brother-in-law of Adolf Hitler, stood bent over a map table beside his benefactor, the Führer, adding his opinion on what would be one of the most important tactical decisions of the Germans in World War II—sending *Das Reich* down to southern France where, along the way, the once-lauded division, now a rump, would perform a few atrocities, including the massacres at Tulle on 9 June 1944 and be forever known as the division involved in the Oradour-sur-Glane massacre on 10 June of the same year.

Next to Fegelein at the map table was *General der Artillerie* (Lieutenant General) Walter Warlimont, senior operations staff officer to General Wilhelm Keitel. In 1940, he was promoted to major general and assisted in developing the invasion plans of France. During the Battle of France, on 14 June 1940, Warlimont was promoted to *General der Artillerie*, and continued to give almost daily briefings to Hitler.

To Warlimont's right at the table was *Generalfeldmarschall* Wilhelm Keitel, a "major war criminal," and *Oberkommando der Wehrmacht* (OKW) chief, the high command of Nazi Germany's Armed Forces. Keitel had signed criminal orders and directives that led to numerous war crimes. At the Nuremberg Trials, he was found guilty and executed by hanging in 1946. Because the hangman's noose was incorrectly tied, Keitel hung suspended for twenty minutes, twitching and turning before he died.

Next, *General* (General) Walther Buhle, chief of armaments. He was imprisoned after the war until June 1947, living in Stuttgart and dying at age sixty-five. He was also briefly accused of being part of the July 20, 1944, conspiracy to assassinate Hitler but was acquitted shortly after.

This is the transcript of their conference regarding *Das Reich*:

WARLIMONT: This movement of the 12 SS Div in this area is also underway, though for the moment, they can be replaced. On the other hand, Student's paratroop replacement and training division which has about 12,000 men, is going into southern Holland . . . being built up here . . . as well as . . . and the front on the south coast. . . .

FEGELEIN: When on contact to 1st Panzer Army has been established, the Reich Battle Group can presumably be withdrawn?

THE FÜHRER: Of course, it should be pulled out—it should move over here.

FEGELEIN: It could be put together quickly.

THE FÜHRER: How strong is this battle group?

KEITEL: Fifteen or sixteen hundred men.

FEGELEIN: No, it's a bit bigger: 2,500 men. They weren't too badly mauled. That's the hardcore.

THE FÜHRER: For over there, it's nothing. But if they're put here, you've immediately got 15,000 men. Then in no time. . . .

FEGELEIN: The *Das Reich* Division has 15,385 men altogether.

BUHLE: The battle group and that?

FEGELEIN: No, that alone.

THE FÜHRER: Then it's ready! Then it's a division again—in fact, an old division!

***

During Easter—9/10 April—four days after the Hitler conference, *Das Reich* prepared to move out to the Toulouse-Montauban area. They knew training and retrofitting could not energetically begin until they reached the Bordeaux area from the East. This training and retrofitting were necessary because they had been badly beaten in the East. From their departure to the war's end, *Das Reich* would be led by *SS-Brigadeführer* (US Army equivalent—Brigadier General) Heinz Bernard Lammerding, his rank at the time, a German SS general officer who would be convicted of war crimes after the war but would not serve his sentence.

On 21 April 1944, the division was loaded on a single, extended transport train. At 0900 hours, the train slowly rolled out to the muscular tones of the overture to *Tannhäuser*—today was also the Führer's birthday; it would be an eight-hour journey. They moved through the bucolic countryside with joy and relief, but the further they traveled through Germany, the more the destruction of their country spread before them, and depression again set in. Few among the men could believe they would ever go home again. Now, moving toward the delights of southern France "Living like God in France" was their new catchphrase. They had survived the suffering and death in Russia and its unprecedented winter weather and moved on to southwest France's beautiful fields and vineyards. This alone boosted their memories back to the glorious days of 1940 when they found most people were relaxed and friendly. No longer was this true. The terrorists' threats made it almost impossible to travel the streets alone. Officers' messes in Toulouse were surrounded by wire mesh to prevent grenade attacks.

Thus, by luck, chance, or good fortune—the troops did not care—Battle Group Lammerding (*Kampfgruppe Lammerding*), one of the most tarnished divisions in Nazi Germany, was now a rump of the finest armored divisions the Germans had. Ordered to abandon the mud, floods, and cold of Russia, they hastened across Europe along a southerly route to the land of wine, fine cheese, and beautiful women. Once there, they would establish an encampment at Montauban in the Tarn-et-Garonne and not far from Tulle and Oradour-sur-Glane, not knowing that they would soon be at the center of one of the worst massacres in the history of France.

On 27 April, the train halted in Montauban.

When *Das Reich* left the Eastern front, they took with them the strong words, ambition, and "hopes" of their Führer, who wanted to show them that the priority now was shoring up the defenses in the West and defeating the Allies. His thoughts were typed down on paper.

Dated 3 November 1943, Hitler's *Führerdirective* No. 51 stated his resolve to win in the West. In part, it stated:

For the last two and one-half years, the bitter and costly struggle against Bolshevism has made the utmost demands upon the bulk of our military resources and energies. This commitment was in keeping with the seriousness of the danger, and the overall situation. The situation has since changed. The threat from the East remains, but an even greater danger looms in the West: the Anglo-American landing! In the East, the vastness of the space will, as a last resort, permit a loss of territory even on a major scale, without suffering a mortal blow to Germany's chance for survival.

Not so in the West! If the enemy here succeeds in penetrating our defenses on a wide front, consequences of staggering proportions will follow within a short time. All signs point to an offensive against the Western Front of Europe no later than spring, and perhaps earlier.

For that reason, I can no longer justify the further weakening of the West in favor of other theaters of war. I have therefore decided to strengthen the defenses in the West, particularly at places from which we shall launch our long-range war against England. For those are the very points at which the enemy must and will attack; there—unless all indications are misleading—will be fought the decisive invasion battle.

Holding attacks and diversions on other fronts are to be expected. Not even the possibility of a large-scale offensive against Denmark may be excluded. It would pose greater nautical problems and could be less effectively supported from the air but would nevertheless produce the greatest political and strategic impact if it were to succeed.

During the opening phase of the battle, the entire striking power of the enemy will of necessity, be directed against our forces manning the coast. Only an all-out effort in the construction of fortifications, an unsurpassed effort that will enlist all available manpower and physical resources of Germany and the occupied areas, will be able to strengthen our defenses along the coasts within the short time that still appears to be left to us.

For *Das Reich*, the situation before departure for France showed substantial losses from whence they were leaving, which had to be replaced with approximately nine thousand men—primarily recruits from February until May 1944. Of course, German troops in the division looked down their noses at them. There was an impurity about these new troops.

Among them were citizens of twelve European nations—a bouillabaisse of soldiers. The largest contingent consisted of men from Alsace-Lorraine and the *Volksdeutsche*—"people whose language and culture had German origins but who did not hold German citizenship." Only a minimal number were volunteers; the rest were draftees. Many said that these men had been "shanghaied." Throughout *Das Reich* and elsewhere, their ranks, equipment, men, and resources had been drastically diluted, and with this, so went the old pride.

Inevitably men from Alsace and Lorraine were allied by upbringing and ties with France and would be used in the coming battle in the West. Each company in *Das Reich* had at least forty men from Alsace and Lorraine in their ranks. They had not one day of training in the German language, not a day in a German barrack. Instead, they had been billeted in local billets in France among French civilians and under the eyes of the *Résistance* movement. Overall, this signaled the beginning of the end for Germany. The dilution was taking effect. The "purity among the SS ranks since Hitler's early days would now begin to dissolve out of desperation."

As they marched from the East through France and down to Montauban, French *Résistance* became pervasive in mid-May 1944. And at the same time, animosity began to burgeon toward each other among both the French citizenry and the Germans participating in the march. What had been a non-confrontational relationship had grown into armed conflict.

According to *SS-Obersturmbannführer* Otto Weidinger's account in his book, one of five volumes, *Das Reich V, 1943–1945*, "Excesses against the German soldiers would provoke, indeed force, the German command to extremely harsh measures against the French civilian population, thereby upsetting the good relations between the German occupation forces and the French and turning them to hatred. *This may have well been the intention in the subsequent battles against the German troops in France* [emphasis added]. In all [*Das Reich*] lost approximately 100 men through murder and abduction alone from March until it arrived at the Normandy front."

The Germans found the methods of the French *Résistance* immensely objectionable. The Germans wore uniforms. The *Résistance* did not and was not easily recognizable. They could pop out of the weeds, forests, and homes and ambush the Germans, who thought they were "not fighting fair." As the hatred increased, the Germans regarded the *Résistance* as "bandits" and "terrorists." The game was changing, and the Germans would become more ruthless and unforgiving. Essentially, French tactics were working, slowing down German efficiency.

Divisions that had been moved to France had either been decimated in Russia or were medically and physically inferior. From these, special battalions were formed of the deaf and diseased. Now, Russian, Hungarian, and Romanian subjects, as well as defectors and POWS of the Indian Army, joined in.

But mostly, the officers and noncommissioned officers were battle proven. No regimental commanders were older than thirty-four; the division commander, *SS-Gruppenführer* Heinze Bernard Lammerding, was thirty-eight. Replacement officers and noncoms had risen from the ranks.

Older personnel had been severely thinned out by death and wounding during the brutal fighting in Russia. By the start of the Allied invasion, every element in *Das Reich* had a backbone provided by men who held the division together. At this point, trust in National Socialism, the military leadership, and Adolf Hitler was still unbroken—it would not survive whole.

Back home throughout Germany, the resultant losses among the civilian population in the towns and villages where the troops were from caused increasing psychological burdens on the soldiers fighting the war. Almost daily, bad news arrived in the letters they received from home informing them of the destruction of their homes and the deaths of friends and relatives, wives, and children.

Many were granted home leave because of "Bomb Damage" and would return to the field heartbroken, shaken, and depressed.

This emotional stress was raised by the new and ever-increasing attacks of the *maquisards*—a French paramilitary organization set up by the Vichy government and then spreading throughout France. It recruited Frenchmen to combat the French *Résistance* and act as informers. Some volunteered to avoid forced labor, but most were opportunistic bullies who enjoyed their treachery. And because of their knowledge of the localities, they were a menace. On the other hand, the *résistants*—a generic word like *maquisards*—opposed the German occupation. The German forces called these groups "bandits" and "terrorists" and went back at them with vengeance, hatred, and extraordinary brutality.

For *Das Reich*, the *résistants* and casualties became more evident in mid-May 1944, approximately one month away from the massacre at Tulle and the heinous military action of *Das Reich* at Oradour-sur-Glane. This sharply contrasts with the easy-going days when the Germans first arrived. Now, the terrorist threats meant the Germans could no longer travel alone or unarmed. In Toulouse, wire meshing had to be used around the officers' messes and the *Soldatenheim* to thwart grenade attacks. No longer did civilians greet Germans with a smile and "hello." A chill developed between them.

The activities of the *résistants* were, for the most part, amateurish and insignificant, but nettlesome and deadly enough for the German command to initiate extreme measures against these groups as well as innocent French civilians. And so, here is the point where the Germans took a turn toward aggression:

Generalfeldmarschall Hugo Sperrle, a morbidly obese officer with a forever scowl on his face who had been appointed commander of *Luftwaffengruppenkommando 3* (Air Force Group Command 3), issued the infamous "Sperrle Orders." The Sperrle Orders would be the impetus to attack and counterattack both civilians and terrorists. After the war, many German defendants in war crime trials would use it to excuse their criminal activities. It never worked.

On 3 February, the first of Sperrle's Orders spelled out the treatment of the French *résistants*; it was unequivocal. The German troops were now emboldened to allow their hellish, pent-up anger and vengeance to flow like the world had not seen since Genghis Kahn.

Sperrle's first order stated:

1. We (the German armed forces) are not in the occupied western territories to allow our troops to be shot at and abducted by saboteurs who go unpunished. The countermeasures taken up to now, despite undenied successes, will not alter the situation substantially if immediate self-protection is not undertaken in instances where we are attacked or presented with insubordination.

2. If troops are attacked in any manner, their commander is obliged to take his own countermeasures immediately, these include: There is to be an immediate return of fire. If innocent persons are hit this is regrettable but entirely the fault of the terrorists. The surroundings of any such incident are to be sealed off immediately and all the civilians in the locality, regardless of rank and person are to be taken into custody.

3. Houses from which shots have been fired are to be burnt down on the spot. A report will not be made until these, or similar immediate steps have been taken.

4. In the judgment of the actions of troop commanders, the decisiveness and speed with which they act are to be regarded as the primary aspects. A slack and indecisive troop commander deserves to be severely punished because he

endangers the lives of the troops under his command and produces a lack of respect for the German armed forces. Measures that are regarded subsequently as too severe cannot, in view of the present situation, provide a reason for punishment.

Then, on 8 June 1944, two days before *Das Reich* hit Tulle and Oradour-sur-Glane, Sperrle issued his second order to the German troops. Whether the order was issued before the massacre at Tulle or the day of to act as a coverup is unknown.

The following order took effect on the issue date and was passed on to the German troops as the Order of the Day. Here it is in its entirety:

> The operations staff of the Wehrmacht expect undertakings against the guerrilla [the German word used here is *banden*, which usually translates as "gangs" and implies criminality] units in southern France to proceed with extreme severity and without any leniency. This constant trouble spot must be finally eradicated. The outcome of these undertakings is of great significance for further developments in the west [the Allied invasion of Normandy began 2 days earlier, 6 June 1944]. Partial successes are of no use. The forces of *Résistance* are to be crushed by fast and all-out effort. For the restoration of law and order, the most rigorous measures are to be taken to deter the inhabitants of these infested regions who must be discouraged from harboring the *Résistance* groups and being ruled by them and as a warning to the entire population. Ruthlessness and rigor at this critical time are indispensable if we are to eliminate the danger that lurks behind the backs of the fighting troops and prevent even greater bloodshed amongst the troops and the civilian population in the future.

On the same day, 8 June, Sperrle added:

The Supreme Command of the Wehrmacht has decided that members of the French *Résistance* movement are to be treated as guerrillas. [This was the day that the Allies broadcast the demand that members of the French *Résistance* were to be regarded as being regular combatants and treated according to the terms of the Geneva Convention on land warfare. This was an odd request—the Germans quite rightly objected to this one-sided declaration, especially as the *Résistance* did not wear any distinguishing uniforms, or themselves abide by the Convention.]

The above quotes come from Weidinger's book *Das Reich V, 1943–1945*. At this point, more about Otto Weidinger is necessary because he plays an essential and significant role in this story.

We see him pictured as a handsome and elegant SS man in his bespoke, bemedaled black SS uniform. Weidinger's good looks could have been misleading and diverted attention from his solid military achievements and decorations, including a Knight's Cross. While a prolific writer—the five volumes are almost two thousand pages—Weidinger partook in the blood-spattered invasion of Poland and the Battle of the Netherlands. Later, he would be awarded the *Eichenlaub* (Oakleaves) to his Knight's Cross. While seeing action in the Normandy Invasion, Weidinger was bumped up to command the 4.SS Panzer-Grenadier Regiment *Der Führer*.

While Weidinger's five-volume record of *Das Reich*'s "heroic" activities in Russia and Europe have been branded an *apologia*, a whitewash of the SS's activities, it deserves scrutiny by students of Wehrmacht history. You have to put the time aside to read it all; it is a snoozer, but interesting to see the Germans from their side of the French. It is often tedious, and the English translation often goes haywire.

Note: Weidinger is quoted extensively throughout this book. Thus, we should note with a "grain of salt" what Jean-Paul Picaper, a French author wrote about Weidinger's observations regarding

Oradour and the surrounding events, that "Weidinger's volumes put forth a tendentious narrative and provide a sanitized revisionist account without any reference to war crimes." Weidinger, by the way, referred to the Tulle and Oradour massacres as "German French tragedies"—a collective indictment without blame for either side. Which is like saying the Battle of the Bulge was just a fistfight.

After the war, Weidinger's volumes were reissued by the right-wing *Nation und Europa*. The books were banned in France. Later, we will see more of Weidinger's participation, verbatim reports, often one-sided observations, and posture regarding Otto Diekmann and the massacres at Oradour and Tulle.

It should also be noted that Otto Weidinger, as commander of the 4.SS Panzer-Grenadier Regiment, *Der Führer*, a component of *Das Reich*, was in constant communication with Lammerding and his daily activities.

***

When the 2.SS Panzer Division *Das Reich* arrived in Montauban, their new headquarters, the invasion news prompted Heinz Lammerding to bring the division to march readiness.

Reichsführer-SS Heinrich Himmler, a close friend of Lammerding's, sent him a note of congratulations for his counter-*résistance* operation in Montpezat-de-Quercy in May 1944.

On 24 April 1943, Lammerding was awarded the Knight's Cross of the Iron Cross, a.k.a. the "tin tie," because it was worn around the neck and hung like a tie. He was a trim man, exceptionally polite in social situations. A ruthless pragmatist as an SS general, he had the reputation of being cold and colorless in character. Many said he would have served Germany better if he were a "desk general." He was a certified engineer by profession. In June 1944, he was transferred to the Tulle Chaumont and Villedie areas. Bloody encounters ensued with the French underground, and individual units suffered heavy casualties in the battle against the "invisible enemy."

In the book *Their Honor Was Loyalty: An Illustrated and Documentary History of Knight's Cross Holders of the Waffen-SS and Police—1940–1945*, numerous apologias are sprinkled throughout by the author, Jost W. Schneider, writing about Lammerding:

> When it was learned that *SS-Obersturmbannführer* Helmut Kämpfe had fallen into the hands of the Résistance on June 9, 1944, and had presumably been murdered shortly thereafter, a young battalion commander [*SS-Sturmbannführer* Otto Diekmann] in sheer frustration attacked the town of Oradour-sur-Glane. . . . Ammunition and explosives were found in all of the houses in Oradour. . . . Since it was clear the town was in the hands of the Résistance [not true] and that the population was definitely on their side, Oradour was put to the torch. . . . The fire spread (unintentionally) [not true] to the church and, since ammunition had been stored in the attic [not true], the church exploded and burned to the ground in a matter of minutes. The women and children perished. No responsible command of the Second World War could have remained indifferent to these attacks and ambushes.

The division Lammerding commanded, by the summer of 1944, had acquired a frightening reputation. *Das Reich* was part of the Waffen-SS, Himmler's "private army" that also controlled the *Allgemeine-SS*, a police force that included the Gestapo and the detachments that staffed the concentration camps.

The strength of *Das Reich* in June 1944 was nineteen thousand. At that time, it was a very different division than the one embroiled in the invasion of Russia. They still wore the death's-head insignia on their caps; the SS sig-runes on their collars, and the regimental bands or "cuff titles" worn on their lower sleeve (*Der Führer*, for example, the name of one regiment within *Das Reich*). However, the quality of the men was far from those who had set out on Operation Barbarossa in 1941. The division attempted to redress these diminishing standards using NCOs and officers to instill the old esprit-de-corps in the new, incredibly diverse group.

There were five officers, in addition to Lammerding, who played a significant role in the Oradour/Tulle narrative:

SS-Obersturmbannführer Sylvester Stadler, head of the division's Führer Armored Grenadiers Regiment, had something to say about Lammerding, and it was not pleasant: "The impression emerges of a man over-promoted and quite unsuited to a fighting command, who would have been much more at ease on Himmler's staff"; *SS-Sturmbannführer* Helmut Kämpfe was commander of the Regiment's Third Reconnaissance Battalion; *SS-Sturmbann- führer* Otto Diekmann was *Der Führer* Regiment's First Battalion Third Company commander. When he was born, he was named, according to SS records, Adolf Otto Diekmann. But Germans often used their second name, in this case, Otto. At nineteen, Otto Diekmann joined the Nazi party two months after Adolf Hitler came into power in 1933. His name has been misspelled in several publications, such as "Dickman" and "Dickmann." He was a tall, lean figure who confirmed the Party's Nordic ideal, blond and blue-eyed. He had difficulty acquiring permission to marry his fiancée in 1940 because her father was mentally ill—such were the criticisms in the SS at that time. In 1940, Diekmann was shot in the lung in France near Saint-Venant. Following recovery, he served as a training officer at Bad Tölz, where his tour overlapped *SS-Obersturmbannführer* Sylvester Stadler. In October 1943, Diek- mann transferred to France. The following year, following Stadler's recommendation, Diekmann assumed command of Stadler's First Regiment *Der Führer*; he was twenty-nine years old. Diekmann was the leading player at the Oradour-sur-Glane massacre; *SS-Hauptsturmführer* (head assault leader, a captain) Otto Kahn commanded the Third Company, and in 1944 was thirty-six years old and had a wife and three children. He had a receding hairline, gray at the temples, and a bony aquiline nose. Comrades said he had less-than-average intelligence, a pinched mouth, and deep melancholy eyes. By D-Day, his section numbered fifty men, most armed with rifles and light machine guns. And *SS-Untersturm-führer* (2nd lieutenant, or SS-Second/junior) Heinz Barth served under Kahn as command of the 3 Battalion.

2

The Gold

THE ORADOUR-SUR-GLANE MASSACRE OCCURRED ON A SUNNY
Saturday afternoon, 10 June 1944, four days after the D-Day land-
ings at Normandy.

Heinz Bernard Lammerding was the commanding officer of
SS Panzer Division *Das Reich*. He would hold this position until
the war's end, despite being wounded and recuperating for a while
before surrendering his once-extolled division to the Americans.

He was a tall, slender man, a standout when he walked into
a room in his bemedaled uniform, especially with the legendary
Knights Cross (*Ritterkreuz des Eisernen Kreuzes*) at his throat. But
most eyes would not be immediately drawn to the general's neck
award and the array of medals and pinbacks on his tunic. Instead,
the scar on his face grabbed the attention first. Such "dueling scars"
had been worn like badges of honor by young men in the upper
classes or the more upper-crust universities throughout Germany
and Austria since 1825. Dueling scars (*Schmisse* in German) were
also referred to as "*Renommierschmiss*," "bragging scars," "Mensur
scars," "smite," or "*Schmittee*."

Lammerding was born and raised in Dortmund. At an early
age, he observed the rising popularity and all-consuming drama
of National Socialism and became an initial member. Thus, he
became an associate of Germany's new Nazi aristocracy. He was

first a director of an SA, or *Sturmabteilung* (Storm Detachment), the Nazi Party's (National Socialist German Workers' Party) original paramilitary wing. Lammerding was soon standing with Hitler through his rise to power in the 1920s and 1930s as part of Hitler's intimidating "protection forces" at Nazi rallies and disrupting meetings of opposition parties—especially *the Roter Frontkämpferbund* of the Communist Party of Germany (KPD) and the *Reichsbanner Schwarz-Rot-Gold* of the Social Democratic Party of Germany (SPD). They often intimidated Romani, trade unionists, and especially Jews.

Colloquially, SA members were referred to as Brownshirts (*Braunhemden*) because of the color of their uniform shirts. They were a rowdy bunch of "hooligans" who did Hitler's bidding, often wielding sticks and whips against people and groups that opposed Hitler.

Lammerding's leadership style and badge of honor did nothing to enhance his reputation as a general officer. Most felt he would have been best suited to a desk job. However, there was a dark side to Lammerding seldom seen or discussed.

In July 1943, Lammerding became chief of staff to *SS-Obergruppenführer und General der Waffengattung* (Lieutenant General) Erich von dem Bach-Zelewski, directing the merciless anti-partisan operations in the rear in Russia. Lammerding's unmistakable signature was on several of von dem Bach-Zelewski's unsavory documents, many ordering the wholesale destruction of entire villages judged guilty of assisting partisans. The barbarity on the Russian front was enormous and hard to fathom. Atrocities were an everyday occurrence.

From the German perspective, few men attached to *Das Reich* during this period believed they would ever see home again. Between July and October 1943, 1 million German soldiers were killed, and in two months of 1944, 350,000 died. In March 1944, Das Reich lost 12,500 of its 15,000 men in the infamous Herkass pocket. And if bullets didn't kill them, there was the appalling cold, frostbite, snow, and ice.

The division tried to rebuild itself, which was not easy. They could no longer go about "cherry-picking" recruits. The SS, by this time, was no longer able to choose only the most qualified, as they had done in their earlier years. To be selected for membership in 1940 into the SS was a high honor. Candidates had to be in perfect physical condition. Imperfect teeth would disqualify a candidate. But after the Russian Front losses, recruits were drawn from wherever they were found. There were at least twelve non-German nationalities in *Das Reich*. The dream of Aryan perfection was now an old dream, cast away in favor of sheer numbers.

Conscripting Alsatians and assigning them to various SS units presented an awkward compatibility problem with the "old-timers." Old-school SS men looked down at them, and German leadership had a problem with their loyalty. There were 2,500 veterans, an elite who stood apart from the rest of the division and frowned upon these non-Germans. Generally, the Germans in *Das Reich* despised Wehrmacht soldiers with almost as much contempt as they did the French.

Lammerding took command of *Das Reich* at the end of 1943. For his work in Russia, on May 22 it was announced with a somewhat subdued celebration that Heinze Lammerding had been awarded the Knight's Cross. He was only thirty-eight. Simultaneously, he was pronounced the governor of Southern France. Because of this powerful position, he would receive occasional shipments of gold bars, presumably to "bribe" and obtain the loyalty of locale Frenchmen.

And so there he was, Heinze Lammerding, an *SS-Gruppenführer*, tall in the shoulders, a man bearing a cumbersome load of responsibility. While this might have seemed remarkable to most, particularly those outside the division, all that Lammerding had achieved did nothing to summon the respect of the men of *Das Reich*.

Many of the men who served with him in Russia had nothing favorable to say about him: he lacked personal presence, had no real gravitas, and possessed no attributes of a born leader. His most significant pluses were administrative competence and a solid friendship with Heinrich Himmler. In many of the *Das Reich* mess halls, it was rumored that Lammerding's friendship with Himmler secured his position as commanding officer of the illustrious division. But the impression that seems most prominent from all accounts of Lammerding in June 1944 was that he was a man over-promoted and quite unsuited to a fighting command, an individual much more at ease on Himmler's staff than as a general officer preparing to do battle with the soon-to-invade Allies.

Many of *Das Reich*'s officers and most of the men said that Lammerding was distracted and that there must be something more compelling swirling around in his head. Their training program and preparation for the battle at Normandy were deplorably behind schedule.

All that spring, their training was interrupted so that units could participate in sweeps and punitive operations against the French *Résistance*. But the sniping, roadblocking, and sabotage campaigns intensified. While these attacks against such a large division could be fended off, they diverted attention from training and retrofitting. For example, an antitank unit had to set off and investigate the theft of a large stock of landmines stolen by the *Résistance*. Gunners were periodically diverted from training to sweep stretches of the countryside where there were reports of weapons and supplies parachuted to the *maquisards*. *Maquisards* covered the entire range of individual *résistants* from dedicated freedom fighters to those simply trying to avoid German attention.

Lammerding was too pragmatic to be a Nazi fanatic. And at this point of the war—almost the end—he was starting to dwell on practical matters, such as "extending his pension" and securing his future, which was tenuous.

This lack of focus was held against him by his men: they wanted more battle training, less pillaging, more equipment, less killing of partisans, and less razing of villages. Such training was seen as protecting *them* and caring for *them* during the upcoming battle—they needed a fatherly approach. Yet, for all the German thoroughness that *Das Reich* applied to these operations against the *Résistance*, they were a matter of exasperation to the divisional staff, who were anxious about the training program. Several protests were made to 58 Corps and Army Group G about the use of *Frontsoldaten* (front-line soldiers) against "the communist bandits": "We were completely unsuited in character and mentality," one officer said, "to this sort of warfare." Adding that "there were specially trained troops for this type of work." Further, it was apparent that a chronic fuel shortage hampered the training exercises at the company and battalion level with an inability to maneuver as a division. Heinze Lammerding was aware of this and felt the finger pointing at him.

But the war situation, Lammerding was certain, was the most worrisome for him—he was taking it personally. What would a *Gruppenführer* do after the war without his uniform and medals? Would he be given any pension by the defeated, chaotic remnants of the government, or would he have to fend for himself? The collapse of Nazi Germany was inevitable, and Heinz Lammerding started thinking of his future in practical terms. And that included the large horde of gold he was amassing.

What could he do now that would help him after the war ended? Would it be every man for himself?

Specifically, he wondered about how to "enhance" his pension.

"The end" was inevitable, and Nazi Germany was falling like a dying duck. Now, the notion of a thousand-year Reich was fast fading. It was an enormous miscalculation by that egomaniacal Hitler, Lammerding thought.

Fortuitously, along came a windfall for Lammerding—one that was hiding in plain sight, and one that he did not have to lift a finger to acquire.

The "thing" that had been consuming his mind for weeks, that he should have realized much sooner. Something that could change his life and settle his mind. And expand that pension.

Just yesterday, another heavy wooden box had arrived at Lammerding's office, marked like the others with the ubiquitous sovereign eagle clutching a wreathed swastika—but with a different serial number. Immediately, Heinze would have his orderly lift the cumbersome box, carry it to his office, and place it on his desk. After the orderly left, Heinze's routine was simple: lock the office door, grab a small crowbar from his desk drawer, and pry the lid off the wooden box; no heavy lifting for Heinze Lammerding. He loved the creaking sounds the nails made as he pried the lid from the crate and the rich scent from the fresh wood and paint used to identify the box. Sometimes the lid on the box was secured with screws, which irritated Lammerding because he would have to spend time unscrewing instead of prying the lid off. But either way, this was almost as exciting as the first time he saw the contents exposed to sunlight—the light glittering off Heinze's future. He wished his men could see the glee on his face now instead of the usual grumpy Heinze, but that would not happen. Then he would lift the contents from the box, taking one at a time—or maybe two, if he was anxious—and carry them over to the safe until the box was empty—maybe one minute's time. And just before closing the safe's door and locking it, he would peek inside, and the smile would return to the *Gruppenführer*'s face.

At this point—late May, early June—*SS-Gruppenführer* Lammerding's safe had accumulated twenty kilograms of gold bars, each bar the size of a cigarette pack, all .9999 gold, neatly stacked, amounting to—well, Heinze was not 100 percent certain what the exact amount was—but his rough estimate of the pile was that it had to be over $500,000. Each bar fastidiously marked DR with an assay number. And Heinze was sure what the DR meant—*Deutsche Reichsbank.*

***

The provenance of Lammerding's gold DR bars was certain—the *Deutsche Reichsbank* (the Bank of the German Realm) located on tree-lined *Jaegerstrasse*, in Berlin. Primarily, they were sent to Lammerding's office to be used as bribes for information and favors. Clerks and management at the bank meticulously noted every bar sent to him. If any accountability was made regularly, it was done after the gold was shipped; the bank was too busy with other matters to apply any further attention. Also, the bank had no way of identifying what bars went where except by the number shipped out; the bars were not marked in any way to provide provenance. In the chaos and confusion of war, explanations for certain lesser matters were secondary to more pressing events. It is not documented whether the gold was a "legal bribe" for Lammerding's loyalty, which was a common practice then, or if it was given to Lammerding to be used to bribe local French officials for valuable intelligence, as Lammerding was also the governor of Southwest France.

Throughout the war, from 1933 to the end, the highest-ranking officers accepted "legal bribes" in "cash, estates, and tax exemption." Of course, in exchange, it was tacitly understood that the recipients would provide unbounded loyalty to Nazism (Adolf Hitler). These bribes were "regularized, technically legal, and made with the full consent of the leading Nazi figures."

Hitler instituted "a secret program of bribery involving most high-command members to ensure their loyalty." For example, a check would be written for a half-million *Reichsmarks.* These gifts from Hitler meant that the recipients would not disobey the

Führer. This arrangement is a sign of how distrustful Hitler was of those around him, including his inner circle.

By 1942, many officers expected the conferring of "gifts" from Hitler and were "unwilling to bite the hand that fed them so generously." It was an unofficial way of buying fidelity and allegiance.

In contrast, around 1940, German infantrymen were paid one Reichsmark ($0.40) "danger pay" for clearing landmines. In several cases, they never got to collect.

If Lammerding wanted his gold under his nose, he had to transport it somehow back to his home after the war and through unconventional means. Along the way, such a burdensome load would indeed be detected. Heinz Lammerding had no idea how he would care for the gold and get it back to his home after the war—or, for that matter, to a Swiss bank. Since he was a practical person, there was also the possibility that he would be captured by the Americans and declared a war criminal. Then, he might as well kiss the gold goodbye.

There was no easy solution.

These matters—the gold, marching to Normandy, the morale of the division—were wearing him down. One thing was sure: he would not allow the gold to get away from him.

Then, an idea, a nub of a plan, began to burnish in his desperate mind.

***

One of the few men in *Das Reich* that Lammerding considered a close friend was *SS-Sturmbannführer* Helmut Kämpfe, a trained typographer, one of the few divisional officers over thirty. He saw service on the Russian Front and commanded the Third Battalion, 4.SS-Panzergrenadier *Der Führer* Regiment of the *Das Reich* Division. He was awarded numerous honors, including the Knights Cross of the Iron Cross for bravery and exemplary leadership during the fighting east of Zhytomyr, Russia. The men under him in his regiment respected and liked him. A venerated combat veteran, Kämpfe, had been awarded Nazi Germany's extremely rare Close Combat Clasp in Gold (*Nahkampfspange*). Hitler regarded it as the highest infantry decoration short of the Knight's Cross to the Iron Cross. He reserved the right to bestow the award personally. By the end of 1944, only fifty gold clasps had been awarded. Most thought the Clasp was more prestigious than the Knight's Cross because it was the only award specifically for bravery. In contrast, the Knight's Cross was often awarded for "administrative achievement" or a profuse "thank you." Kämpfe was just one of ninety-eight men to receive the Knight's Cross *and* the Close Combat Clasp in Gold for his "bravery." On 1 September 1943 he was promoted to *Sturmbannführer* (Major). He and Diekmann saw themselves as allied spirits regarding their decorations and achievements. They both had a penchant for fine wine, good food, and bespoke civilian clothing. Much of their talk revolved around these subjects, along with cigars and brandy. Seeing the two laughing and having a good conversation was not unusual.

In April 1944, just after their march from Russia concluded at Montauban, France, a company of Kämpfe's men was out on *ratissage* (a violent raid) just north of the Montauban area, one of the first for his company. It was a reprisal for an earlier *maquis* attack, and the purpose was to terrorize the local civilians and scare them into not helping the *Résistance*—it rarely worked. In practice, *ratissages* were an arbitrary means of striking terror into the French population, sometimes to discourage *Résistance* and sometimes to filter out forced-labor escapees.

Looting in the towns was relatively standard practice, and when Kämpfe searched through one of the houses on a particular day, he came across a couple of unmarked gold bars.

This was not remarkable, since the French were great hoarders of valuables, particularly gold. They did not trust the local banks, instead preferring the precarious safety of their domestic hiding places over the security of the banks. After the raid, Kämpfe duly turned the bars over to his commanding officer, Heinz Lammerding, who, curiously at that moment, said nothing.

Several days went by, and nothing was said about the gold bars. While Kämpfe found it strange that Lammerding had nothing to say, he let it go as a dutiful officer would.

By this time, Lammerding had already accumulated several gold ingots from the *Deutsches Reichsbank* of Berlin—these were marked with a "DR," nothing else. Lammerding knew that the DR meant *Deutsches Reichsbank*—gold was given to him as an SS general and the governor of Southwest France. The gold was ostensibly held in reserve for bribery and to be used as the Occupation currency then in circulation. And there was the ease and consistency it flowed into the general's hands via an orderly placing it on the general's desk.

What was passing through Lammerding's mind is impossible to know—except that he knew he was in a perilous position. He had to wonder what he could do with this gold arriving at his feet every so often. He knew, too, he would probably be accused of war crimes. His military situation was getting worse, and the optimism that had buoyed him and his men for years was almost nonexistent today.

Some days later, after Kämpfe turned over the gold bars to Lammerding, one of Kämpfe's companies went off on another *ratissage*. Kämpfe took this time to meet and speak privately with Lammerding at his headquarters regarding the gold. Before he got to the subject's heart, Lammerding opened his safe and invited Kämpfe to have a peek. Also, he had a proposition for Kämpfe.

Kämpfe was an intelligent man. It did not take more than three or four seconds for him to figure out what Lammerding had in mind. The proposition was in the air.

They estimated they had a month, maybe two, to collect as much gold as possible before the forced march to Normandy and the subsequent battle.

At the same time, Lammerding permitted Kämpfe to conduct as many *ratissages* as he wished, and the Résistance provided many opportunities.

They both knew without having to say anything. Instead of *fewer ratissage* raids, Kämpfe would conduct *more*. Each raid would produce more gold, and the sparkling towers in Lammerding's safe would soar taller and taller—perhaps as high as the moon! While the plan seemed brilliant on paper—as all plans do—the brilliance would have to be in the execution, that nasty spot where most plans fall apart because the unknown always seems to intervene.

Between them, it was understood that the *ratissages* would not just continue—they would *increase*.

As far as the troops were concerned, the *ratissages* would "officially be part of the division's training program." Of course, they all shook their heads and rolled their eyes.

Of course, the troops would have difficulty reconciling this strange priority with the time, energy, and resources wasted chasing bandits and burning down villages with the invasion of France just weeks away. In the meantime there was an enormous amount of training that had to be done now because there would be no time for it once the invasion began. But what mattered to Lammerding and Kämpfe was accumulating as much gold as possible, and the only way to do that was to increase the *ratissages*.

In their minds, the solution was simple and brilliant, and nothing would get in its way.

Or so they thought.

The *ratissages* became part of the division and were dubbed "training programs."

Kämpfe then came up with an addition to their "special merchandise" plan. He told Lammerding that since they did not know how much time they had before marching off to Normandy or if they would be killed and lose all the gold they had collected, they might include their friend *SS-Sturmbannführer* (Major) Otto Diekmann in their scheme. Diekmann would be a positive addition, and Lammerding agreed; Diekmann was also a close friend of Lammerding's. Lammerding felt that Diekmann's suitability and discretion would be an overall asset to their goals.

Diekmann, the commander of the First Battalion, 4.SS Panzergrenadier Regiment (*Der Führer* of the *Das Reich* division), would be the highest-ranking officer present at Oradour-sur-Glane, France, on 10 June 1944. He was excited to be included in the plot with his two friends—Manna from heaven! He was a good-looking, fair-skinned man with blue eyes, a towhead, and a particularly stereotypical German with an infectious laugh. However—not that it mattered much to their plans—Diekmann's men did not like him. They were fearful of approaching him and always kept their distance. With Diekmann in the scheme, the *ratissages* would increase, and so would the gold bars.

The unmarked bars, after each *ratissage*, ended up piled in Lammerding's safe in the company of the DR bars from Berlin, which were swelling high.

Meanwhile, the systematic looting of the villages continued according to Lammerding's plan and his orders. In early May, the dreadful *ratissage* campaign, an integral part of Lammerding's "special merchandise" plan, began wholeheartedly, and it superseded the needed training and preparation for the invasion.

Today, villages throughout southwest France show evidence of these activities and bear plaques commemorating the deaths of those who died weeks after Lammerding's plan was instigated. Hands continued to fall into secret places; gold bars were withdrawn and passed along to Lammerding's safe.

Unfortunately for Lammerding, as the gold bars increased, his problems rose also.

At the top of his list was his superior officer, *Generaloberst* (General) Johannes Albrecht Blaskowitz, a Wehrmacht officer who despised the Waffen-SS; he started applying pressure on Lammerding to get his division trained, retrofitted, and up to Normandy as soon as possible. With this pressure on his shoulders, Lammerding realized his time to amass as much gold as possible was running short.

And, Lammerding sensed, rightfully so or not, that the general might use the Gestapo to start snooping around *Das Reich* to see what was holding them up—wisely concluding that if Blaskowitz suspected that one fleck of gold was missing, Lammerding would face a firing squad.

Heinz summoned Kämpfe and Diekmann for a planning session regarding their gold.

The subject was, what to do with the gold bars once in their possession?

No easy solution was in sight.

3

Hubris

The "black gold boys" had amassed an astounding six hundred kilos, about half a ton.

Kämpfe suggested hiding it somewhere in the Montauban area, but Lammerding told him that *Das Reich* was unlikely to return. And leaving it with the rearguard would mean widening the secret of the gold's existence; all three agreed that was out of the question.

Another possibility was sending the gold to Switzerland somehow under special guard. This was impractical because even if the convoy escaped or avoided the *Résistance*, the German authorities would almost certainly intercept it before it reached Zurich.

After more brandy, they reluctantly agreed that the only choice was to take it with them on the road to Normandy. It was the only viable option left. It was a chore, and they would have to fend off the *Résistance* on the way. Still, there was no way they would leave that much gold behind.

Lammerding thought it would be possible to get it as far as the river Loire, and then it might be feasible to make other arrangements once there. This soon was cast as the only alternative to a very complex challenge. The question was, how to achieve this task and do it expeditiously, in secret, and in time for *Das Reich*'s march to Normandy?

So, they concocted a plan.

First, special crates would be crafted to fit the gold bars, and the crates had to be the right size so that a man could heft them without too much effort.

Each box would be labeled *"Das Reich Records"* and transported via a half-track on a flatbed railroad car in Diekmann's First Battalion. All the division's records, filing cabinets, secret orders, personnel records, Lammerding's personnel files, and his safe would be aboard this half-track and entrusted to the unimaginative *Oberleutnant* (Lieutenant) Bruno Walter. The half-track would, so they thought, blend in with the long line of tanks sitting on flatbeds. Troops would do all the construction and markings of the crates from the rearguard. Walter would assemble a small unit of trustworthy troops and put together three or four "special vehicles," including the half-track containing the gold. Of course, the eagle and swastika would be stenciled on the crates to give them authenticity.

The crates of gold would be marked 1 of X, 2 of X, etc., and then given a series of fake serial numbers. Since they did not want to draw attention to themselves, Walter's convoy would not be heavily armed.

After a final brandy that night, they started daydreaming about the gold.

Not knowing that a horde of locusts would soon descend and derail their dreams.

4

Leipzig, Germany—Summer, 1933

THE MAIN OFFICE OF THE PRESS AND PROPAGANDA SECTION OF the German Student Union (*DSt*), on 8 April 1933, exercised an "Action Against the Un-German Spirit" that climaxed in a massive literary purge or "cleansing" (*Säuberung*), the so-called and soon-to-be infamous "book burnings." Classic historical images from 1933 show students tossing volumes of books into a massive bonfire, where the books literally and symbolically disappeared in clouds of smoke. The authors were some of the most noted names in history and included Einstein, Freud, Brecht, the Mann brothers, Marx, and Remarque, to name a few. The same year, on 6 May, members of the *DSt* attacked the Institute of Sex Research in Berlin's Tiergarten, invading the institute's priceless archives and setting them on fire at the *Opernplatz* in front of the State Opera House: twenty-five thousand books, journals, and photographs consumed by flames.

In Leipzig and throughout Nazi Germany, these actions were seen as a seismic shift, a new beginning throughout Germany—for National Socialism and the country's new leader, Adolf Hitler, the Reich Chancellor. The book burnings encouraged unchecked members of the Schutzstaffel (SS) and the Sturmabteilung (SA) to go about harassing and beating Jews. The SS and SA, at last, latched on to an idea that would blame all of Germany's economic and other woes on the Jews. Hitler turned his head.

In Leipzig, on a summer afternoon, a boy of ten watched from a hiding place in his father's jewelry shop as they dragged his sister outside. A gang of roughnecks stood outside the store and prevented anyone from helping; they took unhindered delight in this, and no one dared interfere. The boy's father tried to intervene but got kicked and pushed for his effort. Then the ringleader of the bunch, impatient, took the lead and started beating the boy's father with a broomstick. In a few minutes, the man was unconscious.

The mob was relentless, manhandling the boy's sister, tearing off her dress, and taking her away half naked for "corrective" training. Then the crowd dispersed.

The boy never saw his sister again.

His father, in excruciating pain, was helped back inside the store by the boy's mother.

Within days, they left Germany.

The boy was born Raphael Denovicz in 1923 in Leipzig, and his father was a successful jeweler. Jewish harassment was not new to him—he had been persecuted in Ukraine, escaped to Germany, and endured the oppression again.

Despite their hardships and rising inflation, the jewelry store business prospered. Raphael and his sister lived a comfortable life in a large house in Leipzig because of their father's affluence and success. But as the 1920s faded, the virulence of anti-Semitism had a chilling influence throughout Germany. Raphael's father had to sell their house and move to their apartment above the jewelry shop for safety.

Soon, the Denovicz family shop had become a target of aggression, starting with slogans such as "Jews Out!" Blatant shoplifting ensued, but reporting to the police received no reaction except laughs.

***

In 1938, the Denovicz family moved to Alsace, part of France. Raphael changed his name to Raoul Denis, and the family moved to Valence, a small town of about four thousand between Toulouse and Agen. The area overflowed with hundreds of refugees, mainly from the Spanish Civil War. Here the Denovicz family was no exception because, at the time, they all spoke with an Alsace accent and passed for refugees. Raoul's father had plans for him to study engineering in Toulouse, which he looked forward to. To all appearances, he grew up an ordinary French boy. Without ever discussing it, he knew the secrecy and strain the family lived under.

In 1940, France fell to the Germans quite quickly, and the Denovicz family's lives would take on the harshness and cruelties of the German occupation. Under the Germans, Toulouse became part of the Vichy Zone, the so-called Unoccupied Zone, and was removed from the worst of the Occupation. Despite this, his family was comfortable, the black market thrived, and there was no real deprivation. The Vichy police, however, presented a real threat: they sometimes drafted young men into forced labor; for this reason, Raoul's father sent him to college in Pau, a town near Spain. He met and fell in love with Camille, who later became his wife.

Pau, a remote region untouched by the war, is a commune overlooking the Pyrenees and the prefecture of the department of Pyrénées-Atlantiques. It was not long before Raoul drifted into the *Résistance*.

In 1941, he and Camille were asked to act as guides for escaping foreigners crossing the border. At that time, it was not difficult, and for Raoul, it was exciting. The Allied airmen, in particular, were grateful for their aiding them. Soon, the sense of danger and his growing romance combined to make an interesting, unusual life. In this region, the people had a deeply ingrained mistrust of the *Boche*, a denigrating term for German soldiers. But the war, for these people, remained in Paris, and the German argument was with Paris, not the local citizens. This was the right attitude, according to the Germans. As the demands of the Russian Front grew more serious, the quality of the garrison in France deteriorated as troops were called away to shore up the offense in the East.

There were whole parts of France never visited by the German forces until 1943. That was when they arrived in Vichy France, and their presence and the changes it brought were felt immediately.

In February, they introduced *Service de Travail Obligatoire*, the STO, an extremely unpopular law that allowed the Germans to draft French people into forced labor. The lucky ones remained in France, working on coastal fortresses forming the Atlantic Wall. The unfortunate were shipped out of France to work in German factories depleted by the demands of the war.

For Raoul Denis, the choice was obvious. If the STO approached him, his German-Jewish origins would undoubtedly be discovered, and he knew what that meant. So, he went to ground in Bedous, also a commune of the Pyrénées-Atlantiques department. (Pierre Laclède, the Frenchman who founded the US city of St. Louis, was born here.) This was a monotonous place to live, only relieved by several bizarre visits from a French nobleman in fancy clothes who rode an expensive bicycle. Raoul only knew him as Edgar. He never did find out his real name; after the war, he was known as a *Résistance* hero.

Edgar paid Raoul a visit and said he was familiar with Raoul's work guiding escapees across the Spanish border. For Edgar to visit, Raoul understood that he must have proved himself dependable and trustworthy. Raoul learned that Edgar knew much about what was happening in London. He began to suspect that Edgar was associated with British intelligence.

In anticipation of the Normandy Invasion in 1944, Raoul had been selected for sabotage. He found himself in Castelnaus-sur-l'Auvignon, a hundred kilometers north of Bedous. There he spent a week with the deputy mayor, a retired Belgian mining engineer named Gaston, mainly referred to as Hilaire, who taught Raoul how to assemble and use a Sten gun. The Sten was notoriously cheap to manufacture, effective at close range, and tens of thousands were parachuted into France during the war. The British also supplied plastic explosives; they could be molded like putty or clay into various shapes and were safe and easy to transport. Directly applying a match to it had no effect; however, once a detonator was inserted, it produced enormous explosive power. Raoul was also taught the use of a radio.

After his training, Raoul was taken to a rendezvous near Villeneuve-sur-Lot—*maquis* headquarters in a wooded area, approached by an unpaved *route blanche*. Germans seldom moved along these rough tracks unless after something specific. From the thick foliage on the outskirts of the wood, Raoul and his guide were jumped by two "villainous ruffians," according to Raoul, with strong Marseilles accents—they were disappointed when Raoul and his guide knew the password.

The *maquis* leader was a dark young man introduced to Raoul as Soleil. He was speaking softly with two men who were supposedly Englishmen. One of the Englishmen took Raoul aside. He was told that an SS Panzer division would soon arrive in Toulouse, and not long after that, the Allied invasion would commence, probably in the Pas de Calais area. As soon as it did, it would be the *résistants'* duty to harass the division and slow its progress toward Normandy.

The division was *Das Reich*.

It was imperative to cause interruptions and delays while the division was still beyond the range of strafing Allied aircraft. Natural barriers of east and west rivers—the Lot, Dordogne, Vienne, and Corrè—were to be prepared for sabotage and ambush. It was clear that regular *Résistance* forces could do little significant damage to an armored division such as *Das Reich*; nevertheless, it could slow them down, frustrate them, demoralize them, tire them, and force them into costly errors. Every minute of delay could make a difference. These attacks on *Das Reich* were more successful than the *Résistance* imagined.

Raoul asked how the Englishman knew *Das Reich* would arrive when he said it would. By this stage of the war, the Bletchley code-breakers, using the enigma secret of the "Ultra" technique, were intercepting many messages from German sources, and this was how he knew when *Das Reich* would appear. The men of British intelligence knew when *Das Reich* would arrive before the men in the division knew. British intelligence also knew that *Das Reich* could make a crucial difference to the invasion if left alone. It was thought, too, that the division would be in the area within three days. It turned out that it arrived in fifteen days and took a month to regroup before it was back to fighting strength. Historical evidence suggests the delay caused by the *Résistance* helped ensure the invasion's success. Each act of sabotage was often of little consequence, but they added up, slowing down the progress of *Das Reich* and demoralizing its men.

When Raoul returned to Bedous he was filled with excitement—things were now starting to happen.

The instructions he was given were clear: he was to listen to the *Messages Personnels* broadcast from the BBC from London every night. Raoul's personal message was one he would never forget: "*Le pipi est mieux à l'autre côte du mur*"—"It's best to pee on the other side of the wall."

Countless *maquisards*, like Raoul, were also listening for their messages during the spring of 1944, weeks before the invasion. Raoul had no idea what he would be required to do. Since he did so much training with plastics and knew how to operate a radio and a Sten gun, he might be asked to do almost anything relating to sabotage.

But he never got the chance.

A close friend arrived with bad news.

Raoul's parents, he was told, had been denounced by a young *milicien* and sent as Jews to certain death in Germany. Camille begged him not to return home, but she knew he would not listen. It would be reckless to throw everything away that he had achieved for an act of vengeance; he was not listening.

He dreaded that he was going to enjoy the grim task. It would not satisfy him to kill the man once: his training had taught him how to kill someone repeatedly. He would be sure that the man would not die quickly. He was at it for a couple of hours, the screams of agony muffled by a nearby river flush with melting snow. Raoul felt physically sick. After the final sob, he burned the broken remains to prevent detection and then buried them. The man he had just killed was a neighbor in Valence. They had traveled many times together on the school bus to Agen.

While Raoul was in Valence, the first units of *Das Reich* began to arrive from Bordeaux; they set up their headquarters in Montauban, thirty kilometers northwest of Toulouse. This news cheered up Raoul, and he could see that what the Englishman had promised about the division's arrival was becoming more accurate and that he could rely on him more—it seemed reasonable to believe that the invasion and liberty would follow soon.

Then on the last day of May, there it was, the message:

"Le pipi est mieux à l'autre côte du mur."

On his bicycle, Raoul made his way north to Siorac, keeping off the main roads. Just north of Belves, Siorac was a remote site, and there were many parachute drops during the month of May. A quarter of all the drops made in France during the war before D-Day were dropped in May 1944. Many of the weapons in those drops were stored in the church roof "under the protection of God," joked Raoul's host, a carpenter known as *Le Bolchevik*. He said this was done to ensure every *résistant* fighter was loyal and maintained silence. There were two thousand inhabitants in the town, and everyone had to store arms or petrol in their homes. One evening at the carpenter's house, Raoul met Jean-Pierre, a young Englishman who had arrived three months earlier as Commandant Jack's arms instructor. It was a good move because before Jean-Pierre arrived, everyone with a machine gun was likely to be more of a menace to themselves than the Germans. After a while, Jean-Pierre trusted Raoul enough to give him a special mission. He took him to another house and exchanged his bicycle for a different one. The replacement was "special." Jean-Pierre showed Raoul how the frame tubes were packed with explosives. Raoul would be bicycling a bomb—a safe one until it detonated. The next day he was instructed to bike to Le Lardin, a hamlet on the road between Brive and Perigueux about forty kilometers from Siorac.

Raoul lodged in Le Lardin for a few monotonous days, waiting for further instructions.

Although the news was scanty, it was obvious the Germans were also expecting something because their convoys up and down the road between Brive and Perigueux were no longer stopping for bottles of wine and water with the local civilians.

On his third day in Le Lardin, Commandant Jack contacted Raoul. The instructions: Raoul Denis was to go north, staying on the *routes blanches* and around the small town of St. Yrieix-la-Perche, southwest of Limoges. Once there, he was to take charge of six *maquisards*.

When he saw them, Raoul was disappointed; they were not *men*. These were boys that he was put in charge of. Raoul was twenty-one at the time, older by five years of the "men" standing staring at him waiting for instructions—but they were eager, perhaps too eager and blinded with enthusiasm, not disciplined nor cautious, and certainly not mature enough to handle the responsibilities they would have to face. They were boys with bicycles and Sten guns they were not sure how to use, as well as the Gammon grenade, an improvised hand grenade that was used by the Home

Guard, the Special Air Services, and the *Résistance*, and was especially suitable for the destruction of aircraft or vehicles. Somewhat crude compared to regular grenades, it had an explosive charge wrapped in fabric and sewn to an impact fuse for detonation on hard contact. Hand grenades were made of paper, but he would try to make it work. He first told them to use caution in everything they did—this was the first rule for survival. He told them they would travel northwest as fast as possible to St. Junín and there would regroup in a safe house near Chaillace.

Raoul Denis and his "ruffian" boys arrived safely and were hidden in a barn by their new host, a foreman of a glove factory. With great excitement, he took Raoul into his house, grabbed a bottle of cognac and two glasses, and told Raoul they had to have a toast before anything else. A toast?

First, he saluted Raoul's safe arrival. Then, with great fanfare, he saluted all the Allied soldiers on French soil. Raoul was stunned! Did that mean that the Allies had landed in Normandy? Yes! But then again, maybe not. Huh? Raoul was confused—*yes*, or *no*? Had the Allies arrived? Perhaps said his host; he was not 100 percent sure. It could mean, he told Raoul, that it was just a prelude, a feint, or the invasion itself. His host begged him to be patient. That the Allies had landed in Normandy was fact, but to what extent was it questionable? So, Raoul and the others had hope—that the Allies were finally here in France.

However, the foreman said he had good news to counter the uncertainty of the invasion, one that was confirmed with certainty.

After *Das Reich* loaded all three hundred tanks and armored weapons onto the flatcars, the trains started to move tentatively; then they all screeched to a sudden, destructive halt. All the axles on all the trains in all the laagers had been effectively sabotaged—their axles had been drained of oil and replaced with abrasive carborundum—and the trains and their flatcars were irreversibly damaged. All the tanks and equipment on the flatcars had to be offloaded from every flatcar and tediously restored. Repairing all the flat cars would mean *Das Reich* would not arrive in Normandy until several weeks *after* it was promised. Instead of spending time and energy repairing the flatcars, the tanks and heavy armor therefore had to travel by road—an annoying and dangerous alternative. Amid much cursing and condemnation, it took many days before the Germans got them onto the roads to Normandy—and that would present even more laborious, time-consuming problems for the tank crews because heavy tank treads, or links, were not designed for hard road surfaces. Despite their rugged appearance, tank treads, driven on hard surfaces, would grind, wear quickly, and fail sooner than if driven on grass and dirt. If the tracks were not replaced or repaired, the tanks would be as useless as boat anchors. To replace them was a massive undertaking that crews hated. It made them and their tanks susceptible to the ground fire from the *Résistance* and protracted battles. First, the tank treads' tension had to be relieved by several crewmen pulling and yanking at long, heavy cables until the tread was released from the wheels. The damaged links were replaced by hammering, pushing, and slamming until the tread was reapplied at the end—tedious, harsh labor. And nothing on a tank is light. Theoretically, a trained crew could replace a track block in forty-five minutes sitting in the motor pool. In reality, six to ten hours of manual labor were not unusual when you were cold, tired, working in the dark, and in a foot of mud, such as the conditions around Montauban. Multiply this by several hundred tanks—and the possibility of being attacked at any time.

When Lammerding heard this disastrous news, he was incensed.

In addition to the tanks, nearly thirteen thousand men in *Das Reich* had to be moved to Normandy.

Once the flatcars had come to a grinding halt because of the abrasive carborundum, the tanks, and armor had to be unloaded from the flatcars—another thankless and tedious task; they could only advance to Normandy by the local roads. Thus, the journey was slowed by mechanical failure and the waiting *Résistance* along the way.

The tanks would have to join the movement north on the road—and stop when treads needed repair. And if the road weren't wide enough, the disabled tank would cause a roadblock and stop all the tanks behind it. The British knew what they were doing by draining the oil.

For Lammerding's *Das Reich* division, the rail line between Toulouse and Limoges was out of order. *Das Reich* was also effectively cut off from the rest of France, isolated by the sweeping of the Loire River, whose bridges and tunnels, with a single exception, had all been destroyed by the always-menacing Typhoons and Spitfires of the Royal Air Force sniping at anything German that moved.

It was almost eight hundred kilometers from Montauban to Normandy, the destination Blaskowitz insisted on for *Das Reich*. British intelligence's assessment, made before D-Day, calculated that the Second SS Panzer Division would be there by D + 3. It did not arrive until July, indicating the chaotic shambles that marked the following weeks. The problems of the march left *Das Reich* in a shattered state both physically and mentally—particularly Lammerding. Now, they could only get his tanks and the half-track to Normandy via secondary roads, some no more than dirt and mud and littered frequently with "cow dung." Yes, the ubiquitous cow dung, as much as bullets and bombs, would slow down the division's march north toward Normandy and one of history's most significant battles.

On the roads, there were more challenges: the many innocuous-looking animal droppings turned out to be hidden landmines, although not always, so after the first few explosions, every pile of cow poop had to be checked, a distasteful and time-consuming chore because the men had to dig into the piles of cow shit with their hands to detect the familiar shape (and odor) of the mines and then, if lucky, defuse or detonate them.

And the *maquis* would be waiting along the route.

The foreman presented other news to Raoul, this of a local nature.

Partisans had damaged one of the local viaducts, and two Germans had been killed in an ambush.

With that information, the foreman produced a map. In the morning, Raoul was to take his men over the river past St. Junien, then north across the country to a point just beyond an area called Nieul. There were two targets: a railway bridge and a section of road. The thinking was that the SS might try to use Limoges as a railhead and bring the rail transporters down from Poitiers to carry those tanks and heavy armor back up to Normandy.

And more encounters made matters worse: the hilly country of Dordogne, the Lot, and later the Corrèze interfered with radio communications; interference was sporadic. As a result, when Heinz Lammerding arrived at Brive on 8 July, he had no idea where most of his division was situated and that it was in near chaos. Lammerding was facing a dire situation, one he had not encountered before and that undoubtedly interfered with his gold cache and pension plans.

Das Reich was scattered over hundreds of square miles of hostile territory. And already, because of the sabotaged flatcars, 60 percent of Lammerding's tanks were not fit for battle; there was a chronic shortage of fuel, which was increased when another train hauling fuel supplies was obliterated by Royal Air Force fighters.

Now, *Das Reich* was cut off from the rest of France.

5

On the Road to Tulle

OBERSTURMBANNFÜHRER HEINZE LAMMERDING WAS HAVING A stressful time. The Normandy Invasion on 6 June only exasperated and complicated the day.

All of France was joyfully involved—the Allies had finally come and shook salvation's hand. In the meantime, Lammerding had a division to worry about—and, perhaps, more important, the gold. And his life. And his career. And his retirement.

What to do with the gold? A pervasive and nettlesome problem for Herr *Gruppenführer*.

Hide it?

Leave it?

Take it?

Forget it?

To leave such a fortune would be preposterous—stone cold stupid.

Despite the invasion news, some trains were still moving throughout France, most manned by German soldiers. As the news filtered down to the men, it was evident that they would be ordered to move 450 miles north to support the Normandy battle. Yet the German response that day against the Allies moving onto the beaches had been inadequate and uncoordinated and would eventually lead to the Allies' push through France.

Lammerding concocted a plan to thwart the Allied invasion and to favor himself, Diekmann, and Kämpfe—but only temporarily.

Part of the plan he had been crafting before D-Day was to formally state in a memorandum that he intended to retain control of south-central France and suppress the *maquis*. Of course, south-central France was where more unmarked French gold bars were hidden.

On 5 June, Lammerding's "plan" memorandum says much about *Das Reich* remaining where it was, at least temporarily:

SUBJECT: Anti-terrorism Measures:

The development of the *maquis* station in the Cahors-Aurillac-Tulle area represents a threat that, in the event of a landing, could adversely influence operations. The majority of the terrorists are pursuing the objectives of communism and destruction. The population only assists them under duress (especially the moneyed and official classes). The measure taken so far against the terrorists have not had much success. . . .

Lammerding here was making a case for delaying *Das Reich*'s immediate march north to remain in southern France, where the gold in inhabitants' homes was more accessible. Or at least buy more time to stay and pillage more unmarked French gold bars.

He drafted the memorandum on 5 June 1944. He sent it on to Army Group G via Fifty-Eighth Corps, where it was endorsed by its commander, who communicated back: "With reference to the punitive and reprisal measures proposed by 2.SS Pz, the general commanding heartily concurs."

On 7 June, Army Group G dispatched a signal to Fifty-Eighth Corps; it began as follows:

The development of the gang situation in the Massif Central demands unhesitating action by a major formation. To this effect, on orders of the OB West and with the agreement of Führer headquarters, the 189th Infantry Division and the 2nd SS Panzer Division are immediately placed under the orders of the 66th Corps. The 2nd SS Armored Division thus reassigned is to deploy in the Tulle-Limoges area, where the substantial formation of gangs appears to be gathered.

So, despite the invasion the day before, 6 June, a version of Lammerding's self-serving plan was to be implemented, and the division was to move north toward Tulle. Lammerding was surprised but delighted. He'd get Blaskowitz and von Rundstedt off his back and still be able to scour the towns and villages for more gold. This picked him up a bit—but not much.

However, this was a decision that OKW would quickly regret almost within hours after the Allies landed.

OKW would soon discover that more resources—*Das Reich*—at Normandy would be necessary to impede the forward movement of the Allies into France—a need they would never fulfill.

While the battle of Normandy had begun, the highest levels of the German command rebuffed the idea that the Allies had gained the beaches in unanticipated droves. Many thought it was a feint—they did not know what kind. How the Germans, in all their years and experience in astute planning of strategies and tactics, had come to this lame decision was hard to fathom.

For example, on 6 June, Rommel was at home in Herrlingen, Germany, celebrating his wife Lucie's birthday. Later that day, he motored to his headquarters at La Roche-Guyon, France. When he arrived, it was too late for him or anyone to implement an effective plan that would have made a difference at the beaches in Normandy. It was here that the Wehrmacht started to lose the war.

Generalfeldmarschall von Rundstedt was having breakfast in Paris, awaiting orders from the *Führerhauptquartier* (Führer Headquarters)—but no orders were issued because Adolf Hitler was still asleep, and no one dared wake him, despite the grievous situation at Normandy. He remained snoozing comfortably in his pajamas at Berchtesgaden.

These occurrences—the absence of Rommel and von Rundstedt at the beaches, combined with Hitler's staff refusing to wake Hitler on the most important day of the war—contributed to a major disaster for the Germans that they would never recover from. That the Germans, with their historically proficient professionalism and tactical brilliance, allowed this to transpire is inexplicable.

What if Hitler had been wakened?

What orders would he have given?

Could he have staved off the Allies' attack?

What if *Das Reich* were in place at full strength instead of chasing the *Résistance* and hunting for gold and had been prepared to fight the Allies at the beaches?

Of course, we will never know—but it's something to consider. In the meantime, these questions aside, many other failures were afoot.

The first was the Luftwaffe—unprepared to be effective.

Luftflottenkommando 3 (Air Force Command 3) ultimately failed; they had insufficient fighters up in the air, and the sparse number they did have made no difference at the beaches. Some strafing here and there, kicking up sand, and that was it.

Only the *Marinegruppenkommand* (Naval Command), by order of Admiral Krancke, its commander-in-chief, acted on his initiative and issued a coded message: "Large-scale landing in Seine embayment." Which meant that the invasion had begun. But as a naval force long out of the fight, they could not engage the enemy. The entire German navy was useless.

On 7 June early morning, coded orders arrived at *Das Reich* for "Alarm Level II," meaning " establish readiness to move out."

That night, 7–8 June, elements of the division moved to the vicinity of the departure point at the route of advance, the Tulle area.

At 2315 hours, the order arrived by telephone from LXVI Korps:

SS-Panzer-Division-Das Reich is to concentrate on combat-ready elements by the evening of 8 June in the Tulle-Limoges area. Upon its arrival, the division will be attached to the *LXVI Korps.*

But at this point, the troops, the tanks, heavy pieces, and most of its SS troops were going nowhere—at least for the moment.

The 430-mile journey to Normandy by *Das Reich,* if unopposed, would have taken four days—but this would not be a typical movement. Instead, chaos would consume the day. They would not be at the beaches until after 5 July—indicating their trouble moving toward Tulle and farther north into the battle.

The locusts again descended into Lammerding's chaotic world—this time en masse.

The locusts would have their way, ingeniously installed by the British Special Operations Executive (SOE), particularly a gentleman named Anthony Brooks (code name Alphonse) and several teenage boys and girls who came to the fight with lots of courage and love for their country.

There are only two ways for tanks and armored vehicles to travel—either by rail on flatbeds, roads, or fields. (There were no large cargo planes capable of carrying tanks in those days.) The treads, or caterpillars, are susceptible to harsh wear and breaking down on asphalt or cement. Traveling on these roads, particularly for *Das Reich,* meant having to confront the *Résistance* that would engage them along the way—and while they could not stop an entire division, nearly twelve thousand troops, they certainly could slow it down and inflict numerous casualties.

To execute the sabotage, Brooks employed some formidable backup for his extraordinary mission: a sixteen-year-old girl, Tetty, her boyfriend, her fourteen-year-old sister, and several other young people of the same age to spend a few nights conducting sabotage. What an adventure! The courage they had!

If they had been spotted, they would have been shot immediately.

It seems inconceivable that the rail cars bearing the tanks were left unguarded, but unguarded they were. How, one wonders, did the Germans think any idea of interference by the *maquis* was out of the question?

They would be surprised.

Working at night and over several days, Brooks and his teenage saboteurs went to each laager in the area. Crawling under the flatcars bearing the tanks and armored vehicles, they drained the oil from all the axles. Then, they replaced the axle oil with carborundum, a colorless, hard chemical compound composed of silicon and carbon. Also, a semiconductor found in nature as the extremely rare mineral moissanite. Since 1893 it has been mass-produced as a powder and crystal and used as an abrasive. In this case, to change the course of war.

When the time came to mobilize the train, every flatcar's axle, without exception, seized up. The tanks were going nowhere aboard the trains.

It was an astonishing, unprecedented piece of sabotage. The Germans could not move the train more than six feet before stuttering to a screechy halt.

Now, with von Rundstedt hammering at him, Lammerding had no alternative.

On 8 June at 0400 hours, he received the following order. Only the salient points are included here:

2.SS Panzer Division

"Das Reich"

1a/Nr. 750/44/fwh.

Division Command Post,
8 June 1944
0400 hours

Secret

Division Order for Combating Bands [*Résistance* Groups] in the Tulle–Limoge Area

1. The band situation in the Central Massif has significantly intensified. *Immediate ruthless crackdown by strong forces is ordered* [emphasis added].

2. The 2.SS Panzer Division [*Das Reich*] is to be transferred to the Tulle-Limoges area. Accordingly, the *Panzerkampfgruppe* is to move out in the early morning hours of 8 June organized according to Appendix 1 from the present billeting area along two March routes.

   . . .

3. All movements and billets are to be secure for wartime conditions. Protection of conspicuous vehicles requires particular attention. Movement and watches less than platoon strength are forbidden.

4. Enemy *Résistance* is to be ruthlessly dealt with. Excesses against the uninvolved civilian population (particularly plundering) are to be prevented under any circumstance. In the course of combat operations, motor vehicle and fuel supplies are particularly to be confiscated and used to render the troops mobile, and the division is to be notified.

5. Active and passive protection against attack from the air must be a constant concern. Intervals of 100 meters [are to be

maintained] between vehicles. It is entirely possible that the Allies may employ paratroops to reinforce the bands.

For the Division Command
Operations Officer
Signed Stückler

One of the first matters that flashed through *Gruppenführer* Lammerding's mind was the stash of gold—at this point, the cache amounted to six hundred kilograms of gold bars nestled in his large safe standing inches from his desk. And there was still potential for more if *Das Reich* remained and continued the *ratissages*. But *Das Reich* was not nearly at division strength at this precarious moment and were near completion for the journey from Montauban to Normandy.

Days ago, preparations were made to pack up the "merchandise" and have it ready to go with them on the march to the Normandy battle.

This meant immediately packing all the documents regarding *Das Reich*: personnel files, the unit's history, top-secret orders, strategic maps, awards, and decorations. And, of course, several paintings on canvases that Lammerding had filched along the journey from Russia to Montauban. All of this was packed into a half-track, an Sd. Kfz. 25. Something like an SUV, the front portion contained the cab for the driver and two passengers, and the open back portion held the gold nestled among other important *Das Reich* items; the vehicle was armored and driven on treads like those on a tank. Now, like the tanks and armored vehicles, the half-track had to make the Normandy journey via the roads—and be subject to the journey's challenges.

All agreed: they had a plan—except Diekmann: he opposed the half-track containing the gold making the trek northbound on the repaired flatcars; he did not want to have to wait to see those wonderful, handcrafted boxes until they arrived at Normandy. The idea of traveling on the roads with the half-track suited him, and that was what he set out to do—a plan he did not share with Lammerding and Kämpfe; he didn't want push-back on his idea.

Once the half-track was loaded with the gold and the division records, Diekmann would brief *Oberleutnant* (First Lieutenant) Bruno Walter, the young Austrian that would be put in charge of Diekmann's "special merchandise," and double the guard on the Sd. Kfz 251 half-track. Diekmann ordered this without doing or saying anything conspicuous. Walter knew the half-track was necessary—at least he thought he did; he was familiar with the sensitive material it was carrying; he had no idea about the "prohibited merchandise."

The significance of their plan would grow exponentially daily, particularly now with the imminent march to Normandy. The whole matter was depressing, suggesting it was only a matter of time before the inevitable defeat of the Fatherland. Diekmann was concerned, too, that Lammerding had not seen fit to clarify with German precision what he was proposing to do with the "merchandise" at the end of the march when they approached Normandy—how would they get it back to their homes, if they were still alive, after the war? How could they conceal such a load of gold without discovery?

Nor did Diekmann at that moment know where his friend and partner SS-*Sturmbannführer* Kämpfe was.

Was he missing in action?

6

The Hangings at Tulle

EARLY MORNING 6 JUNE.

Sensing an imminent attack, Prefect Trouillé ordered the Tulle schools closed until further notice. Word had reached him that the beaches at Normandy were awash with American, British, and French equipment and soldiers. But right now, four hundred kilometers away, the situation that mattered was the prefect's town and its citizens' safety.

In Tulle this afternoon, street posters shouted: *"JOIN THE WAFFEN-SS!"* and "In the event of fighting or shooting in the streets, shutters must be closed, and civilians must remain in their own homes!"

At Montauban, Lammerding's headquarters was a site of military hustle, antennas, and clerks and signalers scurrying about like frenetic mice, filling gas tanks and making last-minute adjustments. Because of the sabotage of the flatcars by Tony Brooks and his precocious band of teenage saboteurs, the armored vehicles and tanks were not going north on the rails—or at least not until the axles had been repaired. They had to take to the roads to reach Normandy—a dangerous journey because of potential attacks from the *résistants* and the damage that hard-surfaced asphalt roads inflicted on tank treads.

About a hundred gun-mounted half-tracks, armored vehicles stuffed with men and weapons, tanks, ammunition, and trucks carrying nearly five hundred men clanged out of Limoges and Brive-la-Gaillarde. They headed toward their first destination: Tulle—the first of two massacres in the days ahead.

In a thirty-mile radius—including St. Junien, Limoges, Oradour-sur-Glane, and Rochechouart—*Das Reich* came to life for the march to Normandy, where, purportedly, there were eighteen thousand Allied soldiers, tanks, and light-armored vehicles. The division was to position themselves between Tulle and Limoges and, there, to suppress the *maquis* operations, which were an intensifying insurgency against Germans and their interest. This was the personal wish of Adolf Hitler. Some veterans were excited; resting was one thing, and laziness was another. They were anxious to get their blood moving, and now they had an objective.

They swerved out onto the roads lurching and bobbing forward, causing a great clattering and screeching of metal with their caterpillar tracks tearing up the asphalt and defiling the air with thick spirals of blue exhaust smoke. Some men stayed behind and repaired the roads as quickly as possible. Hard to imagine: the SS going around shooting people but also fixing their damaged roads.

SS-Sturmbannführer Wulf oversaw *Das Reich*'s reconnaissance battalion today and the lead element of the *Das Reich* column. He was thirty years old and the oldest son of a north German worker. He joined the SS in 1934, and when France fell, he remained an instructor at the renowned SS-Junker School Bad Tölz (an SS officer candidate training camp) in Bavaria until July 1943.

The officers and most SS men from *Das Reich* were angry and frustrated as they moved out. They felt affronted and irritated for several reasons: They heard General Eisenhower's earlier broadcast demanding full combat status for the *résistants* in arms. This was infuriating. They were not soldiers, they were a gaggle of bandits, terrorists who did not engage by the rules of warfare, and now

Eisenhower had lifted them to the same shelf as soldiers. So tenuous was the German Empire's hold on Corrèze that an SS Panzer *Aufklärungsabteilung*, Wulf's reconnaissance detachment, part of an *Abteilung* (battalion-sized unit attached to *Das Reich*), had to lurch to the rescue of fellow SS troopers because of an annoying group of rag-tag bandits. The *Aufklärungsabteilung* was the eyes and ears of *Das Reich*, their parent division. Now they had to stick their armored nose out, perhaps get bloodied, and make a dash to rescue their fellow Waffen-SS troopers in the Tulle garrison from a band of half-armed terrorists. All felt this was not a division's work and was below the dignity of the elite *Das Reich* and their acclaimed past. A squandering of men and equipment resources for a small cause, and more than likely, men would be killed. A specially trained squad should have undertaken this task, and *Das Reich* should be fighting at Normandy now in a struggle to defend Führer and Fatherland. But none of the men knew what they would see once they crossed the streets of Tulle. They had no idea how angered they would be once they saw the carnage inflicted by the terrorists.

Along the way, many tracked vehicles would have to stop at every suspicious mound on the road, then use their bare hands to check for cow shit or a landmine—a degrading, impossibly disgusting task.

As soon as Wulf's column was within two miles of Tulle, he jutted his hand into the air to signal the convoy to halt. He thought and assessed while his column refueled their vehicles from the jerry cans they carried. A minute passed, and he signaled for the queue to turn off their engines; he stuck his ear in the air. From where he stood, holding his breath, he could not hear any sound of battle. But through his binoculars, he could see a wisp of sooty smoke slowly ascending above the horizon over Tulle.

If the *maquisards*, he thought, had any sense of military operations, tactics, or strategies, they would have cut down trees and blocked the road challenging Wulf's column coming toward them. Still, Wulf and his men had not encountered impediments, blockage, or raids, and the *Aufklärungsabteilung* would move ahead unrestricted to Tulle. As they started their engines and moved out, Wulf ordered the column to close up; every vehicle had to maintain a distance of 100 meters spacing in case of air attacks.

Wulf already had a plan of attack in mind: approach from three points and seal off the entire town—and if innocent civilians were killed or wounded, so be it—and this was following Lammerding's expressed orders stating that "the area was to be secured with all inhabitants and that any house used by the *Résistance* or its supporters, regardless of its owner, be burned to the ground. For every German wounded or killed, we will kill ten terrorists." Lammerding also emphasized that the main goal was separating the *Résistance* fighters from the rest of the French citizens and setting the public against them. However, it did not work out that way for the Germans.

This forewarning would not forestall what was imminent for the rustic, mostly isolated town with the Vizier River flowing through the middle, banked on each side by quays and gray cobblestone streets. On the hillsides above rose three large schools, the barracks, the prefecture, and the town hall. Sitting on the plateau and clustered were the railroad station, the Giat arms factory—the town's primary employer—and a cluster of shops, houses, and small hotels. Architecturally, Tulle was a gray, undistinguished place; some looked at it and thought well of it because it reminded them of a cathedral. This would not be the only day in its history that Tulle endured a mauling; there were others, much less in deadliness: sacked twice by the English in the Hundred Years War, decimated by the Black Death, retaken by Charles V in 1370, and defended by the Catholics in 1585. More than its share of tragedy had visited Tulle.

Now, the *Francs-tireurs et partisans français* (FTP), the best organized of the French *Résistance* groups, initiated by the Communist Party, was frantic and panicky, knowing that today the Normandy invasion had begun four hundred miles from the Tulle area; they had to seize this opportunity now, or communism in Corrèze would be doomed forever. Every protestation of other *Résistance* groups, every order they received from London intelligence, and every rule of guerrilla warfare regarding ordinary prudence would be disregarded in their attempt to take and hold the town of Tulle and wipe out the German garrison.

Around the beginning of 1944, a twelve-member *Sicherheitsdienst des Reichsführers-SS* (Security Service of the Reichsführer-SS), or SD, swept into the Tulle area.

Headquartered in Limoges, the SD unit was under the command of August Meier, an SS-*Obersturmbannführer* (Lieutenant Colonel, or Senior Assault Unit Leader) and a leader in the infamous *Einsatzkommando* 5 of the *Einsatzgruppe* Commandant of the Secret Police and Security Services (AKA Gestapo), or (*GeheimeStatsPolizei*) headquartered in Limoges, a short drive north from Tulle. Directed by SS-*Hauptsturmführer* (Captain) Friedrich Korten, the SD men swarmed into Tulle, accompanied by elements of the North African Legion. They executed a full-force crackdown on the *maquis* to clean them out of the Corrèze department, once and for all, specifically Tulle. The actions were violent and vicious.

This cruel plan of action necessitated forming a temporary composite unit; it consisted of 1.Regiment of the 325th Security Division and the Georgians of the 799th Infantry Battalion "shanghaied" from prisoners of war of the Red Army. Named the Brehmer Division in April 1944 after *Generalleutnant* (Major General) Walter Brehmer. In the village of Lonzac, they arrested 3,000 people. Seventeen inhabitants of the village were murdered, and 24 houses were burned. In Brive, 300 people were deported to work camps in

Germany after having been rounded up and arrested. The Brehmer Division also went after the *Résistance*: 1,500 arrests were made, 55 shootings, 128 crimes or offenses in 92 localities, and 200 Jews were assassinated. In May, after leaving a substantial trail of blood, a devastated Brehmer Division left Corrèze in chaos and ruin.

While we have a good idea what offenses and actions the Germans took, we don't know what specific acts were committed by the French population that may have provoked or caused retaliation—or if there were any.

The *maquis* would not stand for it anymore.

The German SD crackdown, some say, explains the retaliatory actions in Tulle by the *Résistance* wishing to halt the suffering imposed upon them by the SS and the Wehrmacht. When May came around, the commander of the *maquis* FTP, Jean-Jacques Chapou, a.k.a. "Philipp," whose *nom de guerre* was "Kléber," put together a plan. He had been a young schoolteacher and was fired by Henri Philippe Benoni Omer Pétain—known as Marshall Pétain, the Old Marshall, or the Marshall of France—because he was against secret societies and outlawed freemasonry in the Vichy regime. French officials, however, were adamantly opposed to any operations against urban centers.

Although it might seem coincidental, the Tulle attack by Chapou and the FTP was not planned or organized around the Allies' landing at Normandy on 6 June—at this point, the invasion date was still unknown. Chapou's relatively straightforward objectives were to "disarm and destroy the German defense, disarm the mobile reserve, appropriate weapons, and vehicles, and render ineffective the French Militia and known collaborators." Also, they were to "open gaps in the defenses, inspire a healthy fear of its leaders and get them to retreat into Tulle and be unwilling to leave, stopping the Germans, at least for a time, from continuing their efforts against the *maquis*."

Defending Tulle was a garrison consisting of a hundred men of the Wehrmacht's Third battalion of the 95th Security Regiment (not the SS); approximately seven hundred men of the Mobile Reserve Group and the French Militia were added to this number. About another 290 men of the 95th Security Regiment came from the 8th and 13th companies.

Wulf and his forward elements moved cautiously toward Tulle, followed by *SS-Standartführer* (Colonel, or SS-Standard Leader) Stuckler, Lammerding's senior staff officer, a highly effective administrator and military officer.

When *SS-Sturmbannführer* Wulf's Reconnaissance Battalion pressed on toward Tulle, it would soon invalidate Chapou's earlier assumption that no further Germans would be seen in Tulle. Chapou had not received word that *Das Reich* had left Montauban. Radio traffic in the area was notoriously inefficient for Chapou and the SS.

Prefect Trouillé's forecast for the day paid off:

On the morning of 7 June, a few minutes past 5, when the main body of *Das Reich* was still in Montauban anticipating orders to trek north, the FTP fired an 8 cm *schwere Granatwerfer* mortar round that clipped the roof of the *Champs de Maar*, a quaint girls' school, and a building the Germans occupied.

The explosion startled Tulle's residents and jolted them into action. Two hours later, half of the guerrilla army was engaged. For the rest of the day, small columns trickled belatedly into Tulle to join the main attack. Radio communications were poor, and companies fighting in the streets could not judge each other's ragged progress. They were fighting in a fog.

Snaking down over the hills and moving into Tulle's streets came the first columns of ill-prepared guerillas clad in tunics and blue berets, carrying their cheap Sten guns, Brens, bazooka rounds, and mortar bombs in makeshift harnesses. With them went over-confidence and a lack of military tactics.

An hour after the mortar round exploded, the *maquis* began identifying the building where the Germans were hiding out.

The FTP established and secured its command post at 7 a.m.

That flat whoomph from that 5 a.m. explosion was an FTP signal to begin the attack against the garrison of the 95th Security Regiment, commanded by a fifty-five-year-old dentist *SS-Hauptsturmführer* (Captain, or Head Assault Leader). Another five hundred men were members of the *Milice Française*, the *Groupes Mobiles de Réserve* (GMR), or mobile reserve groups—paramilitary units created by the Vichy government during World War II, and the German SD security force.

A fierce but ineffective gun battle lasted for three hours without either side gaining much except gun smoke and spent brass shell casings.

Finally, at about 11 a.m., a Tulle civilian, white flag in hand, approached a *maquisards* company commander in the street. He had a message from the GMR and the *gendarmes* in the beleaguered *Champs de Mars* barracks—they had enough. Could they please move up to Limoges under a white flag? Reluctantly the *maquisards* gave permission, and a long procession of trucks filed out from the barrack's yard, each bearing a white flag. Many of the *maquisards* were incensed when they saw this. They did not understand this act of mercy.

The afternoon droned on without any further progress on either side. The Germans were holding out in the *Ecole Normale*, the Giat arms factory, and a school in front of the factory.

Two German reconnaissance aircraft appeared, scrutinizing the town; then they rounded back and strafed the *maquise* with machine gun fire. Aside from the clatter of their machine guns and the drone of their engines, it was a waste of much time and resources.

As evening approached and the light grew gloomy, it was still impossible to move about the town because the Germans held the positions on the heights above. The first hours of the assault taught Chapou and the *maquisards* a terrible lesson in warfare: The *maquisards* falsely assumed that the Germans would quickly surrender when they saw the enemy forces opposing them. Not so. At this moment, it seemed the attack had emboldened them. Two hours later, the *maquisards* were pinned down in a deadly firefight.

A wispy spiral of smoke continued to curl from *Champs de Mars*, the security forces' barracks where the mortar nicked the roof earlier in the morning.

Two hours drifted by, and barely half of Chapou's guerrilla force was engaged in the battle. This has never been understood, except as probably due to their lack of understanding of military tactics, training, motivation, and leadership. At the same time, Chapou did not have solid intelligence and knew not of *Das Reich*'s ferocity.

By now, the German garrison in Tulle had occupied all the strongly fortified buildings: notably, the *Souillac École Normale*, where most of the garrison was holding out; the *Champs de Mars* barracks, the girls' school in front of the Giat factory—all were well armed and supplied. By contrast, the *maquisards* were short of arms and ammo, and had no heavy weapons or solid tactical plans. Of the 1,400 who were supposed to participate in the attack, an estimated 450 were late to the battle.

At the train station, the *Résistance* found eighteen watchmen and one railway employee, Abel Leblanc; they invited him to join the *maquis*.

At 11:30 a.m., forces of the *Milice*, the Germans, and the Mobile Reserve Group strung up a white bedsheet on the barracks of the *Champs de Mars*. Negotiations followed, then at 4:00 p.m., they falsely assumed they would lose the battle.

Eventually, the *maquisards* succeed in setting the *École Normale* ablaze. Some of the Germans escaped through windows and the side streets—they were gunned down by *maquisards* waiting for them behind a stack of wine bottles, and their bodies started stacking up.

Here, one of the controversies begins and, some say, it initiated the slaughter of Tulle's residents on that stormy day, the day before the historic massacre of 642 people at Oradour-sur-Glane.

Around 5 p.m., the Germans tried to escape for unknown reasons, one raising a white flag. They were immediately cut down at close range as the *maquis* opened fire with their automatic weapons, spraying the Germans who were rushing out of the building. Some of them were blown to pieces by their hand grenades stuffed in their belts, which explained their mutilated bodies. Later, the Germans would claim the mutilations were inflicted by the *maquis* by hand. Traditionally, because they had long wooden handles, the German soldiers stuffed grenades behind their leather belts—a bit risky because if a bullet or shrapnel hit the grenade, it could cut a man in half. Nine members of the SD were killed. Except for two small holdouts, Tulle had been liberated.

The Germans would claim that forty German soldiers had raised a white flag and surrendered and yet were gunned down by machine fire, coming out of the *École Normale*. The FTP's response to this claim, dubious or not, was that the Germans had tried to make a run for it—and had not attempted to surrender as they said they had; they were fair game. The absolute truth will never be known. But a lot of Germans died with their hands in the air.

Tulle's Prefect directed the Red Cross and the monks of a local seminary to remove the German bodies from the area of *Souillac École Normale* and transport the wounded to the hospital. Of course, neither the townspeople nor the *maquisards* were happy about treating wounded Germans. And the Germans' claim that the FTP had mutilated the German corpses would remain a highly controversial issue for the balance of the war and would be an item in a war crimes trial after the war concluded.

At 4 p.m., a white flag appeared at the door held by a girl, Louise Boucheteil, a courier for the FTP who had been captured ten days earlier and been held prisoner in the building cellar with about twenty other *maquisard* captives, all expecting death at any moment. Behind her, weaponless and with their hands held up, were forty surrendering Germans in uniforms and civilian clothes.

Maquisards recognized one of the men in civilian clothes; he shouted: "*I have seen you before—in the Hôtel St Martins!*" It was an SD Gestapo agent in mufti; he instantly broke away from the group, running for his life. A blast of fire cut him down And a *maquisard* ran after him and shot him in the head.

Now the only Germans remaining in Tulle were in the arms factory and the small school in front of it. Silence overtook the town.

People started to come out of their homes, applauded the exhausted attackers, and congratulated them on their victory over the Germans. They brought out food and drink and tended to the wounded.

But their victory was stillborn.

Das Reich would now enter the reckoning.

The Waffen-SS went to work.

At around 9 p.m. on 8 June, the first tanks of *Das Reich* arrived at Tulle from the three defensive areas Wulf had earlier established, effectively sealing the city from anyone entering or leaving. This surprised the *maquis* with its suddenness, and its forces immediately began fleeing the city for the hills.

The Waffen-SS set up a command post adjacent to the weapons factory, then moved on 9 June to the Hotel Moderns. The highest-ranking officer there was intelligence officer *SS-Sturmbannführer* Aurel Kowatsch, the divisional 1c or third-ranking staff officer from the division headquarters. He stated that in the past two days, the citizens of Tulle had not been uninvolved in the events. This assurance was repeated several times at various levels. Kowatsch said mercy was shown by the Germans "because of the care with which the German wounded had been treated in the town hospital." All night, 8–9 June, the SS patrolled the town, ensuring that it was sealed.

The following day, 9 June, the SS found the prefect, Trouillé, and threatened to execute him. For security reasons, they began by rounding up the men in Tulle and locking them in the courtyard of the Giat ammunition factory while considering what punishment would suit the horror they would eventually inflict. Some of the men, not knowing where they were going or for how long, had their overcoats draped over their arms and held loaves of fresh bread. A German intelligence officer singled out those who were not residents and those subject to suspicion. The remainder were intermittently freed throughout the day.

***

At 10 a.m., while punishment for the "atrocities" was still being pondered, some three thousand bewildered Frenchmen of every age stood about in suffocating heat in the courtyard of the arms factory under the muzzles of fidgety troops and *SS-Schütze* (SS Rifleman/stormtrooper) Sadi Schneid, an SS platoon leader. He ordered the town fire engine and crew to drive slowly through Tulle reading a proclamation.

As this antiquated machine moved slowly, the engine's ringing bell drew the attention of the townspeople. The fire chief—who was in tears, according to Scheid—read aloud a brief German announcement in French:

> Because of the indescribable murder of forty German soldiers by communist maquisards, the German authorities have decided that three Frenchmen will pay for each German killed, as an example to all France.

During this period in the war, reprisals were legal and condoned by the Americans, French, and British, but with limitations. The Germans, at that moment, were undoubtedly proceeding within the legal limits of the rules of warfare. After all, the FTP "mutilated" German soldiers, so the Germans were operating within their rights and were going to start doing some mutilating themselves. Of course, it would go too far.

An hour later, a local printer was dragged from his home, and a formal proclamation was hastily printed and hung everywhere:

It said that because forty German soldiers were killed, 120 *maquis* or their accomplices would be hanged. The Germans called the murder of their soldiers "cowardly." Then, the announcement declared that if a German soldier were wounded, three *maquis* would be hanged. This was posted at Tulle on 9 June 1944 and signed by "The General Commanding the German Troops."

Now, the Tulle massacre commenced with an intensity.

The hornets had been jostled, and there would be poison in the air.

To this day, controversy flourishes regarding many details, and mystery shortens the reach for the truth.

Who to believe?

The definitive truth is beyond discovery.

We have the words of survivors and controversy on both sides—the SS and Tulle survivors.

SS-Obersturmbannführer Heinrich Wulf and his SS colleagues stated that on the morning of 9 June, a group of forty German bodies had been discovered, all mutilated. Their faces had been staved in, and their testicles cut off and shoved in their mouths.

This act, Wulf and others alleged, rather than the *résistants'* attack on the Germans, prompted the drastic reprisals that were initiated.

SS-Schütze Scheid (Private, or SS Rifleman) claimed he heard the same story from his friend, the "Sani" (medical orderly or sanitation man).

One of the primary controversies surrounding the Tulle reprisals covers *SS-Gruppenführer* Heinze Lammerding.

Postwar narratives have struggled to indict Lammerding of war crimes definitively. After all, the Tulle and Oradour massacres were committed by *Der Führer*, an element of his division, *Das Reich*, and were overseen by Diekmann. Lammerding repeatedly asserted after the war that he did not arrive in Tulle until late afternoon 9 June, when the hangings had already abruptly stopped.

He said, "I am still ignorant of the source of the order for executions at Tulle. But I do not think it was given by a higher authority."

Pointing his finger, Heinze indicated that the Tulle hangings were the responsibility of his senior staff officer, *SS-Obersturmbannführer* Albert Stückler. In attempting to pardon himself, Lammerding stated that he could not have been at Tulle because he was in Uzerche, "conducting an entirely separate hanging of his own." Further, he was accused of approving and signing the so-called proclamation of doom of 9 June outlining the reprisal ratios and signed by "The General Commanding the German Troops." Lammerding stated, "If it had been my signature, I would have naturally signed myself—'Lammerding.'"

Lammerding, present or not at Tulle during the hangings, bore full military responsibility according to many, as is evident in the text of the division's anti-guerilla memorandum of 9 June. Incredible as it seems, this senior SS officer who commanded anti-partisan operations in Russia persuaded a postwar generation that he did not authorize a divisional mass execution at Tulle.

It would be absurd to accept the words of one man unless that man were a reliable witness that he was at Tulle at that moment. Perhaps we should listen to all and then take what they said as "an impression." But some impressions, unlike our memories, are more reliable than others.

At this point, begrudging voices seep into the narrative. Wulf asserts that he was affronted when he was ordered to assemble an execution squad: "I protested that this sort of thing was the responsibility of the *Feldgendarmerie* (military police)." But the men necessary for the task were found anyway. According to "Hascha" Kurz, the execution was to be by hanging, which was more humiliating than a firing squad. The executioners were chosen from among the Pioneer company. This turned out to be a challenge. Not many men wanted to hang people from lampposts; they felt it dishonorable for soldiers in the SS. They had to be reminded what these *maquisards*, these communists, had done to their fellow soldiers.

At around four that afternoon, detailed arrangements for the hangings began.

Then Schneid and twenty of his fellow Waffen-SS men took to the street at the lower end of Tulle, close to the courtyard of the Giat arms factory—to better control the lives inside.

This was when the cruel tragedy unfolded that day in Tulle.

That morning, before Schneid and his group arrived at the courtyard, *SS-Untersturmführer* (Lieutenant) Walter Schmald and his colleagues had been screening the crowd of Frenchmen in the courtyard of the arms factory. Schmald was one of the prime players in the massacre. A member of the *Sicherheitsdienst* (SD), the security police, Schmald was the son of a mechanic from St. Vith. He was a chemistry student who had served with the SS for the past five months. Both he and his colleague, Beck, knew that after the school caught fire, they had no chance of surviving. Beck put a Luger to his head and killed himself. But Schmald found a hiding place in the school kitchen on the night of 8 June. He almost suffocated to death but managed to stay alive. When he came out later, he was extremely bitter. He stated that most of his colleagues were among the mutilated bodies found by the SS; in his heart, he swore vengeance and went about it today with fervor.

Haughty, Schmald strode among them, asking stark questions: "Why are your shoes so dirty? If you were a decent citizen, they would be clean." In the process, he could not hide his disdain, his craving for revenge for the days of terror the *maquis* had inflicted on him and his *Waffenbrüder*. Then Schmald felt compelled to resort to methods that were reprehensible even by SD standards. One by one, he picked individuals and directed them—arbitrarily, it seems—to a specific courtyard wall. Many had been allowed to depart (why we do not know). By early afternoon, some 400 remained. They were transferred to the Tulle armament factory. Finally, 120 men had been selected by Schmald; the youngest was seventeen, the oldest forty-two.

Before the hangings commenced, Schmald said, "We were almost all Rhine Catholics. We would very much have liked a priest to comfort us." As soon as it became known that many of the four hundred prisoners would die by hanging, *Herr* Brenner, the German director of the factory, intervened. Some in the courtyard, he said, were key workers, almost irreplaceable. Could they not be excluded? Twenty-seven were released. Brenner said that now the difficulty was that two men in the courtyard were *maquisards*. Perplexed but persevering, Schmald arbitrarily chose fifty victims and asked Abbé Espinasse to address them. The priest said, "My friends, you are going to appear before God. There are Catholics among you, believers. Now is the time for commending your souls to the Father who will receive you. Make an act of contrition for all your sins, and I will give you absolution."

The overall operation was led by *SS-Sturmbannführer* Aurel Kowatsch, thirty, a large man, a former policeman before joining the SS. Witnesses claimed that Kowatsch taunted the condemned before their executions.

A squad of young Vichyite *chantiers de la jeunesse* was recruited to assist in the hangings. The *Organisation des Chantiers de la Jeunesse Française* (CJF) was a French paramilitary institution active from 1940 to 1944. Today at Tulle, they gathered ladders and ropes for the execution because the SS found that the cables on the SS vehicles were too heavy for the purpose.

The hangings themselves were carried out by a pioneer NCO from Saar, Germany, Staff Sergeant (*SS-Oberscharführer* or Senior Squad Leader) Otto Hoff, thirty, who, later in the war, would be awarded the German Cross in Gold and was now attached to the *4. Regiment* of *Das Reich*. "Because our wounded were so well-treated," Hoff told Prefect Trouillé, "we shall be merciful and not burn the town."

The captives were walked to the first lamppost in the street—a hangman's noose was already hanging, fastidiously and excitedly knotted by the SS and the enthusiastic *chantiers de la jeunesse*. Leaning against the lamppost, two ladders that the victims would be ordered to climb.

The prisoners did not need any explanation; they knew what this was about, that they were facing their deaths in an appalling manner of execution.

Each captive was escorted to a noose hanging from a lamppost.

Since there were not enough lamp posts, ropes were hung from balconies.

After a while, looking down the street, lamppost after lamppost after lamppost and balcony after balcony after balcony had a body hanging, swaying, dead or about to be dead in the clammy air. Some of the SS laughed as they worked, but others found it disturbing and unacceptable. As the lampposts filled along the street and the nooses were knotted, the prisoners tentatively mounted the ladders until they reached the top.

Hoff adjusted the noose around their necks. Then he pushed the man off the ladder. With a kick from other SS boots at each of the lampposts, all the ladders were shoved away—in military unison. Most died instantly. Some twitched and spun, flailing their arms and legs. This irritated the SS, and they would run up to the victim and splatter him with a burst of machine gun fire.

Then, a moment of drama: one of the prisoners broke away, dashed for the bridge, and leaped on the rocky bed. An NCO emptied his Schmeisser, and the Frenchmen's body drifted in the water until it was caught at the foot of the bridge, where it floated for some time.

One prisoner's rope snapped, and he fell heavily onto the road, his neck broken. One of the Germans watched him twist and shake for an endless time, trying to breathe as he gazed into the man's eyes, pondering for whatever reason. Then he shot him.

And so, it went.

A routine was established.

It was a scene from Hades: a cloudy, humid, gray sky, bodies hanging and swaying and twisting down a mournful town of whimpering, crying, beseeching victims.

A few prisoners sobbed as they waited. Some went submissively, others screaming.

Others twisted and convulsed futilely for several minutes, striving for the last minutes of life. Occasionally, this would irritate a German, and he would give the victim a shot from his Luger, a *coup de grâce*.

Some of the *chantiers de la jeunesse* found this amusing and twisted the hanging bodies or swung them back and forth. Some, half-hanging and half-standing on the ladders, broke off and ended their lives themselves.

The hangings began around 4 p.m. At 7, Schneid was ordered to the arms factory courtyard, take a count and report if there were more to come because "there would not be enough rope to continue." He glanced over the three hundred remaining, terrified, and condemned. Ninety-nine, by 7 p.m., had been hanged. The Germans decided that was enough.

The hangings were abruptly halted. This has never been clearly explained. Of the three hundred remaining, twenty-one had been condemned but were spared. Perhaps Abbé Espinasse's request for mercy had been granted. Others suggested that Maurice Roce, the secretary-general of Corrèze, who had the advantage of speaking fluent German, persuaded the division staff to desist. Or perhaps the sudden stop was because they had no more rope to continue. Later, the twenty-one were loaded onto trucks and taken to the Hôtel Moderne for further identity checks. The ninety-nine bodies were cut down by the *chantiers de la jeunesse* and loaded onto lorries. French officials persuaded Aurel Kowatsch that if the SS carried out their earlier promise to dump the bodies in the river, they would pose a serious hygienic threat to the town and the garrison. It worked: the bodies were thrown onto the two rubbish heaps on the Brive road, where they were later buried.

Thirty-six years later, *SS-Sturmbannführer* Wulf said that the "French officials expressed their satisfaction that the business had been correctly and cleanly carried out."

Interestingly, every German officer of *Das Reich* interviewed after the war, including several nonparticipants, approved of the action as "a correct and legal response to the FTP's activity and the killing of so many SS men in Tulle." Wulf was shocked and mystified by the force with which war crime charges were pursued against him and others for "a day's work." The SS, he was saying, were the victims. From his perspective, the killings were a legal reprisal leveled against the murders of his comrades and the others who were all acting fairly. "We let them have a priest," he said. "Where else have you heard of people being hanged in the war who were allowed a priest before they died?" Heinrich Himmler had given them their cue: "One basic principle," Himmler had said, "must be the absolute rule for the SS man. We must be honest, decent, loyal, and comradely to members of our own blood and to nobody else. What happens to a Russian, to a Czech, doesn't interest me in the slightest."

**

As darkness fell on Friday, 9 June 1944, Raoul Denis and his band of six teenage *maquisards* left the barn's safety in Chaillac, where they had been hiding for the past twenty-four hours. Raoul had been told that the Germans rarely ventured down country lanes like the one they were on. As Chaillac fell behind them, overconfidence began to creep into the young men following him. Unlike Raoul, they had no idea of their place within a strategic plan and little to no experience in sabotage or combat. As far as they were concerned, they were on a long overdue adventure, a holiday away from their boredom, eager to kill SS, shoot their weapons, and throw hand grenades. They had no idea what war and bloodshed were like.

Raoul had to repeatedly order them to keep quiet as they chattered excitedly about the brave deeds they would be performing before daybreak. Now Raoul was having serious second thoughts about going out on this mission with this band of immature boys; they had the potential to jeopardize the mission.

Meanwhile, *SS-Oberleutnant* Bruno Walter was preparing a special unit following an order from *SS-Sturmbannführer* Diekmann. At midnight, Walter gave the command to move out. He climbed into his car, a Citroën 2CV, beside his driver. The convoy of three vehicles and the German guard detail moved down the dark road.

Once they passed the village of Limousine, the young French *Résistance* fighters' confidence resumed. They started getting chatty again, which annoyed Raoul—he called them "hooligans" and disliked them for their lack of discipline and maturity. This time, the hooligans' confidence was turning to noisy arrogance, and they began talking about killing Boche and how they were going to bloody their noses and kick their asses—their blood fever was surging.

Everyone in this area knew the sound of tank tracks on the road; it was ominous.

Raoul ordered the French boys off the road and into the drainage ditches.

Bicycles were flung into the hedgerows. Sten guns were cocked, and the young men leaped for the shallow ditches for meager cover.

Then, Raoul heard the sound of a heavy vehicle changing gears to take the hill above Les Remejous—that was the half-track shifting gears.

Raoul ordered the group to shut up, saying that this convoy was not their concern and that they had to save themselves for their objective that night.

Again, one of the young Frenchmen started to make banal patriotic sounds and how there were only three vehicles, and with surprise on their side, they would kick the Boche's asses and destroy their vehicles—it was too good a chance to miss, he muttered.

Raoul's resentment rose.

Here they were, facing a German column of three vehicles and SS men.

In a stage whisper, he repeated that their objective was the village of Neil and that this convoy was none of their business. A few curses emanated from the hooligans; further argument was not possible.

Now coming over the rise, Raoul saw them: the Citroën 2CV, the truck, then the half-track.

From their crouched positions, the sound was loud.

Raoul saw the car swinging slowly high, round the curve, the driver's eyeglasses glinting in the moonlight. Raoul called upon

Jesus Christ to come down and keep them safe. His heart was drumming.

He found himself holding his breath, and when he looked up again, he could see the officer beside the driver looking back, presumably checking to see if the truck and half-track made it up the gentle hill.

And then, to his dread, Raoul watched as one of the French hooligans did the worst thing he could do at that moment.

The worst thing he had done in his short life.

7

The Ambush

Now, back to *SS-Gruppenführer* Heinze Lammerding and the perplexing situation he was entangled in regarding the war and his gold—the "prohibited merchandise."

Tactics were one worry that Lammerding could work through. But the extraordinary amount of gold, its weight, and its mass presented a complicated dilemma. If exposed, Lammerding would be jailed or, worse, face a firing squad. There was no question of leaving it in Limoges—an absurd thought. Of course, Lammerding was not thinking clearly. The brightness of the gold was indeed blinding his reality.

He took an accounting of his woes: the list was short but impactful: he still had no clear idea where 40 percent of his tanks were. And *Das Reich* was spread out over a fifty-mile area. The training of his troops preparing to engage the Allies at Normandy was not nearly completed. And, short of saving his neck and career, there was the matter of the "prohibited merchandise" he was to share with *SS-Obersturmbannführers* Diekmann and Helmut Kämpfe—which, he was starting to imagine, was becoming more challenging to manage than the tactical problems *Das Reich* faced here in Corrèze. He could account for Diekmann, yes; he knew where he was and engaged, but where was Kämpfe? He had not heard from Kämpfe in a while, and now this was also causing him to lose sleep. Kämpfe, after all, was more than one of his command-ers—he was an integral part of the "pension" program and could add value to the disposition of it, the handling, and so on.

Heinze Lammerding had transferred his divisional head-quarters to a villa on the outskirts of Tulle. A series of urgent conferences immediately arose for discussion and decision and to determine the division's next movement; the list of items to address was endless. The notion of conducting a major operation to clear the route to Clermont-Ferrand was examined. Wulf was sent for, and Lammerding instructed him to immediately prepare the companies in his reconnaissance battalion to advance eastward the following day, 10 June.

Several minutes later, before Wulf was out the door and, on his way, Lammerding abruptly canceled the order after an adjutant handed him a sheet of paper.

Finally, the OKW and Army Group B had come to their senses regarding the disposition and orders for *Das Reich*. The battle in Normandy was consuming a dreadful toll of tanks, guns, and the lives of his men. It finally dawned upon their commanders that it was absurd to deploy an entire SS division to pursue terrorists across Corrèze.

Part of the OKW War Diary for that day regarding the Nor-mandy invasion reads:

> The third day was again distinguished by the continuous activity of the enemy air force, which swept the forward area and deep into the support areas, suffocating our tank attacks. . . . Rein-forcements were brought in from the west and from the Reich. . . . But it was evident that these forces would not be sufficient to drive the enemy back into the seas. The Führer ordered the following units to be moved in: 2 Pz Div, I Pz Regt of the 116 Pz Regt, 2 SS Pz Div [*Das Reich*] (which had been on clearance operations in southern France).

The signals shot out from OKW to Army Group G, even as Barth, the hangman, was doing his business up and down the main street in Tulle: 2. SS Pz Division's tacked vehicles were to be entrained immediately, regardless of present operations.

This was von Rundstedt's *cri de coeur*, entreating Lammerding to move north, demanding *Das Reich's* heavy armor presence—a necessity and a burden that Heinze Lammerding's shoulders could hardly carry.

Von Rundstedt's orders were more easily issued than executed.

***

Regarding Kämpfe's disappearance: Facts slowly started to resolve into a problematic picture.

On 9 June, while the hangings were proceeding in Tulle, Helmut Kämpfe's SS-Panzergrenadier Regiment, *Der Führer*, advanced to Guéret. They moved out midday before reaching a thick, wooded area and ran into two trucks with armed Frenchmen that immediately opened fire on the Germans. A single bullet to the head severely wounded the German squad leader. As it turned out, the other people in the trucks were German—one was a female staff assistant who had been shot in the stomach. One or two of the other Germans were killed. Kämpfe ordered *Obersturmbannführer Doktor* Müller to drive to the local hospital where the wounded women and the Germans could be treated.

At 8 p.m., Müller dashed away in his SPW—an eight-wheeled *Schwerer Panzerspähwagen* (heavy armored reconnaissance vehicle). A minute later, Kämpfe, alone at the wheel of his much faster French Talbot sedan, whizzed past the SPW, giving a jaunty wave and characteristic smile as he went. Kämpfe had decided to move ahead; in a benevolent gesture, Kämpfe wished to meet the mayor of a locality to thank him for repairing a bridge the SS had destroyed, an order that Kämpfe had previously given. A few minutes later, after darkness fell, Dr. Müller caught up to Kämpfe's empty Talbot at the edge of the deserted road; the engine was running, and the driver's door was open. Müller, and his men, it was dark now, checked the area and found no blood or any other evidence; some speculated that Kämpfe was answering nature's call and perhaps became disoriented in the dark going back to his vehicle.

By now, the lead elements of Kämpfe's battalion had arrived at Guéret, a light industrial town in the prefecture of Creuse in the Nouvelle-Aquitaine region in central France. The battalion adjutant, *Obersturmbannführer* Weyrauch, who had been driving the SPW in the lead armored vehicle, ordered the wooded area combed, despite the darkness, and had troops spread out. Weyrauch sent Dr. Müller to Limoges to make the necessary reports to the regiment. But the search for Kämpfe was for naught, and there were no other traces of him.

To all, Kämpfe's disappearance seemed to be a kidnapping, and he was probably dead; disbelief spread through the division for the well-liked Kämpfe.

But for Lammerding, it was another nettlesome worry adding to his pile of woes—a kidnapped, dead SS commander. Kämpfe was an intelligent, diligent, decorated officer who would have been invaluable in helping Lammerding and Diekmann hide and transport their black gold. His absence was now problematic, and he had no idea how it would end.

The news of the missing Kämpfe spread throughout *Das Reich*, enraged Lammerding, and spread down the ranks. This was a severe loss to the regiment and the division from a military and human viewpoint. All units were informed, and an investigation began—initially, efforts immediately proved fruitless, but they continued. In the meantime, the Limoges *Sicherheitsdienst* office informed the regiment that, according to reports from French informants, there was a *maquis* command post in Oradour-sur-Glane.

When Diekmann arrived at SS headquarters in Limoges on the morning of 10 June, he was informed of Kämpfe's disappearance by Gestapo officer Schmald, the supervisor of the Tulle hangings the day before. Everyone knew that Diekmann and Kämpfe were best friends, so they passed off his extraordinary action and sorrow to the loss of his friend.

There in Limoges, Diekmann also met with *SS-Obersturm-bannführer* Karl Gerlach, a recipient of the German Cross in Gold (*Der Kriegsorden Deutsches Kreuz*) and the Knight's Cross (*Ritterkreuz des Eisernen* Kreuzes) awarded on May 3, 1945.

The previous day Gerlach, now in Nieul, had been inspecting a planned billeting area for the Third Company, two or three miles from Oradour, when the *maquisards* encircled him and his driver. Gerlach's driver was shot and killed immediately.

That morning Gerlach, an ordnance officer, arrived at the regiment's command post exhausted, wearing nothing but his underwear. There, worn out, he reported on what had just happened to him. Present was a German attorney who took Gerlach's report.

According to Gerlach, on the morning of 9 June, in Limoges, he received a mission from regimental commander Stadler: find quarters for the *Sturmgeschutz-Abeitlung* (assault gun vehicles) in the Nieul area. He was also warned of active *Résistance* fighters in this area.

Gerlach took off and drove to Nieul accompanied by six men in three automobiles slower than his. However, since his car was faster than the other two vehicles, he turned around occasionally until they caught up to each other. At one point, he was far out from the other vehicles and was stopped by a truck with people in military uniforms. He thought for a split second that it was a truck full of friends. Not so. Before he had time for second thoughts, seven or eight uniformed men jumped down from the truck pointing their weapons at Gerlach and his men, shouting, "*Hands up!*"

They dragged Gerlach and his driver out of his car, tore their uniforms off, struck them in their faces, and said, "*SS—immediately kaput!*" Meaning "we are going to kill you."

Gerlach, feeling hopeless standing in his underwear, was sure they would be executed immediately. He tried to explain to one of the Frenchmen, who, luckily, seemed to speak good German, that he was an *Ordonnanzoffizier* in *Das Reich*. If they brought him to the *maquis* leader, he would provide important information and proof that he was not on combat missions. This did not seem to make an impression on anyone.

They were dragged back to their automobile, ordered in, and drove off under guard. In a short while, they stopped at a street sign that said Oradour-sur-Glane. This was one end of Oradour's main street.

Ordered out of the car, they were surrounded by *maquis* and many curious people. Some became belligerent, threatening and cursing at them. A few came with ropes, and Gerlach thought for sure they were going to be hanged right here.

Then, a battery from a restaurant was brought out—probably to torture or execute them. Gerlach and his driver were again wrenched down from the truck and bound with ropes, the knots secured with wire. For forty-five minutes, Gerlach and his driver stood like that.

Again, they were ordered back into the truck and drove away from Oradour.

Fifteen minutes later, they stopped in front of a house that bore a telephone sign on a wall indicating it was available for the public. After going into the house and making a phone call, one of the *maquis* returned to the truck and spoke to his commander in French, which Gerlach did not understand.

Back in the trucks, they drove another three to four kilometers and were then unloaded, untied, and given something to eat. The last meal? Probably. Because both Gerlach and his driver were picking up a bad vibe—imminent execution.

The truck with the escort party drove off and then returned two or three hours later. They were tied up again and ordered back into the truck.

It became apparent that the *maquis* did not know what to do with them, or at least were waiting for orders to execute them.

They drove eight to ten kilometers, stopped, and were yanked down from the truck and beaten.

Then, one *maquis* screamed at them: "*SS nix Verhö, Sofort kaput!*" "SS, no interrogation, immediately kaput!"

The vibe they got was accurate: the French were not going to waste time interrogating the two men. They were going to kill them, intending to walk them into the woods, out of sight, and shoot them.

Gerlach's driver understood the situation quite clearly. They would shoot them and leave them not far from the road.

And Gerlach's driver wasn't waiting for the bullets to hit him.

He spun and dashed away, zigging and zagging through the woods and waist-high brush. Gerlach sprinted after him. He heard several shots and saw his driver fall lifeless. He kept running; several bullets buzzed past his head, but he kept changing directions until he was out of sight.

It seemed like hours lumbering along in his underwear until he arrived at Stadler's headquarters and reported what had happened. Stadler told him he was not the only SS man attacked and kidnapped the day before. Surprisingly, Gerlach was shocked to learn that the commander III.A Battalion of SS-Panzergrenadier-Regiment 4, *Der Führer*, Kämpfe, still had not reported back; he had probably been killed.

Stadler then ordered Gerlach to get cleaned up and sleep; there were still wearisome marches ahead.

An hour or so later, after Gerlach arrived at the command post of 1.SS-Panzergrenadier-Regiment 4. *Der Führer*, he showed Diekmann on a map where he had been captured and the spot where his driver had been shot.

Diekmann soon left afterward with a *Kompanie*, commanded by *Hauptmann* Kahn.

Their objective was Oradour-sur-Glane.

Based on Gerlach's report, Diekmann returned to St. Junien, where he conferred with the Gestapo and *Milice*. It can be safely assumed at this moment that Diekmann was putting together a plan for sweeping into Oradour-sur-Glane for one purpose: disguising his intent to find the gold.

How lucky! The perfect cover.

And it was not for taking revenge for the death of *Bruder* Kämpfe.

The world would come to think that the reason for Diekmann massacring the town was for revenge. This theory, among others, would dominate others for years. Diekmann, without this excuse, could not arbitrarily march into Oradour without a solid intent. He knew he could not ask permission either.

***

Raoul leaped to his feet.

As the Citroën blocked his view, he knew what would happen.

The boy, one of the "hooligans," the one who earlier made the inane remarks, the one with the cough and runny nose, in his fist a Gammon grenade made of paper and shaped like a pear, threw the explosive toward the Citroën's open passenger window.

The Citroën 2CV disappeared.

In a glaring explosion.

Blistered the night sky.

Slamming the air with shards of metal, glass.

The driver's skull fragments.

A squeal of brakes.

Pandemonium.

Raoul's face took half the force of the Citroën's blasted glass windshield, cutting his cheek and bloodying his shirt collar.

He fumbled for a grenade, a Gammon like the one the kid had, and tossed it into the truck's window. The inside burst into a wreath of orange flame and thick smoke. Now the French boys were caught in the crossfire. All the hooligans were firing aimlessly—at the Germans and at each other.

The soldiers leaped out of the half-track.

Raoul took them all down with a sweep of his Sten gun. The two French boys on the other side of the road were dead, and the third nearly. His head was almost severed from his body, and Raoul thought of putting a bullet into his face to stop his misery. He was trying to say something, but all that emerged was an awful gurgling and ropes of thick blood. Then he died. Raoul hastened to the tailgate of the half-track to be certain there were no more Germans.

The open bay looked like a moving van.

Strapped to the shattered bulkhead and sides were two tattered canvases—Lammerding's nicked war booty. One, a large painting, was on the floor, and next to it were several rows of small stout cartons; there were approximately thirty, all stenciled black and bearing consecutive numbers. It took effort, but Raoul pried one open with a knife.

What he saw in the box almost knocked him off the half-track.

Then, the sound of boots running on gravel.

He looked up.

Running down the road was a single German soldier. Raoul aimed and fired his last round, but he missed the soldier as he disappeared into the thick woods. Now, he had to act as quickly as he could. Although it would take a while for a lone survivor to contact his comrades, once he did, they'd descend upon this ambush site and start an extensive investigation.

He crouched down.

He could not comprehend what he was gazing at.

This was absurd—hundreds of gold bars in the back of a German half-track in the middle of a war—and surrounded by smoldering vehicles and scorched corpses.

He estimated about a half-ton of gold was there at his feet.

He paused and counted the boxes—thirty!

Dear God, help me understand this!

His first thought was to treat this as an enormous windfall and think of it as poetic justice for what the Germans had done to him and his family.

But now what?

Raoul decided: he had to do something fast.

He could not just leave thirty boxes of gold there.

What could he do? Take one box on his bicycle? Impossible. How could he transport the cartons and not be caught?

He couldn't.

He grabbed a spade from the truck. Dashed into the thick woods not far from the smoldering vehicle and corpses.

He started digging.

He told himself, *Raoul, you dumb donkey, you do not have a hope in hell to succeed. Any moment, someone will come along and discover you.*

But he continued struggling, cutting, slicing the shovel into the ground.

The digging took almost thirty minutes to scrounge out a rectangular hole big enough, he imagined, to hold thirty cartons of heavy gold.

Then, back to the half-track and hefting the cartons into the hole. Raoul covered up his work with dirt, leaves, and branches. And prayers.

When he was done humping all the cartons from the half-track into the rectangular hole, he glanced down, out of breath, and felt something unusual.

Raoul Denis was exhausted but smiling,

Still, he felt half-sure he stood zero chance of getting away with this. When he pried open the first carton, there was a mix of marked and unmarked bars, a notion he'd have to ponder later. Now, he thought of taking one box and bicycling away, but he banished the thought: bicycling with the box and getting stopped would cause an insurmountable problem.

He ran over to the road's edge and looked back at where he had buried the cartons. But he had concealed the area well enough so that it was not visible. No one would ever find it. Maybe not even himself.

One final distasteful chore remained that Raoul had to do immediately.

At the same time, another unpleasant dart shot through his head: he wondered if, after the war, he would come back. *Then what*, Raoul, *how would you get thirty cartons of gold and take them home—anyplace?* He did not believe he would return and find the hole. He would be too fearful.

Now, the distasteful part.

He could not leave the corpses of the eight Germans and six young French boys, which, once identified, would mean certain death for their relatives. To be sure they were all dead, he pumped a round into each of their heads, using one of the German's Walther P.38 9mm pistols.

Then he grabbed the jerry cans of gas from the truck and half-track, pulled the boy's bloody, tattered bodies and Germans closer to the truck, and soaked them with the gasoline.

He reached into his pockets—no matches! So, he dug through the Germans' uniforms and found some.

He dropped a match on the pile of corpses and dashed toward his bicycle, not to get away from the *whoomph* of flame so much as from the horror and sweet, sickening stench of burning flesh.

He cycled away, pedaling fast, glancing back.

Trying to memorize the location.

Thinking of all that gold.

Smiling again.

8

Confrontation

AT 6 A.M., 10 JUNE IN JUNIEN, ABOUT THE SAME TIME RAOUL finished bicycling away from the smoldering ambush, an adjutant wakes Diekmann and tells him to contact Lammerding in Limoges immediately. This cannot be good. It takes twenty minutes before Diekmann's call connects properly to Lammerding's office—the weather, the mountains, etcetera. As usual, the phone lines are unreliable, and Diekmann is pacing back and forth in his room like a nervous drake about to be shotgunned for dinner.

Diekmann, weary, manages to pull himself together and gets his uniform on correctly a moment before he hears the snarl of Lammerding's voice spike his ear.

The *SS-Gruppenführer* sounds agitated, yes; Diekmann has never heard this tone of voice from Heinze Lammerding; he orders Diekmann to report to him at Limoges within the hour. He wants to discuss the "divisional records" and "what the hell happened to them during the night."

Diekmann cringes at what the general is saying between his words. If something has happened to the "divisional records," something has happened to the "prohibited merchandise" because they were packed together in the half-track that Raoul and the *maquis* had just sent off to the stratosphere.

Lammerding hangs up, and Diekmann slams the phone and swears loud enough for the veins to pop blue in his neck. Heinze's call could only mean that Bruno Walter—the not-so-brilliant Bruno Walter—and his elite unit had run into a substantial shitstorm, probably an ambush they could not break through.

Diekmann sees his life pass before his eyes—or at least his career. He'll never see home again. He will never embrace his wife again or lay down with her. There will not be any more family dinners or celebratory occasions.

He is brain whipped.

Diekmann does not care about Lammerding's damned divisional records, fuck them, or the fucking half-track, or Walter and the burning fetid corpses, or anything else.

Fuck everything!

What upsets him, what he can't understand, is how the information got to Lammerding first. If he had found out before Lammerding, the news would have precluded much difficulty with the general. And the gold?

Diekmann will have to face Lammerding's wrath and possible accusations of stealing the gold himself. After all, he took to the road and avoided loading the half-track on the train to Normandy with the other vehicles. What else would it look like to Lammerding?

What the fuck happened to the gold?

He is certain now that Heinze will accuse him of being an irresponsible SS officer—worse perhaps, stealing the gold for himself—because he had, without authorization and on his own, dispatched a small unit with insufficient security—and without Lammerding's approval. This meeting is not going to be pleasant. If there weren't enough problems with the regiment, now this shit! The gold is becoming more problematic than the regiment and the march north.

Limoges's roads are glazed with morning dew and overnight drizzle.

The more Diekmann thinks about the matter while driving to meet Lammerding, his anxiety intensifies.

Why Lammerding asks himself, did Diekmann take it upon himself to assemble a small convoy and go his separate way, detached from the impressive security of *Das Reich*? Where was he going? Why did he not consult with him?

The implications and the questions are piling up—and the answers are diminishing.

Ten to fifteen minutes into the trip, Diekmann spots a wispy spiral of black smoke painted above the trees and gray sky. He braces himself. His combat experience tells him what he is about to see.

He sniffs the pungent air.

Burnt corpses.

Scorched armor, smoldering rubber.

"Slow down," he orders the driver.

They move warily over a hilly curve on Les Remejoux road, the same road Bruno Walter was instructed to take by Diekmann in their earlier briefing.

And the same road that . . . well, you know.

God damnit!

He has pictures in his mind of what he is about to see.

And there, just over the little hill where Les Remejoux flattens and straightens, there it is—a corrosive pile of melted metal, burning tires, and charcoal-broiled bodies in postures of agony. If Diekmann rolls down the car window, he will smell the piles of smoking flesh and uniforms. He orders the driver to be slow enough to study the festering half-track—absent are the gold cartons fastidiously packed in fresh-smelling sawdust. He slams his fist on the dashboard.

When Diekmann arrives in Limoges, Lammerding tells him his friend Kämpfe is missing, making this meeting even more painful. Until now, Diekmann was unaware of Kämpfe's kidnapping by the *maquis*. Patrols were scouring the area all night, searching diligently for Kämpfe, an SS *Bruder* they all cared for. Indeed, dear *Bruder* Kämpfe is now up in SS heaven—shot, tortured, toasted alive, handcuffed to the steering wheel in an ambulance. Lammerding tells him a survivor of the ambush had been discovered waving his arms at an approaching German patrol. There was a flesh wound on his shoulder from the bullet fired by Raoul.

***

With the door to Lammerding's office closed, the switchboard operator in the vestibule hears bits and pieces of their stormy conversation but not their exact words. The "discussion" is certainly not about Kämpfe's disappearance. The shouting thunderstorm between an *SS-Sturmbannführer* and an *SS-Gruppenführer und Generalleutnant der Waffen-SS* is unthinkable and unheard of in the ranks. Lammerding's point, it can be assumed, is about Diekmann's decision to send the invaluable, lightly guarded three-vehicle convoy at night carrying precious cargo on a minor road *"unattached from the protection of the Das Reich column!"* Diekmann shouts back vehemently, defending himself and his decision—he wasn't taking crap from anyone, including an SS general, a particularly hazardous posture—especially after what he had been through these past few days. We can assume he received no clear orders from Lammerding before Walter left for Normandy—as such, Diekmann made an executive decision. At the same time, Lammerding is entangled with logistical matters about the movement of *Das Reich*. And so it goes for ten minutes, back and forth. Both under severe stress—particularly Lammerding. And now an orderly enters Lammerding's office and hands him an urgent message: *Generalfeldmarschall* von Rundstedt is demanding *hourly* reports regarding the division's progress toward Normandy.

In Lammerding's mind, there isn't any time for suitable vengeance against Kämpfe's abductors—he has to be focused on the gold and his future.

It is unknown what was in either man's mind, but surely, they had to have come to think of the gold as their pension fund, a matter they now took very seriously—and they were not going to allow anything to interfere with getting it back.

This, Lammerding tells Diekmann, is *your* responsibility—*you* find it. And get back *before* eight tonight.

However, a new thought arrives with a certain ironic pleasantness: With Kämpfe's absence, their shares of the thirty boxes of gold now amount to a fifty-fifty split, fifteen cartons of gold ingots apiece, a considerable hefty uptick in what they had when Kämpfe was part of the equation.

Sometime after their heated scrum in Lammerding's office, they probably calmed and started reasoning that the gold could not have gone far. Perhaps they stuck a finger on a map and pointed to Oradour-sur-Glane as the only place for the thirty crates of gold to be immediately stashed; we will never know for sure.

Oradour, two kilometers from the Raoul ambush site, was the only community of any size in the area that could accommodate and hide that many cartons. The people that took the gold from the convoy could not have any previous plan to steal it—they fell upon it accidentally and had to hurry to hide it. Diekmann and the SS had enough heft, power, and intimidation to turn Oradour upside down to find it.

Of course, they had no idea that the gold was hidden in a different location, resting in a hole fifty feet from the half-track it was being transported in.

Since Lammerding now felt sure about the gold's probable destination—Oradour—he wouldn't allow anything to stand in his way of getting it back. He would use the Kämpfe kidnapping as an excuse for keeping *Das Reich* in the area for at least the rest of the day—to buy time, if necessary, to find the gold. Even with von Rundstedt's insistence to move the division immediately hanging over his head, the Kämpfe kidnapping was a matter that could not be left without some retaliation. It would entail a significant and immediate investigation that needed the division's focus and effort. That would buy them some time. And it would be difficult for von Rundstedt to deny. Going after lost or kidnapped soldiers in any army always had precedent over other matters.

Gruppenführer Lammerding ordered Diekmann to report back to Limoges that evening at 8 o'clock. The *SS-Sturmbannführer* was given less than twelve hours to take whatever steps necessary to find and retrieve the gold. One wonders what threat, implied or otherwise, Lammerding had in the back of his mind if Diekmann had not recovered the "prohibitive merchandise" within the twelve hours Lammerding ordered.

Because right now, Diekmann was Lammerding's only hope for "extending their pensions."

After the war, many wondered why Oradour-sur-Glane had been chosen for a massacre; there was no logical reason for the action.

The town sat only two kilometers from the ambush. It was a small, remote town without a history of the *Résistance*'s involvement. Conclusive answers have never evolved; hearsay answers remain abundant. The SS would frequently visit Oradour, eat at restaurants, and enjoy the wine at the outdoor cafes. They befriended some of the people that lived there.

After meeting with Lammerding, Diekmann talked with *Oberleutnant* Karl Gerlach. If you recall, Gerlach had been kidnapped the previous day, stripped down to his underwear, escaped, and wended his way back to the division, where he gave a lengthy statement. He said in his report and told Diekmann in person that after his kidnapping, he had been taken to Oradour-sur-Glane. In Diekmann's mind, this might have indicated that Oradour was brimming with the *maquis* but he did not know this with certainty.

The division was now proceeding to a rapid and lasting cleanup of these bands from the region, intending to become speedily available to reinforce the fighting men and join the line on the invasion front.

Das Reich, at last, was on the move again.

***

After Diekmann dashed out of Lammerding's office, the general took more than a moment to assess the situation, both the gold and the state of *Das Reich*—and himself and the gold.

He reviewed the orders he had received from the insistent von Rundstedt for the division's urgent move north. This and the gold situation gave him little satisfaction. His only consolation now was, with Kämpfe dead, the gold would be evenly divided between himself and Diekmann, his fifty-fifty "partner"—and the specific investigation into the Kämpfe matter would allow *Das Reich* to remain in place for at least one more day.

Elements of *Das Reich* were spread across Lot, Corrèze, and Haute-Vienne. Along the roads from Tulle to Montauban, broken down tanks and destroyed assault guns were a testament to the *Résistance*'s effectiveness. The general's staff's warnings about the technical cost of moving heavy armor on the asphalt roads had been justified. The steep hills and tall trees made unit-to-unit communications sporadic and unreliable. But with the trains sabotaged, there was no other choice.

Lammerding felt a need to immediately write a report assessing the matter and pass it on to the 58th Panzer Corps. The report is a tribute to the effectiveness of the *Résistance*'s ability to slow down *Das Reich* at a time when the division could have done much to blunt the Allies at Normandy.

In a testament to the *Résistance*, Lammerding wrote an accurate, truthful "state of the division" memorandum. It explained *Das Reich* was dispersed over three hundred kilometers and lacked advanced preparation for operations and supplies. Much of the division's woes resulted from the *maquisards'* persistent attacking and slowing down the division. Sixty percent of Lammerding tanks—an unprecedented number—and towing vehicles were unserviceable and could only be back in service after the division received spare parts—and those parts were nowhere to be seen. Further, none of the vehicles or tanks could be functional without fuel—which was also out of sight. Only the division's wheeled vehicles were capable of joining the fight. The *maquis* held certain areas along the march to Normandy and stood ready to pounce immediately. This, coupled with the French government's capabilities, had become stagnant. When associated with the division's complex reorganization and supplies are obtained, operational orders can be issued and their goals achieved.

In this instance, unlike others, Lammerding signed the memorandum and passed it on.

***

At this point, a review of Heinze Lammerding's career might be helpful.

First, he received a degree in engineering before the war began. This partially held him together through the end of his career to war's end—his engineering degree would, he figured, provide job security and, hopefully, success. He was uncertain, though, about a potential pension once discharged. He indeed had to know that soldiers convicted of war crimes did not receive a pension—thus, he had to do everything he could to plan for this possibility. But when things started to go badly for Heinze as the war began to falter for Germany, he knew that things would not end well for him; he had many hurdles to overcome. Thus, pursuing gold at this moment was paramount in his mind. And there was the matter of his signature on orders issued by *SS-Obergruppenführer* Erich Julius Eberhard von dem Bach-Zelewski the *Höherer SS- und Polizeiführer* (Higher SS and Police Leader, HSSPF), and SS Army Group Centre Rear Area Chief for occupied Europe. Dem Bach-Zelewski held control and issued orders for the infamous *Einsatzgruppen* (deployment groups) and the murder of thousands of Russians. Lammerding knew this, signed orders relating to these executions, and knew he would be prosecuted as a war criminal.

So much depended on the gold that it made Lammerding a desperate man.

***

Sturmbannführer Diekmann's First Battalion drove into Limoges at around 6:30 a.m. on 9 June, four hours after the rest of the *Der Führer* division.

For Diekmann, it wasn't easy driving into Limoges. They suffered numerous losses and had to clear tree barriers. Diekmann seemed tense and strained.

We emphasize "tense and strained" because we believe that Diekmann's focus, his feelings, were indeed not based on the kidnapping of his friend, Kämpfe. However, he cherished their friendship, but not now—*now* was about the gold he believed was secreted somewhere in the Oradour village. What to do about securing that treasure had been paramount to his mind. Undoubtedly, Diekmann had the resources to scrub the whole village—he would use his troops and provide a veiled excuse to tear the place apart for multiple boxes enigmatically marked. There was no other way for Diekmann. He could not do it alone. Also, like

Lammerding, Diekmann, who had ordered atrocities during the march from Russia to France, knew, like Lammerding, that there was a strong prospect that he would eventually be tried for war crimes.

Early the following day, 10 June, Diekmann was back at *Der Führer* HQ in Limoges, where he met with Weidinger. According to Weidinger, Diekmann appeared "nervous and abrupt." Diekmann told Weidinger that while in St. Junien, two French civilians approached him, saying that "a high German official" (Kämpfe, more than likely) had been captured and was being held prisoner in Oradour. Diekmann's ears perked. The Frenchmen stated that the prisoner was being tortured for information and could not say anything to satisfy his captor's questions; they continued to beat and torture him. Later that day, the German prisoner would be executed in a brutal and sadistic manner: he would be publicly burned alive amid a celebration in Oradour. Further, the two Frenchmen said everyone in Oradour was working with the *maquis*, which was also untrue.

Nevertheless, Diekmann wasted no time requesting permission to enter Oradour, search for Kämpfe, and determine if there was any truth to the rumors. The regimental commander then informed Diekmann of the other events in the Oradour area on the previous day (the capture of Gerlach). It took him no time to grant Diekmann permission to enter Oradour. But there was a caveat.

If Kämpfe was not found, Diekmann would bring back prisoners for negotiations with the *Résistance* to release Kämpfe in exchange for the prisoner. Diekmann agreed.

Diekmann had inadvertently stumbled upon a perfect reason to invade Oradour and stated so in Weidinger's report: "*Sturmbannführer* Diekmann," Weidinger wrote, "requests permission from the regiment commander to take a company there [Oradour] to free the prisoner [Kämpfe]." This would be an excellent cover to rip Oradour apart and search for the gold; without it, Diekmann might have had a hard time explaining why he attacked such an insignificant town as Oradour—and wasted precious resources.

From what we know about the gold, *Sturmbannführer* Diekmann, and *Gruppenführer* Lammerding, it seems clear that Diekmann drove into Oradour focused on his objective and certainly nothing else.

And it had nothing to do with massacring 642 people.

Find the gold.

All else was irrelevant.

Theories purport to show why Oradour-sur-Glane was the target of such a horrendous unadulterated massacre. All the theories bear little or no truth. Today, based on what has been learned of Diekmann, the gold, and *ratissages*, there is no longer a possibility of discovering the definitive truth about Diekmann's motive; only Diekmann knew.

But this is true:

Diekmann did not purposefully direct his battalion into Oradour and order them to massacre 642 Frenchmen; strategically, there was no reason for this. When he discovered the gold missing from the ambushed half-tracks, he had to report this to Lammerding. Where did the gold go? Both wanted to know immediately. And lest we forget: Time was running out.

In some regards, that much gold was a much more significant concern than *Das Reich* and the battle at Normandy. Lammerding and Diekmann had to have decided after their heated, unprecedented shouting match that the most likely place was within the geographical boundaries of Oradour-sur-Glane.

For what other reason did Diekmann and the SS select Oradour and kill 642 men, women, children, and babies on 10 June 1944? Some who knew are now dead. Others always had solid motives for lying, especially amid imminent war crimes trials and firing squads. Certain colleagues of Diekmann's knew the answers but have never revealed them.

No terrorists were hiding in Oradour.

Oradour was hundreds of miles away from Normandy.

It was a peaceful town in a pastoral setting known primarily for the food served in its restaurants.

An attack by terrorists had never originated from the town.

Diekmann's reason for entering the town?

He wanted to tear it up with the SS resources he had to find thirty cartons of gold that would secure himself and Lammerding their "extended pensions."

The propensity of German soldiers to receive pensions at the end of WWII was granted for their service and obedience to Germany, for following orders as they had sworn they would. However, in some cases, an individual of the Waffen-SS did not get a pension if he was guilty of war crimes. Lammerding knew this, where his career was going, and that he might eventually be classified as a war criminal after the war and was looking out for himself.

Here are more prominent hypotheses:

First: many asserted that the massacre was a tragic error—Diekmann and his battalion attacked Oradour-sur-Glane, whereas the *maquisards*, some suspected, were in Oradour-sur-Vayres, a town twenty miles southwestward near the forest of Rochechouart where the FTP had killed several German soldiers in recent weeks. Because of the alleged attack perpetuated on the Germans in Oradour-sur-Vayres, the Germans felt obligated to conduct reprisals. Evidence to support this does not exist.

Second: some allege that the *maquis* had perpetrated a horrendous atrocity against a German ambulance convoy adjacent to Oradour. This bears a bit of logical consideration because Kämpfe and three other German soldiers were found locked in a bullet-ridden German ambulance, where they were doused with gasoline and burned alive. Kämpfe was found tied to the ambulance's steering wheel and set on fire with the other German soldiers while they were still breathing.

Third: the zeal and enthusiasm the young SS men had for National Socialism was something they were born into, that they grew up with, and that propelled them to select Oradour as a killing place arbitrarily, demonstrating their zeal for Führer and Fatherland. This zeal is a radical thought; while young German soldiers were enthusiastic about fighting for Germany, the act of slaughtering 642 people was beyond their thinking.

The SS was evil in many ways—brutal, heartless, ruthless—but they never arbitrarily selected a raid out of thin air. In their Germanic ardor for planning and perfectionism, they set about in an orderly manner and planned their attacks, which were justified according to their logic. In their savagery, the SS often viewed their actions as warranted, a form of revenge against the *maquis* for killing and torturing unarmed SS men—from their perspective, another logical step.

And finally, one more wrong reason: Diekmann acted upon poor intelligence from French sources that might have had a score to settle with Oradour. When Diekmann led his detachment into Oradour that afternoon, his officers expected him to do what he had done many times before: make examples and conduct salutary executions and burnings.

***

By mid-morning on the tenth, Diekmann was back in St. Junien and held discussions with Kleist of the Gestapo and the *Milice*.

Afterward, he ordered his Third Company, commanded by *SS-Hauptsturmführer* Otto Kahn (soon to be a significant player in the massacre), to move out for an operation at Oradour. Around 1:30, Diekmann, the reluctant Kahn, and 120 men in a convoy of two half-tracks, eight trucks, and a motorcycle drove east of St. Junien, taking an indirect route to Oradour-sur-Glane. Diekmann rode in his commandeered Citroën Deux with his young Alsatian driver and Lange, his adjutant.

After the war, some stated that Diekmann halted his detachment to give his men a hurried briefing or "pep talk" about their imminent "search and destroy" operation. Perhaps he notified them of the mysterious boxes with the enigmatic lettering, not revealing what was inside but bringing them to him. One officer in the group, *SS-Obersturmbannführer* Heinze Barth, said to a group of recruits, "You are going to see some blood flow today! And we'll also find out what the Alsatians are made of!" Barth had an excellent notion of what Diekmann had in mind before rolling into Oradour that day. A few minutes later, the column moved out toward Oradour, taking the N41 as far as Loubier and then the D3.

They arrived at the south end of Oradour-sur-Glane around 1:30 p.m. where, true or not, according to Diekmann, they came upon three dead German Waffen-SS men. This sight of three dead comrades, some said, was what set off Diekmann's massacre. Now, it was told, this was cause for a reprisal, these three dead Germans. Here, the German point of view applies: "Reprisals conformed with international military law under the second Hague Convention." Following the trial conducted in Belgium on the execution of hostages by German troops and one conducted in Italy for the Ardeatine massacre, "one can conclude that the Tulle massacre violated the law of armed conflict," wrote Bruno Kertheuser, who made a study of the slaughter, and disputes the word "reprisals," particularly in the case of the Tulle massacre: "The death and deportation of hundreds of inhabitants of Tulle on the 9th and 10th of June *are very clearly a war crime* [emphasis added]. Any other name for Tulle and Oradour, like that of reprisals, is a whitewashing, an absolving measure, belonging to the jargon of perpetrators of these crimes and participants in their logic with them."

Without knowing Diekmann's true motive—finding the gold for himself and Lammerding—many landed on what they thought was the one valid reason for the massacre at Tulle, "that it was carried out to punish the capital of the *Résistance*, Corrèze, in order to terrorize other regions, this in accordance with the established practices of the Wehrmacht and the Waffen-SS on the Eastern Front."

Massets farm was the place *Sturmbannführer* Diekmann set up his command, situated between Oradour and the village of Bordes. There, he drafted a plan of attack.

Then SS troops surrounded Oradour, starting first at the bridge.

Soldiers in pea green and tan smocks spread throughout the village. To complete the encirclement, SS troops from Diekmann's detachment were positioned outside the village.

Oradour was now locked in an unyielding vice.

The initial phase of Diekmann's chilling plan was to assemble the population on the town's fairground, thus preventing escape.

Meanwhile, according to several witnesses, no antagonism emanated from the SS at this moment. Their pretext was to conduct "identity checks," which seemed to calm everyone, as it had done dozens of times before. Simultaneously, the German trucks and half-tracks were going about the town loading people and dropping them off at the fairgrounds—a sort of German taxi service that seemed to calm the people. German discipline and duplicitousness prevented panic among the citizenry making the SS's task easier.

According to Robert Hébras, an Oradour massacre survivor from Laudry's Barn, as time passed, the crowd kept expanding to the point that Hébras could not recall such a large crowd in the village. To assuage the group, the Germans kept telling them it was only for an identification check. At this point, German half-tracks were disgorging people they had previously picked up around the village. The soldiers, meanwhile, were positioned around the square, leveling machine guns at the assembly while the bright sunlight and heat were becoming unbearable. Despite this, the crowd was lively and chatty, as if this were just another routine check—little did they imagine what would happen. At that moment, approximately six hundred people gathered, most showing no sign of panic.

On March 1, 2023, *The New York Times* reported the death of Robert Hébras; the headline said: "Robert Hébras, Last Survivor of a 1944 Massacre in France." His death, at ninety-seven, was reported by President Emmanuel Macron via Twitter.

"The bullets," Hébras said, "had passed through the others, and by the time they reached me, they no longer had the power to go in deep." The *Times* wrote "that the massacre, which occurred days after the D-Day invasion, traumatized France. The ruins of the original village were declared a memorial, left in their burned-out conditions as a reminder of the atrocity."

Mr. Hébras, in an interview for the Associated Press, said, "Everyone makes money from the name Oradour-sur-Glane." His words were not that distant from the truth.

***

To the British and Americans, Oradour-sur-Glane was a small quaint town, not a bustling village. It included 254 buildings, two small hotels, several shops, and charming cafes. Before it was built in 1911, the tramway to Limoges was protested by the people because they felt it would mar the old-world appearance of the main street, Rue Emile Desourteaux, with necessary overhanging cables and pylons—but they provided electricity and brought the village within easy commuting distance of Limoges. The structures were twentieth-century architecture with privet hedges. Because of Allied bombings throughout Europe, the town had been burgeoning since the war started with ragtag refugees, as did other French rural cities.

Today, as in all of France, the news of the Allied landing promised an end to the long, painful struggle, but the fighting was distant enough to pose no threat or cause fear. Many people came into the village to collect their tobacco ration, issued every ten days, or to do the weekly shopping. The three schools were full; it was the day for vaccinations and a medical inspection. The boys' school opposite the tram station held sixty-four children. The girls' was divided into three classrooms and held 106. And there was also a special school for the little Lorrainer refugees.

By the time Diekmann and his detachment drove in, Oradour would have come to full life. Fishermen took the tram from Limoges to catch fish in the Glane. People from around the area sought readily available food. The sky had cleared, but the sun shone harshly, filling the air with humidity. Oradour, at this hour, was an unprepossessing town, but in the middle of a war that would hopefully end soon. Oradour was a haven for many, considering what was happening in Normandy. Initially, this German intrusion appeared less lethal than those in the past.

But on 10 June, around 2:15 p.m., Oradour would never again be seen like this—a tableau frozen forever.

The normal population of 330 had enlarged to about 650, driven to this figure by the pressures of war, and never resumed what the clock said before these last moments.

In his diary, Michel Forest wrote, "This place is pervaded by classical tranquility, in which one can live as a human being should. Everything here is done in moderation in the word's best sense."

At this hour, 2:15, the air was shattered by the metallic snarl of Diekmann's trucks and half-tracks rattling along the streets of Oradour, the vehicles bristling with steel helmets and camouflaged smocks of Waffen-SS men covering the houses with their weapons—this caused immediate bewilderment and surprise.

Until now, there had been no battles in Oradour, no gunfights or killings, no engagements with the Boche, no suspected terrorists, just an easy tranquility unmarked by mayhem or massacre.

Until now.

While some in Oradour were calm, some were terrified of the Germans. The sight and sound of soldiers cocking the bolts on their weapons was alarming.

Soon the troopers fanned out, firing their weapons in the air, smashing the doors with rifle butts, firing in the air, and pushing and dragging families into the streets. Families from outlying areas were trucked in and dropped off at Champs de Foire by impatient German soldiers.

The town crier, M. Depierrefiche, walked up to Diekmann and was hastily pushed through several streets by two SS troopers—he was ordered to beat his drum telling the people that the Germans said to assemble immediately in the Champ de Foire, the small central square, and to take their identity papers with them. Most of the townspeople were relieved to hear this because, well, this was turning out to be just another rude, inconvenient identity check.

Like his father, Dr. Laternser Desourteaux, the mayor of Oradour, tried to assure a young boy that ran to him that all was okay, but he was not persuaded; he fled home and hid in the loft. He tried to persuade his parents that they were in danger, then he ran to the fields and stayed there all afternoon.

Other parents shouted, "Hide, hide!"

A Jewish couple staying at the Hôtel Avril desperately took their daughters, eighteen and twenty-two, and their nine-year-old son into a bolt hole under the staircase by the garden door. A Jewish dentist ran as fast as he could into the fields.

Men were being driven from the fields. Mme. Binet, the girls' school principal, had been ill in bed but now appeared with a coat over her nightdress. A sick old man was carried by his two sons.

The Abbé Lorrainers was pushed out of his house with his sister and a friend.

SS troopers, menacing and relentless, burst into classrooms at the girls' school yelling, "*Alle raus!*" The teacher obeyed without haste and mustered her pupils like a snake toward the square. Some children were crying but obeyed because everyone in Oradour was compliant.

Still, around 2:45, Oradour's entire population, except for some old, *infirmes*, still lingered in their beds or hiding places. At the Champ de Foire square, it was quickly seen and understood that the men and women had been separated.

German machine gun teams had set up their Spandau guns—the formidable Maxim LMG 08/15 and nicknamed "the Devil's paintbrush"—were covering the square, the gunners on their stomachs at their weapons, the brass cartridges sparkling gold in the brilliant sunlight, snaking into the breeches. Many there seemed calm, others bewildered, clutching each other's hands.

The men were standing around, most in faded blue overalls, gray or black suits, many wearing much-mended shoes. The local *gendarme*, Duquerry, wore his uniform. The baker, Boucholle, was standing shirtless, anxious to get back to his customers.

Dr. Jean Desourteaux, the medical doctor and the mayor's son, had hastened from his car to the corner where his father was talking to a German officer. The officer—either Diekmann or Kahn—demanded that the mayor select thirty hostages—"I cannot do that," he replied. In the mid-distance, the sound of erratic gunfire erupted in an uneven pattern. They did not know that isolated civilians were either dead or dying here and there throughout Oradour, but they were acutely aware that danger was filling the air.

By now, the nave in the church began to be choked with clumps of women and whimpering children, the air thick and humid.

Till now, the Germans moved about casually, some laughing, smoking French cigarettes.

But suddenly, they started to move furtively, decisively, tigers straining for the kill, announcing that all women and children that remained here would go to the church. With their rifles at the port, the SS detail directed the long procession of old and young, mothers and their babies, and grandmothers supported by their families. They shuffled across the road and went a few yards down the hill to the tall church with red Romanesque tiles and a turreted spire. The crucified Christ up on the outer wall stared down at them, sadly as dumbfounded as they were.

Meanwhile, Dr. Desourteaux again informed the German officer that "I cannot nominate hostages." He was seized and escorted to the town hall (in the same building as the boys' school opposite the tramway station). He was returned to the German officer ten minutes later. Again, the officer demanded hostages. Desourteaux replied, "Very well, I nominate myself, and if necessary, my family too." The officer ignored the answer, and the mayor was ordered to join the rest of the men.

Two hundred men waited for the next thirty minutes in the broiling sun and humid air. Some could not stand any longer; they sat. Some were talking. The soldiers appeared relaxed, some laughing. Finally, the officer who had addressed the mayor told the men, through an interpreter, to stand up and be quiet. He asked if they owned guns. The officer did not appear interested when some said they owned hunting rifles. The officer insisted that terrorists owned weapons and munitions in Oradour and that a search would be conducted through the whole town, and "God help you if we find an unreported gun." While this was being carried on, the villagers would be put into barns, garages, and other holding areas, and as soon as the weapons were found, those not implicated would be set free. The men, hearing this, were relieved—because no amount of searching would produce weapons that did not exist in Oradour.

The Germans knew how to act duplicitously when they wanted to.

But the men were not stupid. They knew the Germans were being deceitful and suspected something ominous would fall once the false smiles and soft words diminished.

About two hundred men were separated into five groups of varying sizes—the largest around sixty—and marched off with their German escorts to the Laudry barn. There, they were ordered to drag out farm wagons and bales of hay. The Germans had machine guns and stretched out beside them. Other soldiers had light machine guns, two sub-machine guns, and two rifles, and the NCO in charge was holding a pistol, a 9 mm Luger with a long barrel and shiny black finish. Some of the captives sat on the ground, others on bales of hay. Fifteen minutes passed, and it became sweltering and humid. But the men were not that concerned because they knew that the search of the village would take time. But the calm ended abruptly: Joseph Berman, the barber who understood German, said that he heard one of the soldiers say they would shoot everyone. When they heard this, they were unconvinced.

Before the men could react, a shot rang out from a pistol coming from the direction of the village green. This would have been Kahn's pistol firing in the air.

A signal for the executions to begin.

The machine gunners in the front of the barn opened fire with their Spandaus, the "devil's paintbrush," so-called for its rapid fire. The soldiers with rifles and submachine guns let loose. They deliberately aimed at the victim's legs to prevent them from escaping. The noise of the firing was brutal and deafening; many soldiers filled their ears with cotton. There were screams, but many died so quickly that they could not cry out. When the shooting ended, the barn was filled with dust and muted beams of sunlight. Moans and cries clawed the air. Marcel Bissaud, whose head rested on a dead body, cried, "The bastards! They have cut off my other leg!" (He had lost a leg in WWI).

The Germans hauled straw, kindling, ladders, wagon wheels, and any combustibles that they could find and heaped them on top of the bodies. Finally, the soldiers retreated down the road. They returned fifteen minutes later and were yelling like "savage beasts."

The survivors in the barn knew what was pending.

The soldiers took the animals and guided them from the barn; some using pitchforks started poking as they clambered over the bodies to finish off the wounded.

Two Germans standing outside the barn had to step away from the heat of the fire that was building.

As the fire increased, Robert Hébras, an Oradour survivor, managed to extricate himself from the dead bodies and expected to be shot immediately. He made his way to a door and escaped.

Soon, two soldiers made it to the woodpile, and one climbed a ladder into the loft with a box of matches and lit some straw. Climbing down, he fired a few incendiary rounds into the roof. Soon, embers began falling on the victims below; five villagers managed to escape. When looking down Cemetery Road, soldiers were there blocking off their escape. They quickly took cover in the first of three brick-and-tile rabbit hutches.

**

The men, the women, and the children were separated and herded to the church and directed inside; the Germans closed the doors. Some Germans came in and inspected the church's interior like prospective buyers. There, approximately 250 women and 200 children were crammed into a church with a seating capacity of 300; they waited in silence, anxious. More than 60 of the children were under six years of age; some were in baby carriages, and some were in their mothers' arms; they waited for about ninety minutes. At 5:00 p.m., two Germans walked in carrying a box about a foot long with several "tangled white strings" attached. The box appeared heavy, and the Germans placed it on two chairs before the altar, removed the cover, and untangled the fuses (the white strings).

Then, without saying a word, the two Germans lit the fuses and exited via the Sainte Anne chapel to the right of the nave. There was no panic among the woman and children because most could not see the box and the smoldering fuses. Soon, there was a loud explosion blowing out the stained-glass window. Acrid smoke filled the church. The smoke was causing asphyxiation, and now the women and children cried in panic, screaming and trying to escape the fumes. Near the locked door in the Sainte Anne chapel, a crush of bodies was trying to escape the horror looming behind them; some ran. Outside, machine gun fire was directed at them, and many fell dead and wounded.

Opening the church doors, the soldiers came in as far as the sacristy and sprayed them with machine gun fire. Soldiers first shoot at people's legs to prevent them from running—an old trick learned on the Russian front. Simultaneously, other soldiers were in the basement shooting up through the floorboards. Mme. Rouffranche's unmarried daughter, Andrée, was shot in the throat and killed. The Germans then threw grenades into the sacristy basement igniting the wooden floor. Shortly after, Mme. Rouffranche's older daughter, Amélie Peyroux, and others were burned to death.

The children and women were locked up in the church; the soldiers of the Third Company went about looting and setting fire to the buildings in Oradour. *Sturmbannführer* Diekmann, the highest-ranking officer in Oradour that day, did nothing to stop them. Mainly, he kept going about searching for specially marked boxes with gold. Some who stayed in the building were burned alive. When the soldiers arrived, the Beaubreuil brothers hid under a trap door in the Mercier house. They could hear the sound of looting and the crackle of flames. They crept out of their hiding space, crossed through the fire on the floor, and escaped out the back.

When news of the Oradour massacre spread by word of mouth on Monday, 12 June, a Wehrmacht convoy drove into the town and worked for several hours digging two mass graves. Before they left, the Germans helped themselves to the overlooked fowl. Many volunteers, doctors, nurses, sanitary workers, civil defense teams, and priests began arriving. They started the dreadful task of removing and identifying bodies already degraded by the awful heat and humidity. Their task was to work on the bodies of an entire community—the burnt-out homes, shops, garages, cars, crockery, cutlery, scorched living rooms, stray cats and dogs, and children's toys.

On Sunday morning at about 11 a.m. Diekmann's men drove out of Oradour, loaded with pillaged loot and livestock. There is no record of how he appeared or his demeanor or mental state after the slaughter. We can only say that the *Sturmbannführer* had to have been distraught. There is no indication anywhere that he found his "extended pension" nestled in the rubble and ash before or after the murder of 642 people and the razing of the town. However, within days, Diekmann's actions were met with a surprisingly negative push-back for what was committed under his command.

The toll of death and destruction was inconceivable.

In all, 642 people had been massacred (245 women, 207 children, and 190 men). All 328 buildings had been destroyed.

Oradour-sur-Glane no longer existed.

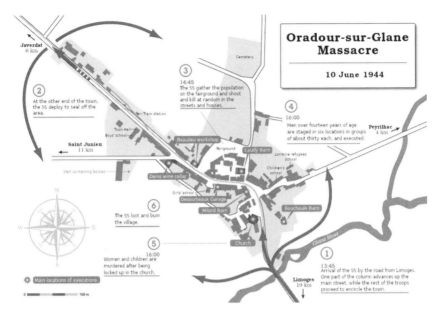

Oradour-sur-Glane Massacre

10 June 1944

Javerdat 6 km

(2) At the other end of the town, the SS deploy to seal off the area.

Saint Junien 11 km

Cemetery

(3) 14:45 The SS gather the population on the fairground and shoot and kill at random in the streets and houses.

(4) 16:00 Men over fourteen years of age are staged in six locations in groups of about thirty each, and executed.

Peyrilhac 4 km

Tram station

Town Hall

Boys' school

Beaulieu workshop

Laudy Barn

Lorraine refugees school

Children's school

Well containing bodies

Denis wine cellar

Girls' school

Desourteaux Garage

(6) The SS loot and burn the village.

Milord Barn

Bouchoule Barn

Glane River

N W E S

(5) 16:00 Women and children are murdered after being locked up in the church.

Church

(1) 13:45 Arrival of the SS by the road from Limoges. One part of the column advances up the main street, while the rest of the troops proceed to encircle the town.

Limoges 19 km

Main locations of executions

0 ▬▬▬▬ 100 m

Timeline of the massacre.

SS-Gruppenführer Heinze Lammerding, 38, shown here wearing the rank gorgets of a major general, one rank below lieutenant general. At his neck is the lauded "tin tie," the Knights Cross awarded for his leadership in the Russian campaign before moving on to southwestern France.

Otto Weidinger. A much-decorated officer, Weidinger was a regimental commander in *Der Führer,* a component of *Das Reich.* After the war, he wrote a voluminous but dubious five-volume *apologia* regarding the activities of *Das Reich* in Russia and France. He was peripherally involved in the Oradour massacre, tried, and found not guilty. Pictured here as an *SS-Sturmbannführer* (Major).

During the march from Montauban, France, to Normandy (left to right): The popular *SS-Sturmbannführer* (Major) Helmut Kämpfe, days before the *Résistance* murdered and burnt him alive while shackled inside an ambulance; *SS-Sturmbannführer* (Major) Ernst Krag, artillery regiment officer and later Knight's Cross recipient; *SS-Sturmbannführer* (Major) Albert Stuckler of the SD; and *Das Reich* division commander *SS-Gruppenführer* (Major General) Heinze Bernard Lammerding. A dueling scar is barely visible on Lammerding's cheek. Note the variety of uniforms from Stuckler's white shirt, tie, and black leather overcoat. His SS "crusher cap" was a favorite look and deliberately shaped this way. Some said the higher the peak, the more arrogant the wearer.

A week after the massacre.

Aerial view of Oradour.

Gravestone of Adolf Diekmann.

Multiple bodies stacked together. Most of the victims died from asphyxiation or burning. There were many others that were shot. Teams of doctors and local citizens spent days trying to identify them, a daunting task.

9

Court-Martial

On Sunday, 11 June, *Sturmbannführer* Diekmann's convoy drove out of Oradour weighed down with livestock and pillaged loot taken from the homes and shops in the town—not unusual for soldiers of all countries. One of the last trucks to pull out was towing a stolen car. The cable snapped, and the car careered into a cement pylon, injuring the SS driver, the final Oradour "victim." Then, they were gone. Leaving behind death and devastation.

So, what happened in Oradour?

What was in Diekmann's mind as he left behind a colossus of killing, destruction, and unparalleled grief?

What psychological thoughts prompted those terrible moments can be explored for naught. It would take hundreds of psychiatrists, psychologists, and sociologists a hundred thousand years to discern, evaluate, and conclude how one human could have been so cruel; there are no words.

The gold, in the end, motivated Diekmann to toss the town upside down and, if he was lucky, to find the boxes of "prohibited merchandise" that would somehow have given him a worry-free path through his retirement—if he ever outlasted the war and lived a long life. He and Lammerding came upon an opportunity to abandon their morals and seize an opportunity many other humans would also have taken. It did not matter that such a load of gold—approaching $5 million at that time—could have been in their possession through the remainder of the war without discovery. Of course, if they thought about that, the notion was abandoned in favor of success. Because, at this time, nothing much mattered more than the possession and protection of the gold both had dearly coveted and considered theirs.

But regarding the massacre at Oradour, and with their knowledge of Auschwitz, Buchenwald, Bergen-Belsen, and numerous others KZ camps, Diekmann and Kahn could, with a clear German conscience, easily repeat such horrific acts—they had precedent on their side. These were men who, since their earliest years growing up in Germany, were imbued with National Socialism, with Adolf Hitler's guiding spirit and elitism. Diekmann attended a National Socialist Cadet School and was said by his comrades (and the men in his regiment) to have a pleasing, infectious laugh. But on the other side, he was a ruthless, easily agitated officer from whom his men kept a distance.

After the massacre, at 5:30 p.m., Diekmann handed in his only report of the action to his commanding officer at the Regimental Headquarters in Limoges.

The following pertains to Diekmann's actions at Oradour and comes from Otto Weidinger's book *Comrades to the End*:

The Company had encountered Résistance in Oradour, and the bodies of executed German soldiers were found. It then occupied the village and immediately conducted an intensive search of the houses. Unfortunately, this failed to turn up Kämpfe [a popular officer who was missing from the day before, when he was apparently abducted while doing a route recon]; however, large quantities of weapons and ammunition were found. Therefore, all the men of the village were shot, who were surely *Maquisards*. The women and children were locked up in the church while all this was going on. Then the village was set on fire, as a result of which the ammunition that was stored in almost every house went up. The burning of the village resulted in fire spreading to the church, where ammunition had also been hidden in the roof. The church burned down very rapidly, and the women and children lost their lives.

These are the only memorialized words of Diekmann—terse, evasive, somewhat self-serving, painting a less than a thorough picture of his involvement and motivation at Oradour and void of informative detail concerning a monumental event in WWII history.

On the road through Dordogne on 8 June, Diekmann would command the first of several Oradours: he commanded a *ratissage* at Frayssinet-le-Gelat, while *Das Reich* was still quartered at Montauban: 400 civilians had been assembled in the central square much the same way as Oradour. An older woman, frightened and nervous, fired a shotgun, intentional or not, at the German intruders and was hanged, along with two nieces who shared her house. Their bodies were thrown into a bonfire. Ten hostages were shot, and a father begged to embrace his fifteen-year-old son for the last time. Kahn quickly devised a solution: he shot both of them as they stood in each other's arms.

It can be said that neither *SS-Gruppenführer* Lammerding nor *SS-Standartführer* Stadler gave Diekmann a direct order to destroy Oradour. However, throughout their years in the SS, there is no doubt that Diekmann and his fellow officers and NCOs had been shooting and killing civilians almost routinely. If you recall, on 3 February 1944, *Generalfeldmarschall* Hugo Sperrle issued a notorious order—the Sperrle Orders—to the Occupation forces in France; it decreed the most ruthless attitude toward civilians at the slightest sign of attack or implacability: "There will be an immediate return of fire . . . immediate burning down of the houses. . . . If thereby innocent people are hit, that is regrettable but entirely the fault of the terrorists." And Lammerding had issued numerous similar orders demanding savage reprisals in terrorist areas.

At this point in the narrative, we would be remiss if we bypassed the question of the gold: What happened to the hundreds of gold bars between 10 June 1944 and the war's end?

We believe we have the answer, as you will see later.

***

In his regimental history of *Der Führer, SS-Sturmbannführer* Weidinger wrote of the first news of the Oradour tragedy concerning Diekmann; he wrote that Diekmann returned on 10 June to the Regiment and had met with resistance in Oradour. Upon entering Oradour, Diekmann had encountered several murdered German soldiers, which incensed him and caused him to order the occupation of the entire town. Immediately, they began searching the town for terrorists. During this procedure, they did not come upon any. According to Diekmann, they then determined that the entire town could be identified as *maquisard* and shot. This would be their retribution for the murdered Germans.

Women and children had been locked in the church during this time, the town was set on fire, and the hidden ammunition began cooking off.

When Diekmann's command officer, *SS-Sturmbannführer* Stadler, heard of this, he was shocked:

"Diekmann," he said, "you could pay heavily for this. I shall request that you be court-martialed immediately by the division! I cannot let something like this rest on the shoulder of the regiment!"

Stadler was also enraged that Diekmann had not carried out his order to bring back *maquis* prisoners should Kämpfe not be found. Deeply disturbed, he sent Diekmann off to write a detailed report.

It needs to be noted here that Diekmann had painted himself into a corner between this accusation and his desire to find the gold. Diekmann did not defend himself but, at the time, was expected to explain the event at a military hearing. Stadler reported this to Lammerding—the events at Oradour—and recommended Diekmann's court-martial after the arrival of the divisional commander, *Brigadeführer* Lammerding. As such, preparations were being made to organize the procedure.

Intelligence officer Kowatsch overheard a radio message sent by a senior *maquis* staff officer after the events of Oradour and Tulle, ordering that all fighting against the Germans was to cease until the division *Das Reich* left central France. Another message on an enemy wavelength claimed that Kämpfe has been shot and burned alive to avenge the destruction of Oradour.

Weidinger, however, felt that Diekmann went far beyond his commander's orders and took a personal initiative *that could not be regarded as an excess*. First, according to Weidinger, it must be realized that Diekmann wanted to free his friend Kämpfe. If he did not find Kämpfe and did not take hostages, as he had been ordered to, he must have concluded that Kämpfe could no longer be alive and, therefore, could not be released.

In Weidinger's judgment, Diekmann also had to consider the general instruction of OB Westphal: the Sperrle Orders and the special order of the corps concerning terrorists. Eyewitnesses reported that Diekmann did not take the decision lightly. The destruction of Oradour by Diekmann, again according to Weidinger, could not be blamed upon the leadership of the *Der Führer* regiment, the *Das Reich* division, or any other German authority.

Here, the reports should be adjudged by the reader. Weidinger is naturally looking at the matter to protect his *Bruderschaft* (brotherhood) and Diekmann and to excuse the actions of *Der Führer*. There are several points of contention here: Weidinger implies that there were numerous ammunition stores in *all* the homes at

Oradour, as if it were okay, because of this mistruth, to kill 642 people and set off ammunition supposedly stored in the church steeple. This might have been the case, but there seems to be no proof that Oradour's residents were storing ammunition in their edifices. Beyond secreted ammunitions, Weidinger passes a magical wand across Diekmann's brow, stating, "*The fact that Diekmann went far beyond his commander's orders and took personal initiative can no longer be regarded as an excess.*" Here Weidinger stops short of saying that Diekmann should be given a decoration—perhaps the Knight's Cross?—for his actions and that what he did in Oradour was not only correct but laudable; he took the initiative as any good SS officer would have.

Further, Weidinger adds, "In his judgment, Diekmann also had to consider the general instruction of OB West, the Sperrle Orders, and the special order of the corps concerning terrorists." This might be true because the Sperrle Orders had to be obeyed. Weidinger's report is nothing short of a whitewash. Further, the report suggests that *Das Reich* made nothing of Diekmann's involvement at Oradour until Vichy forced statements from the division and army headquarters caught up with the division in Normandy for an explanation. Until then, no investigation had been initiated to investigate Diekmann and the Oradour massacre.

If the armed *résistants* had never attacked the Germans the moment they stepped onto French soil—May 10–June 25, 1940— there would never have been reprisals. Most of the young men in the German army believed they were in France as an occupation force—policemen—not killers of women and children and babies. At the time, not all killings were illegal; some were accepted by the rules of law. Reprisals, within reason, according to the Geneva Convention, were not outlawed by the SS elite force.

Eisenhower, a seasoned soldier and a brilliant tactician, could not expect the Germans to accept his broadcast demanding that all captured *maquisards* should be treated as prisoners of war; he knew better and was good at politics. In combat, civilians who take up arms against an armed force have always been liable to summary execution—whatever the Hague Convention might say. It is foolish to overthink German looting when Allied forces throughout Europe were equally liable to grab anything not nailed down. Think of the thousands of American soldiers who, after the war, took "bring backs" home—Nazi daggers, medals, artwork, uniforms, personal items, etcetera. Today's demand is insatiable, and their values usually increase about 10 percent per year. The Liberating Armies—American, British, Polish—were no more popular among civilians in many parts of France—particularly Normandy—than were the occupiers. They "leveled everything in front of them" and then, to show their "benevolence," distributed Hershey's chocolate, chewing gum, C rations, and Lucky Strikes.

The Germans in French-Occupied France always had a problem with the Allies viewing them as killers. Wehrmacht officers, for example, always asked, "If it was just for the British to shoot Sinn Feiners in 1921, why was it unacceptable for the Germans to shoot French *résistants* bearing arms and killing Germans."

Yet, despite this, the march of *Das Reich* will always be recalled as the most dreadful episode of World War II—a storm leaving a hellish path of fire, smoke, and blood in its wake.

In the years following Oradour, there were many accounts of what occurred and the motives of the men who did those horrible things to innocent people. World War II developed a fascination all its own that it still has today. Tune in to Netflix: see dozens of World War II movies, series, documentaries, Nazi stories told from every angle imaginable. Hitler and SS fascination is unequaled in any other evil presented on the channel. And there is a reason why Netflix posts so many Nazi films: the audience wants it, and it brings in revenue.

Twenty-one men from Diekmann's company were tried at Bordeaux after the war. One stands out, a former Hitler Youth member, forced by his father—an ardent Nazi—to join the Waffen-SS in February 1944. Joseph Busch deserted *Das Reich* in Normandy in July, approximately one month after Oradour. His words from a court transcript might help further an understanding of the Oradour slaughter:

"When we were one kilometer from Oradour, all officers and NCOs were called forward to Major Dickman [*sic*] and Captain Kahn, from whom they got instructions."

"What instructions?" asked the Court President.

"We couldn't hear what was said. But some papers were passed to them.

"Then what?"

"My squad drove directly to the marketplace. We picked up the people we met along the way, and then we helped separate them into groups and stood guard over them. I was there when a group was led off to Desourteaux's barn. We had orders to shoot them when Captain Kahn fired his pistol."

"And then you fired?"

"Yes, Herr President."

"Then what happened?"

"Well, people fell over."

"Yes, but what did you do next?"

"Well, then we threw timber and brushwood in on top of the people."

"Were these people still alive?"

"Well, they may have been, Herr President. I didn't pay too close attention. . . . I was not especially interested."

"All in accordance with orders?"

"Yes, sir, Herr President."

"Then what?

"We were ordered to go to the church, where I was placed on guard duty."

"Did you see anything there?"

"Yes. Two women came looking for their children. We told them to get out of there or they'd be shot. But then Sergeant Boos and a German came along. They dragged the women into the barn and shot them."

Brigadeführer (Major General) Sylvester Stadler, his rank at war's end, ordered Diekmann's court-martial proceedings. Only thirty-four years old at the end of the war, Stadler was one of the youngest German army generals and a recipient of the Knight's Cross with Oak Leaves and Swords.

A note here about Stadler: First, we must ask ourselves if Stadler is showing a strand of decency in this otherwise awful moment. Almost immediately upon hearing of Diekmann's killing spree and sensing it most egregious without further investigation, Stadler reacts with a wave of integrity—he has heard about the massacre, he finds it wholly repugnant, and he puts forth to Lammerding that he sees fit to court-martial Diekmann, starting the process immediately.

This presents a broader picture: At the very least, we see a crack in the SS armor, which is very much anathema to the cold-hearted Waffen-SS ethic as it has been viewed in history books—they want justice in the case of Oradour to be served. A refreshing moment, perhaps? Lammerding agrees to the court-martial; despite this, he did not suspend Diekmann or confine him to quarters awaiting his court-martial. Lammerding, in signing off on the court-martial, is placing almost all the blame on Diekmann and indicating he, Lammerding, had nothing to do with the matter—which is mostly true.

During this time, the 2.SS Panzer Division lost two-thirds of its fifteen thousand men and endured sixty-four brutal American attacks. *Hauptmann* (Captain) Kahn lost his right arm and had to endure the rest of his life with a false eye and an artificial arm.

News of Oradour spread with uncanny speed along with Stadler's initiated court-martial proceedings; by all accounts, Lammerding's chief of staff seemed appalled at Diekmann's action.

Hearing the news, *Generalfeldmarschall* Erwin Rommel was outraged and embarrassed: that a member of the German military could have performed such a heinous act should not go unpunished. He endorsed Diekmann's court-martial and volunteered to lead the proceedings. Lammerding gave his tacit approval but, for some odd reason, allowed Diekmann to remain in command of his battalion, something never done in most armies. Perhaps this was some sort of reward for partnering with him in search of the gold?

It would seem evident that Lammerding wanted Diekmann to be free to hunt for the stolen gold and have the needed resources. Protests at Diekmann's unilateral action followed from the German commander in Limoges *General* (General) Walter Gleiniger, and no less the Vichy government. Diekmann, in his defense, said "the atrocity was retaliation for the partisan activity in nearby Tulle (the hangings) and the kidnapping and murder of SS commander Helmut Kämpfe," viciously burned alive in "a German field ambulance with other German soldiers while handcuffed to the steering wheel."

But nothing came of it.

A little more than two weeks after Diekmann's involvement in Oradour, at the age of twenty-nine, Adolf Otto Diekmann, a German SS officer who had a pending court-martial for Oradour, stuck his head out of his bunker without his helmet at Caen, Department du Calvados, on 29 June 1944. A splinter from an American mortar round slammed his head, and he died instantly. Diekmann's comrades stated, "He did not seem to care if he lived or died anymore." No one admitted with certainty that Diekmann felt he committed a war crime at Oradour. Many of Diekmann's comrades thought that the burden of Oradour, the killing of 642 residents, *perhaps*, weighed heavily on him, and his death was a suicide. Of course, presumably, none of his comrades knew that Diekmann was searching for gold ingots.

One survivor of the massacre, Robert Hébras, in his book *Oradour-sur-Glane: The Tragedy Hour by Hour*, wrote that "Diekmann was a 'blood-thirsty man' and that Major Diekmann was a man whose callousness had earned him the reputation of a cold, cruel butcher, and a drunkard besides." Hébras, however, had no idea that these attributes of Diekmann's rose through a hunger to get gold ingots that would secure his life forever—a matter most of us only dream of. Also, one wonders how Hébras knew this about Diekmann, whom he never met.

Diekmann was buried temporarily at Bonneville, France. After some time, his remains were disentombed and brought to La Cambe German Military Cemetery in Normandy, with its granite grave markers cut into somber gray Iron Crosses. He shares a gravestone like most dead German soldiers, to save space, with Georg Bossel, a seventeen-year-old grenadier.

Some say *Das Reich*'s actions at Oradour could have been mitigated had the SS publicly announced that the massacre was initiated because of a search for the kidnapped and murdered Kämpfe—this could have been seen as justification—and that their action was a reprisal for his death. In other words, if *Das Reich* had announced immediately that their action in Oradour was a justification for crimes committed against German forces again. (Don't forget, in 1944, reprisals were legal, which sounds harsh, but is true.) But think of it this way: if reprisals were not allowed, then civilians could have murdered German soldiers arbitrarily without suffering any punishment. Also, the average Frenchman felt the *Résistance* was responsible for reprisals and that Germans would not have carried them out if they did not occur.

When Diekmann was killed, he took his knowledge about the plot to steal the gold. But he died having no idea where the gold was after he passed by Walter's ambushed vehicles. His search around Oradour came up empty. He indeed had to have been enraged not finding the cartons containing the neatly packed ingots that would have guaranteed a peaceful life if he survived.

Driving out of Oradour that day, Diekmann probably no longer cared if he lived or died: he had not found the gold that would have made his future placid. At his orders, he was responsible for killing over six hundred people within four hours. At his direction, his troops burned down a village. And he was going to face a court-martial that would probably find him guilty and hand down, most likely, a death sentence.

Such a massive number of ingots, a windfall, had slipped through his fingers like the sand falling through our fingers we never touch but can almost feel.

And *Gruppenführer* Lammerding?

SS-Gruppenführer Heinze Lammerding was wounded in the kidney and legs by a mortar round on 25 (or 26) July 1944 in Normandy. He resumed his command after hospitalization in mid-October until January 1945, when he was appointed the chief of staff of the Army of the Vistula (its commander was his old friend Heinrich Himmler, a wholly ineffectual tactician with no tactical military experience that a desperate Hitler had assigned the task).

After Easter 1945, Lammerding was made commander of SS Division *Nibelung*. He was captured by the Americans on 2 May 1945 and imprisoned in Bavaria but released relatively soon. He maintained his real name but concealed his rank and lofty position. He returned home to Düsseldorf and obtained an identification card from the United Kingdom zone officials in his name. In a statement, he said he was taken by Americans in civilian clothes and released two hours later. A secret but recorded conversation between two German officers in February 1945 indicated that Lammerding was involved in another crime for which he was not indicted. *SS-Obersturmbannführer* (SS Senior Assault Leader) Friedrich August Freiherr von der Heydre, commander of the Sixth SS Airborne Regiment, had captured two American doctors in Normandy. They were from the First American Paratroop Division. He said that they were handed over to *Das Reich* and summarily shot; Lammerding, it seems, gave the order.

After the war, Lammerding lived openly in Dusseldorf but faced numerous troubles regarding his service. Using his background as an engineer, his innumerable connections, and the administrative skills he picked up during his SS days, Lammerding ran his own lucrative construction business—the state of Westphalia was his biggest client. While he was not a defendant even *in absentia* at the Oradour trial, he was condemned to death three times for other war crimes.

One of the reasons, some say, that Lammerding was never extradited to France was that the Americans protected him. This could have been possible at that time but was never proposed with certainty. The Central Intelligence Agency defended many scientists, for example, Dr. Werner von Braun, one of the fathers of NASA's space program. In an affidavit in 1962, Lammerding stated that at the Bordeaux trial, his lawyer negotiated with the Americans to gain permission for entry into the US zone in Schleswig-Holstein, which he subsequently did.

Some said that Lammerding's escape from justice was the fault of the French; they made little or no attempt to seek his extradition during the extraction period between 1947 and 1949. This left the Alsatian members of parliament incredulous. The Tulle citizens' position was that Lammerding's notice of the hangings, signed "By the Commanding General (Lammerding)," constituted proof of his involvement. Lammerding, in turn, said that his name and rank were not on the order—this was true.

Lammerding, in 1951, was indicted by a French Tribunal specifically to investigate the hangings at Tulle. He refused to attend the proceeding, and the British declined to hand him over. The reason: Since 1948, murder had to be proven, and if not, there would be no extradition.

Two years later, the Oradour matter came up before the same tribunal. This time, Lammerding sent an indignant notarized letter half praising and half denigrating Diekmann; he said the soldiers under Diekmann had no choice but to follow his orders and that Diekmann had, in a moment of enthusiastic zeal, "grossly exceeded his orders." The German press attacked Lammerding for being a coward and writing and hiding from the safety of Germany instead of facing the Bordeaux court full-on. His distaste for journalists inspired Lammerding and, in 1965, twelve years later, he unsuccessfully sued a reporter who had written about Lammerding's connection to Tulle and Oradour.

Lammerding blamed the horrors of Tulle and Oradour on *SS-Sturmbannführer* Kawatsch *and* Diekmann. Even though the Oradour case was known as "*L'affaire Kahn et autres*," Khan's name was not brought up because Lammerding knew that Diekmann and Kawatsch were dead and that Khan was alive and could stir up more legal trouble for Lammerding.

On 27 February 1953, the trial in Bordeaux ended.

The British authorities in Germany issued an order for Lammerding's arrest. At that point, Lammerding and his wife were one step ahead; they left Düsseldorf and went into hiding in the lowlands of Schleswig-Holstein in the American zone. Later attempts for extradition were fruitless because the West German constitution in 1954 prevented extradition. Lammerding died at age sixty-five from cancer on 16 January 1971. His funeral was a reunion for several hundred SS *Bruders*, including his old *Das Reich* colleague *SS-Hauptsturmführer* Otto Weidinger busy writing five volumes of *Das Reich* apologia.

Otto Weidinger, the suave and handsome author of *Das Reich V: 1943–1945–2.SS Panzer Division Das Reich*, was the division's commander-in-waiting. He took over the regiment *Der Führer* from Stadler on 14 June 1944, after he was promoted and transferred. Weidinger's only admitted involvement in Tulle or Oradour was when he was sent to Tulle from Brive on the night of 8–9 June to obtain an in-person report because radio communications had been sporadic at best. He also wrote *Comrades to the End*, which included many unverified stories of a German medical unit found murdered outside Oradour (Kämpfe?); that the 3rd Company was met with fire when they arrived; that *Résistance* munitions were stored in the church; and that two collaborators had told Diekmann that a German officer (Kämpfe again?) was being held in Oradour and was going to be executed.

Rebutting allegations, Barth and Kahn, in postwar depositions, stated that there were no German bodies at the peripheries of Oradour when Diekmann entered the town; that no one fired at them from the village; that no search for Kämpfe had taken place; and that the SS had placed the explosives in the church at Diekmann's direction.

US intelligence files show that Weidinger was extradited from the American zone on 12 August 1947 after a French request.

He was then sent to Dachau, where, ironically, he had served as a prison guard in the infancy of his career. Weidinger and seventy-six others were tried and acquitted by the Bordeaux Military Tribunal; they were released and returned to Germany for lack of evidence. Weidinger died in Würzburg in 1990. His funeral was copiously attended by his *Bruder* SS men that could overcome their infirmaries just this once to attend and pay their respects to a brother.

The Tulle and Oradour massacres intended, theoretically, to do two things:

The primary purpose was reprisals for military actions committed against the German occupiers—a tit-for-tat situation. But near the end of the war, the French finally realized that for every attack against the Germans, they could expect *ratissages*, and most of the time, they would be dealt three-fold in copious devastation. They soon realized that their attacks against the Germans would certainly not stop or push the Germans out of France; in the case of *Das Reich*, they would only slow down the advance from Montauban to Normandy.

Otto Kahn, an *SS-Hauptsturmführer*, commander of the First Battalion of the Regiment *Der Führer* when Diekmann was killed at Normandy on 29 June, lost an arm, and was hospitalized. He later served in a noncombatant role in Czechoslovakia, was imprisoned in Russia, and then released in 1945.

Before entering Oradour, he said to the Alsatians, "You are going to see some blood flow today! And we'll also find out what the Alsatians are made of!" A statement many heard that would come back to bite him. Kahn was condemned to death at the Bordeaux trial in France after the war, twice *in absentia*, and once by the Bordeaux Tribunal also *in absentia*.

Kahn was a significant participant in the Oradour massacre, albeit reluctantly throughout, and even questioned Diekmann's order to "burn the village down." In fact, Kahn tried to go around Diekmann—something that is anathema in all militaries and designated as an "end run"—to Stadler to confirm the order to raze the village. In the chain of command in *Der Führer*, he reported directly to and took his orders from Diekmann.

After the war, in addition to being tried and found guilty twice *in absentia*, on 13 December 1962, Kahn, an Oradour participant, made one of the most significant, detailed, revelatory statements regarding Oradour; it renders a fair, sober-minded picture of what occurred because he was not only a witness but also an involved participant who actions had several credible witnesses.

The salient points are presented here and are particularly informative, presenting a much wider picture of his involvement, as well as a more detailed picture of the massacre itself.

At the beginning of his statement Kahn tells us that the mission began on Wednesday 7 June at Limoges, their first objective.

When they arrived, Kahn and his company checked into a hotel, and he reserved a room for himself and tried to go to sleep.

Almost immediately, a messenger arrived ordering him to present himself to Diekmann, who was in Oradour.

Diekmann told Kahn that his company had a mission: they were to go into Oradour and burn it down and annihilate all the inhabitants, this according to Kahn. This was a lie. No one told Diekmann to take this action—not Stadler or Lammerding. But who was lying? Diekmann or Kahn in relating this in his statement prior to the trial? We will never know. It seems likely that it originated in Kahn's head. Nevertheless, Kahn said that Diekmann ordered this annihilation of the village and ordered Kahn to carry it out.

Kahn, on the other hand, states that he was amazed when he heard this from Diekmann. In fact, he says, Diekmann *repeated* the order without explanation. Kahn felt this was a strange order coming from Diekmann. Kahn crossed the line when he asked Diekmann if the matter had been raised at the regiment. Should it not be verified, or at least postponed for review, he asked?

This was a bit unusual because German soldiers, particularly SS men, did not question their superior's orders. Kahn must have believed that his unit under Diekmann's command, was to embark on something criminal. Frankness between ranks in the SS was encouraged. Perhaps Kahn was trying to indicate his reluctance to participate in what he thought was leading toward a potentially serious war crime. Diekmann, however, became extremely indignant. He directed, no, ordered that Kahn should immediately make the company ready for a march to Oradour. A refusal on Kahn's part would be fruitless and very risky.

And so Kahn assembled his company, but simultaneously made an attempt to get clarity from his Regimental Commander too.

At this point, Diekmann became most indignant and in a sharp tone again ordered Kahn to prepare the company to march for Oradour.

Kahn here decided to contact the Regimental Commandeer to receive transparency over this troubling (to him) issue, but in the meantime, he assembled his company in compliance with Diekmann's direct order. The matter, Kahn would state later, was troublesome. We can only assume Kahn had a guilty conscience or was trying to put his innocence—truth or not—on the record.

When Kahn's combat group was ready to set off to Oradour, he still had no clear idea for immediate action or if the order was legal. And Diekmann was unhappy with Kahn; he told him that he was a careless SS man and told him that he, Diekmann, was taking command of Kahn's company—further telling Kahn that he did not trust him to do a good job. For Kahn, this must have been devastating. Normally such a lack of faith in a subordinate—Kahn in this case—would have been regarded as a grave insult and worthy of a reprimand, or release from his command. However, Kahn did not seem to have been as one might be under the circumstance. Kahn then placed himself at the head of his column.

As they broke out of a forested area, there was Oradour in the mid-distance.

Kahn now portrays himself as a man willing to abandon and suffer the consequences of disobeying an order and thinks of driving off to Limoges and speaking with Stadler regarding the situation at Oradour. Kahn, it appears, wants us to consider that he stands on the good side of the matter: he wants to spare Oradour's citizens from Diekmann. This move, if carried out, would have been considered disobedient.

Four hundred meters away sat Oradour, a nonaggressive, tranquil picture. According to Kahn, there were no humans visible. It seemed to Kahn, driving in a Volkswagen staff car at this moment, like a peacetime march. Far from it.

Now, they came upon a truck lying on its side at the edge of the road with about eight to ten partially burned corpses. This scene has been claimed by many witnesses, including Otto Weidinger, that bodies of German troops had been part of this carnage. But here is Kahn claiming not to have seen such a thing, and he says that if he had, he would not have objected to attacking Oradour.

In his trial testimony, Kahn seems to be trying to put off his involvement in a potential war crime or at least diminish his participation. At one point, he challenges Diekmann and asks if his intent is to raze the whole village.

Kahn's putting a question to his superior officers not only sounds unusual but very risky—though not impossible, as he obeys Diekmann's orders and directions to the end of the massacre at Oradour. But when Diekmann initially ordered the convoy to be assembled, Kahn paused, thought about this, and gave up a chance to disobey.

After Diekmann had planned the configuration of the action, he ordered Kahn to stay with his vehicle; then he moved on to Oradour. With Diekmann gone, Kahn thought about taking his troops back to Limoges and contacting Stadler, informing him of

Diekmann's orders to destroy the village and asking for direction. Instead, he decided he would drive on to Oradour and thus disobey Diekmann's order to remain in place.

But after approximately forty-five minutes a messenger came from the village and told Kahn that Diekmann wanted to see him immediately, thus forestalling his intended disobedience.

Kahn met Diekmann at the center of the village and stood between two groups of rounded-up villagers. On one side, men were gathered, while the women and children stood on the other side.

At this point, Kahn stuck his neck out again—at least according to his statement—and asked Diekmann if he wanted to execute his earlier order, annihilate and burn down the village. Diekmann's answer was blunt: "Orders are orders." He led the women with the children to the church approximately three hundred feet away. Then Diekmann ordered the men into groups of thirty and led them in nearby barns. (Note: a barn here is not necessarily a place for automobiles or animals but often a storage area.) Kahn estimated that there were 180 men.

As they entered the barns, Kahn again tried to disassociate himself; he knew what was about to transpire: "I moved myself away, and I heard shooting in the barn." He added that no one tried to escape.

A messenger approached Kahn again: Diekmann was at the church and wanted to see him. Kahn asked Diekmann "what he wanted to do now, that enough had transpired": the church was burning, and there were many dead. At the same time, he suggested that the women and children should be allowed to leave and be chased into the wood. Diekmann said, "That is out of the question."

Then Diekmann asked Kahn if he had explosives. "No," was his reply.

Behind Diekmann stood an *Untersturmführer* (SS junior squad leader), the equipment manager for arms and ammunition; he answered, "Yes, *Sturmbannführer*, I still have something on the wagon." He had a cache of explosives. Kahn turned and said, "Idiot."

Diekmann ordered the *Untersturmführer* to get the explosives and asked the *Untersturmführer* if he was qualified to handle munitions of that sort; he was. On Diekmann's orders, the *Untersturmführer* took the explosives from the wagon into the church after being told by Diekmann where he wanted them placed.

The *Untersturmführer* did not have the experience he stated on his certificate; why he lied is unclear. When the explosion occurred in the church, the *Untersturmführer* was blown through the church door, severely injured, screaming, and covered in blood. His name was Knag, and that day, he was the only SS casualty in Oradour; he died a few minutes later.

After the explosion, Diekmann assembled teams with machine guns and took off for the church; there, they started shooting anyone alive.

Kahn said it was a terrible scene and, with his messenger, left the area. They went to a house at the edge of the village and stayed for an hour until Diekmann ordered Kahn to assemble his company. During this time, the entire town was ablaze, and they could hear explosions and what sounded like fireworks—"probably ammunition cooking off in the houses," according to Kahn.

As soon as Diekmann departed, Kahn ordered his company to stop shooting civilians. If they continued, he said, he would not hesitate to draw his pistol out and shoot them; they stopped.

Kahn's lengthy statement in court, which often strives to diminish or deny guilt, sharply contrasts with eyewitness testimony at the 1953 Bordeaux trial.

Some of Kahn's SS troopers testified that, at the church, "he was behaving viciously." On the orders of *Hauptsturmführer* Kahn, some witnesses said, "We shot 20 men; it was all over quickly." Another witness told the court that "at the church, when one of the women attempted to escape, *Hauptsturmführer* Kahn shoved her back into the flames. At that moment, Kahn had said, 'I am not going to have any witnesses turning up later.'"

Dieckmann arrived thirty minutes later and told Kahn he did not need to write an after-action report—he would do it himself.

Kahn states that he could not have had personal knowledge of, nor at any time seen, an order to attack Oradour. It was the old refrain: "I know nothing," he said, "of murdered German ambulance teams in Oradour, whose corpses would have lain at the side of the road. Anyway, I myself saw no dead German soldiers lying there."

Diekmann said that at the approach to Oradour, they found dead soldiers and officers by the roadside. Some stated that this might have been an excuse for Diekmann to shoot the villagers and burn it to the ground. Taking the same road Diekmann took, Kahn saw no such scene.

On 1 August 1944, Kahn was wounded a second time, resulting in the loss of his arm.

Walter Schmald, in the summer of 1944, was a member of the *Sicherheitsdienst* (SD) with the 8.Company of the Ninety-Fifth Regiment, stationed at Brive and Tulle. He sheltered in a cellar during the battle at Tulle and almost died of asphyxiation on 10 June. He was nicknamed "the Hunchback" because of a fault of his spine. He escaped the fighting for the liberation of Tulle by the *Résistance*. He was probably the only survivor of the local section of the SIP0-SD—the *maquisards* shot nine members at the Cemetery of Puy Saint-Clair after the surrender of the German troops embedded in the normal school. On the morning of 9 June, Schmald appeared after the roundup of the men while they were gathered in the courtyard of the arms factory.

He appeared like a character from an old "Frankenstein" black and white horror movie to many.

He was dressed in a huge, frightening hood, greenish, wearing green socks in big troop shoes, his face low, *chafouine* (sly or scary), his back hunched. He snoozed like a hunting dog. He had long blond hair pulled back, a shaved face, matt complexion, about thirty years old, eyes always half closed, and especially the upper-right half-lip always raised, as if swollen with venom, to see better; he spoke little, questioned a lot, not showing deference to any authority. His outfit was very funny. A huge hood, very simple, fringed on the edges, like the one given to the reservists without crest, without a badge, without any mark other than that of the SS insignia on the right arm.

Schmald made the decision to hang a hundred inhabitants of Tulle and was responsible for the selection of prisoners doomed to death.

The intervention of Canon Jean Espinasse ended the executions after ninety-nine had been killed. Why did he do this? His answer was ambiguous, but the imminent end of a lost war and the legal actions resulting from defeat had something to do with his attitude. Schmald also selected men to be deported to concentration camps on the morning of 10 June.

On 16 August 1944, members of the Secret Army arrested Schmald. On 22 August he was shot by a *gendarmerie* platoon at La Vialle. The execution by the *gendarmerie* gave the proceedings "a legal air" rather than the action of vigilantes. It was done quickly for fear the German troops would be coming back.

10

Bordeaux Trial

ON 12 JANUARY 1953, NINE YEARS AFTER THE ORADOUR MASSA-cre, the war crimes trial started in Bordeaux, France. Before the courtroom doors opened to allow in the overflow crowd, there was much hope that, finally, justice would be achieved. Not far from Bordeaux, a day's drive, the village of Oradour remained as it was the day of the deadly massacre. The French government, specifically Charles De Gaulle, saw it proper to leave the burned-out buildings precisely as they were when Diekmann and his men left the village a ruin. If the residents were massacred that day, the village would appear torn and fragmented beyond recognition after the flames died out.

Days before the judge's gavel fell, the trial's onset contained a hope of closure and long-sought justice. But this would not be.

To demonstrate the tenor of the trial and the judge's objectivity, or lack of it, his "first statement in the courtroom was for the *gendarme* to 'let the guilty enter.'"

A most inappropriate way to start justice in a courtroom. This did not promote an air of objectivity among anyone.

There were over two hundred SS men on 10 June participating in the attack and murder of 642 residents, ordered to do so by *Sturmbannführer* Otto Diekmann. Of the 200 SS men involved, sixty-five were accused and on trial. Out of those, only twenty defendants were convicted of war crimes. This did not endear the court to the French people; they saw a strong bias. While Diekmann was dead, he was still found guilty of ordering the killings that day.

After seventy years, soldiers from Diekmann's command were still being pursued and investigated. Fortune fell upon them: On 8 January 2014, an eighty-eight-year-old-former member of 3.Company, Werner Christukat, was apprehended in Cologne and charged with twenty-five counts of murder. To the world, the name used to identify the suspect was Werner C. If the case went to trial, it would have been held in juvenile court. At the time of the massacre, the suspect was only nineteen. Werner C's lawyer, Rainer Pohlen, stated that while the suspect acknowledged being at the village, he certainly was not the cold-blooded killer the prosecution portrayed. The case was dropped for lack of evidence.

None of the key players was present at the trial in Bordeaux. Diekmann was the most notable—a piece of American shrapnel killed him on 29 June 1944 in Normandy, France. If he had heeded his own orders to all his troops to keep their helmets on, perhaps he would still have been alive for his court-martial and trial at Bordeaux. The French, of course, held a bloodthirst for Diekmann. They wanted him on trial, and at the same time they also wanted to see him dead at their own hands, not those of Fate.

Heinze Lammerding was living and thriving in Stuttgart, Germany, as the head of his own construction company, and he effectively fended off several extradition attempts by French authorities. While he never admitted to participating in Oradour or ordering the action—and this was never proven otherwise—he nevertheless stated that the massacre fell on the shoulders of not him but his old friend Otto Diekmann, whom he admired enough, for a time, to invite him to join in his thievery of the gold. He never acknowledged, of course, that Diekmann was not at Oradour to massacre people but was instead searching for their "retirement" funds. Lammerding was tried *in absentia* while living in Germany; the Germans denied the French extradition to France several times.

When the trial ended, no one was satisfied. No one in the courtroom felt satisfied. No one in France.

The trial's end was a shamble of misapplied justice, bigotry, anger, and hostility.

Today, the trial is almost forgotten and relegated to the back pages of history books, but, on the other hand, it is remarkably modern regarding its raised dilemmas.

Today, the relating of the Oradour massacre is a complex cat's cradle with an unsavory pile of unanswered questions and impossible-to-comprehend scenarios. Almost all accounts agree on *what* happened but not *why*—although many concede that some "facts" are nothing more than subjectivity and speculation.

One of the main areas of contention, a seriously problematic one, had to do with the Alsatians within the ranks of the SS. Obviously, one must wonder just how trusting the SS had to be to bring Alsatians into their ranks.

Because of the passage of time, the prosecution failed to present the unclouded truth, and facts began to blur and fade. A familiar problem of the Bordeaux trial was the issue of pretrial detention. Seven Germans and two Alsatians had been in jail for nine years when the trial began. Lammerding, on the other hand, had been residing in the British Zone of Dusseldorf. As the saying goes in almost all militaries: R.H.I.P., Rank Has Its Privileges. After 1948, British policy stated that "extradition could only be effected if the accused was involved in a murder." At any rate, there was no successful extradition request by the French—possibly through an administrative error.

Lammerding, it seems reasonable to assume, might have received CIA protection in exchange for intelligence and everything they thought he knew.

Only one of the accused did not hesitate: he immediately admitted his involvement in the massacre. However, to the judge's astonishment and disbelief, others said that while they had been there, they had not taken an active part in the killings and had "not heard explosions or gunshots." It should be noted, however, that most of the Alsatian defendants and Alsatian recruits were not Nazi fanatics.

From the beginning, the German General Staff was vehemently opposed to the inclusion of Alsatians into the Wehrmacht. After military engagements, their weapons were often examined to see if they had been fired. Why, looking back now, did the Germans place so much trust in them? Desperation? This is hard to fathom now. But, at Bordeaux, witnesses testified how difficult and risky it would have been for any of them to oppose orders or desert the SS. The argument had been made that the Alsatian defendants were not obeying orders as much as they were fearful of being shot if they refused to obey. That they were being recruited had to have meant that there was no other way to salvage a dire military situation without their warm bodies.

Heinze Barth had been "hiding in plain sight" in East Berlin for fifty years. The sole surviving SS officer implicated in the massacre lived under an assumed name in one of the biggest cities in Germany. In his lengthy court statement, Barth never denied his involvement. Life imprisonment was later amended for medical reasons. He died ten years after his release.

Adding to their sense of injustice, the sentences handed down to the Alsatians were less than those given to the Germans— twenty-one NCOs and men of the 1.Battalion of *Der Führer* were indicted for participating in the massacre. Diekmann was dead, and Kahn could not be found. Other senior officers, such as Stadler, were never tried.

In 1953, in the United States, people were oblivious to Oradour, what happened there, and the trial. There was, instead, a swath of historical matters passing from coast to coast. Americans had become numb to war crimes, trials, war criminals, and the hunt for Nazis. They had other things on their minds: Dwight David "Ike" Eisenhower was inaugurated as the thirty-fourth president. The game "Scrabble," devised about twenty years earlier, was now enjoying popularity. Joseph V. Stalin, premier of the Soviet Union, a key WWII figure, died. Books that were popular included *The Power of Positive Thinking*; *Life Is Worth Living*. Fiction: *The High and the Mighty*; *The Bridges of Toko-Ri*. Big films included *From Here to Eternity* and *Peter Pan*. On television, NBC presented the first coast-to-coast broadcast of the Academy Awards with Bob Hope hosting. CBS and NBC covered the coronation of Queen Elizabeth II. The most popular songs were *Rock around the Clock*; *It's Alright with Me*; *Stranger in Paradise*; and *That Doggie in the Window*.

In Bordeaux, France, the Military Tribunal delivered its verdict.

The Alsatian volunteer, Sergeant Boos, was sentenced to death; nine other Alsatians received hard labor and four prison terms, none exceeding eight years.

After the trial ended, there were protests throughout France. Cries of "*Souviens toi!*" (Remember!) were heard everywhere.

No one was satisfied.

11

Dresden and Oradour—What Was the Difference?

FROM ADOLF HITLER'S MAP TABLE IN THE *FÜHRERHAUPTQUARTIER* (Führer Headquarters) in East Prussia and down and down through central France and its encampment in Montauban, the march of *Das Reich* will be remembered as among the most dreadful episodes of World War II.

In fact, there is not a great deal anyone other than a psychiatrist or philosopher can say about the men who carried out the heinous massacres at Tulle and Oradour. These men—Diekmann, Kahn, the leaders of the Waffen-SS detachment from *Der Führer*—were capable of ordering mayhem and murder without guilt or reluctance, and they did so with the blessing of the Third Reich. They were the spirit, the flame, of Nazism. Their enthusiasm and idealism were such that it allowed the murder of civilians in Yugoslavia in 1943; the murder of 920 Jews in Minsk; and the Tulle and Oradour massacres.

From its inception and beer hall days, *Das Reich* had been instilled with a ruthless, hardened carapace of duty unseen in any other force at the time. The young ideal SS men knew they "could get away with murder" and were emboldened by Hugo Sperrle's orders. They said so there on paper: On 3 February 1944, the

157

morbidly obese *Generalfeldmarschall* Sperrle signed two of the most cold-blooded orders of WWII, a.k.a. the Sperrle Orders, decreeing the most ruthless attitude toward civilians at the slightest sign of resistance or recalcitrance: "There will be an immediate return of fire . . . immediate burning down of the houses. . . . If thereby innocent people are hit, that is regrettable but entirely the fault of the terrorists."

There it was, in writing, with Sperrle's signed authorization. Thus, it was never hard to believe that Lammerding or Diekmann would tolerate savagery to suppress the partisans. That they did not specifically order the massacre at Tulle and Oradour is probably true; their tacit approval was there. Their troops had unstated permission to do what it took to murder and destroy to get the job done. Throughout the years, murder, executions, and burnings had become the norm, de rigueur.

No authority, no officer, no order had suggested to Diekmann and his men that there was a specific number of expected executions or burnings—no precise moral or military score to be kept, no scorecard.

Previously, in Frayssinet, Diekmann killed thirteen people, which had been considered a proper performance of his duty and a good day's work for which medals were often handed out.

In Tulle, ninety-nine people were hanged without protestation or procrastination from a signal officer, none of whom even suggested impropriety.

So, why should Diekmann have supposed that killing 642 people was exceeding his authority?

Many found it surprising that Diekmann's young recruits so readily carried out his terrible order on 10 June. But the chief motive in almost all armies is the example set by one's colleagues; the fear of revealing personal weakness to one's associates is paramount in young men's minds. Had any of them flinched when the orders were issued, they would have most likely found themselves with their brains splattered about their feet.

For the young SS recruits, obedience was a fetish, and they took this throughout their careers in what all considered to be the most elite armed force in the world, which undoubtedly led to the perversions of Tulle and Oradour.

For Diekmann, who had learned his soldiering in Russia, these slaughters were the norm, not the exception. They were the storm that overtook them and pressed them and blew them forward.

War crimes and atrocities—Oradour and Tulle—were carried out by the SS with deliberation and forethought, similar to the attack on Dresden, Germany, a city without substantive tactical value sitting calmly in the waning months of the war.

None of the Allies, the pilots, the crews, or higher authorities paid any criminal costs for the deliberate killing of almost 25,000 people in Dresden. Collectively, the air raids on Dresden were a war crime of the first rank. Probably second only to the Holocaust.

Between 13 and 15 February 1945, the British and American air forces mounted a joint bombing attack on the charming city of Dresden, a major transportation hub in Germany. The world was astounded. That such a city could have been victim to a staggering 3,900 tons of high-explosive bombs and incendiary devices was hard to comprehend, particularly with the war's end months away. The unprecedented firestorm and bombing flattened 1,600 acres of the city center. Between 22,700 and 25,000 Dresden civilians were killed. On 2 March, three more USAAF air raids occurred at the marshaling yard. Then, on 17 April, one more attack was aimed at the industrial areas.

Forty-two percent of the bombs fell more than five miles from their targets.

Because there was an urgency to protect the skies elsewhere in Germany and Dresden was considered not a priority target, flak units were sent elsewhere; the city was now mostly defenseless.

Seven hundred ninety-six British bombers participated in the raid. Six were lost and three hit by bombs dropped from above. Only a single US B-17 bomber was shot down

The flight from England to Dresden was eight hours, sixteen hours round trip. By the time the bombers approached Dresden the exhausted crews were anxious to go home as soon as possible. This caused "creep back": bombs were dropped early, short of their targets.

Since the structures in Dresden were not stone but mostly wood, they burned rapidly.

A family in their home, sensing a lull in the bombing, decided to leave. When they got outside, the tar in the streets was percolating.

Indeed, the raids on Dresden, the "Jewel Box" of Germany, presented an unprecedented atrocity compared to the relatively diminished massacres of Tulle and Oradour—even with its cumulative death toll of seven hundred over a two-day period. And yet, after many years of studious, scholarly examination, no single person has been held accountable for the horror of Dresden.

Unlike Diekmann, no single soldier, planner, or general officer, was held responsible for the unjustified slaughter of so many civilians.

Why?

Simple.

The Germans lost the war.

After the war, the major question focused on the morality of the raids, whether they were justified. This soon evolved into a moral cause célèbre of WWII, which lingers today and will, more than likely, never be resolved. But critics were flabbergasted. That Dresden was a cultural landmark with little strategic significance, and that the bombings were indiscriminate and disproportionate to the military gains, and that the German surrender was only months away, was impossible to comprehend. Unquestionably, the attacks were a war crime. (Many far-right Germans refer to the attack as "Dresden's Holocaust of bombs.")

Joseph Goebbels's Ministry of Propaganda and Public Enlightenment took the statistical reports he received regarding the day's bombings and personally added zeros to the casualty numbers.

Dresden was difficult to defend because of a severe shortage of experienced pilots and fuel. Meanwhile, the Royal Air Force had an advanced system of electronic countermeasures. The result: a serious inability to shield the city. The horrors throughout Dresden were ineffable, and many could not find precise words to explain what they were living through.

Dresden's destruction provoked unease among the leaders in Britain—as well as Britons themselves. It was easy for them to imagine the horrors of Dresden because of the bombing they had endured earlier in the war.

In February 1945, the author Max Hastings, wrote that "attacks upon German cities had become largely irrelevant to the outcome of the war." He added that "the bombing was the first time the public in Allied countries seriously questioned the military actions used to defeat the Germans."

When the smoke cleared after the war, many thought that the bombing of Dresden was wholly unjustified and the killing of nearly 25,000 people—mostly civilians—had been unwarranted and criminal in the pursuit of an Allied victory three months away.

And while the pursuit of justice in the bombing of Dresden went ahead with unabated vigor, investigation of the Tulle and Oradour massacres was impotent and mild by comparison.

If Oradour was an exceptionally grisly event in the history of WWII, it was a trifling of what the British and Americans did to the people and the historic city of Dresden. For Oradour, there was a half-hearted pursuit of justice that did not fully meet the enormity of the crime committed.

For Oradour, justice never seemed to be a worthy pursuit or concern and, unlike Dresden, was never fully pursued.

***

In his defense after the war, Heinze Lammerding gave a statement for Weidinger's book and brought some clarity to a foggy situation, one that he had been peripherally involved in but certainly did not order. He said: "It was a crime. I recognize it."

That the Wehrmacht at Normandy was getting whacked was incontrovertible. German wireless networks were overwhelmed with pleas for a variety of essential resources. On average, Hitler's once elite military forces were losing a staggering 2,500 to 3,000 men a day; on the beaches at Normandy, German casualties might have been diminished if not for Allied enemy fighters picking away at them. German forces often lapsed into confusion and were reluctant to glance up at skies choked with enemy fighters on their bombing runs. On average, the Allies sent up six hundred fighter bomber sorties daily. Because of the state of the rails, German armor had to use roads, presenting themselves as rich targets for the almighty Allied air attacks. Speaking almost for all his troops, *Generalfeldmarschall* Irwin Rommel, one of Germany's most capable tacticians, wrote, "Our operations in Normandy are rendered exceptionally difficult, and in part impossible to carry out, by the . . . overwhelming superiority of the enemy air force." Almost every German who fought at Normandy conceded that Allied air attacks were the decisive factor that led to the Germans' defeat.

Near Fléche, on 14 June at dawn, a convoy was halted; an SS orderly handed SS-*Sturmbannführer* Stadler a note saying that the commander of the 9.SS Hohenstaufen Panzer Division has been killed in action.

Stadler immediately appointed Otto Weidinger as commander.

Weidinger and others that day expected to take part in a great, historical counterattack and force the Allies back into the sea. Instead, astonished and dismayed, they were ordered to plug a crack in a line that, at that moment, was not prepared to accept repairs.

As mentioned previously, on 30 June, Diekmann moved out of his bunker without his helmet, and an American shell fragment caught his skull and killed him. There was some speculation that it was an act of suicide, but it is difficult to believe that he was stricken by a sense of remorse for his actions at Oradour. More likely, he was exasperated by his actions, a looming court-martial, and the loss of the gold that had slipped through his hands.

Coincidentally, on this same day, 30 June, Von Rundstedt had a telephone conversation with Führer headquarters. A frustrated Keitel asked, "What shall we do? What shall we do?" Von Rundstedt shouted back in what is now a piece of WWII history: "Make peace, you idiots—what else can you do?"

Three days later, Hitler sacked von Rundstedt.

By now, at war's end, most of the *Das Reich* survivors were in Hungary or Austria fighting alongside a jetsam of Dresden fire-fighters. They were there, they had said, because there was nothing left to go home to. Some of the SS reacted adversely to the surrender, like a wireless operator who put one bullet into his radio set and the second into his head. Most soldiers, of course, saw it as the end of the killing and a return to home and building a normal life.

In 1951 and 1953, the war crimes trials of 2.SS Panzer Division finally came around—and they proved unsatisfactory to everyone.

None of the verdicts, positive or negative, made anyone happy. Everyone was angered.

There was outrage.

Twenty-one NCOs and men of the 1.Battalion of the *Der Führer* were indicted for their part in the massacre at Oradour. But

Diekmann was dead, and Kahn could not be found. Many senior officers, Stadler among them, were never tried.

On 12 February 1953, the military tribunal at Bordeaux presented its verdict after hearing weeks of horrifying evidence: Sergeant Boos, an Alsatian volunteer, was sentenced to death; nine other Alsatians received hard labor and four prison terms; none exceeded eight years.

France was shocked by the verdicts; a storm ensued. One German was acquitted, the remaining five received ten to twelve years; forty-two others were sentenced to death *in absentia*.

PART II

12

Fox Face

1982. BONNEVILLE, AT THIS TIME A FRENCH ALPINE TOWN, HAD a population of about seven thousand; it sits almost halfway between Geneva and Chamonix. Lyon's new route ran to the west of the town. This new route brought positive change to a city steeped in history, sitting at the junction of the Rhône and the Saône Rivers and often referred to as the "gateway to the Alps." Now, it was barely a fifteen-minute drive from Chamonix and Geneva. No longer was Bonneville a small, isolated Alpine town but a place of enormous potential and prosperity, nestled against a spectacular landscape with a panorama of the massive Mont Blanc; commuters and skiers moved there. *Frontaliers* (cross-border workers) could easily travel to work in Chamonix. French citizens living on the border could travel daily to Geneva.

Because of this influx of *frontaliers*, the DNRED had to add more manpower to Bonneville. The *Direction Nationale du Renseignements et des Enquêtes Douanièrs* is a French intelligence agency founded on 1 March 1988. The customs service of the French Republic is the Directorate-General of Customs and Indirect Taxes, commonly known as *Les douanes* (customs). It levies indirect taxes, attempts to prevent smuggling, surveils French borders, and investigates the origination of counterfeit money. It was also a coast and border guard, a sea rescue organization, and customs service;

it casts a wide, always suspicious net. It had acquired a somewhat glamorous reputation as the drug-busting operation that resulted in two *French Connection* films with Gene Hackman. But the *douaniers* (customs office), as they are more colloquially known, are France's fiscal authorities whose work is much less admired than movie stars and drug-busting police; they are the butt of many jokes.

Frenchmen, more than anywhere else, "manipulate" so much of their tax returns that, to most, it has become a national pastime and, as such, one that is particularly unpopular with the *douanier* and the DNRED.

Traditionally, the French try very hard not to share their money with the government—the greater the amount, the craftier the means to conceal it. Conversely, the DNRED resorts to similarly devious methods to outwit such deceitfulness—a cat and mouse *jeu.* And, generally speaking, the *douaniers* had developed a reputation for not going by the book and going loose and easy with the laws and regulations—it was a game of cat and mouse—sometimes the mouse wins, sometimes the cat licked his chops. As such, the DNRED had a disreputable reputation as an organization that is clandestine, devious, much disdained, and, above all, feared.

In 1981, a socialist government devised a new peril and obstacle to taxpayers—a capital tax. The French citizens were incensed. This they saw as state confiscation. Caving in a bit, President Mitterrand announced a grace period for France's citizens to declare secret hoards; few bothered to abide by this. Almost everyone went about hiding their illegal money in more "creative ways."

Further, French currency controls forbade French citizens from holding foreign bank accounts; many ignored this regulation. Beautiful was nearby Switzerland with its wonderfully secretive banking arrangements, "lack of state control, absence of reporting requirements, and, with the new autoroute, its accessibility." And they spoke fluent French—at least in Geneva and Lausanne. Also, the Swiss banks knew about global investments undertaken with absolute secrecy. At the start of the 1980s, luring Frenchmen was irresistible and ubiquitous, and their funds began to vanish in more significant and larger amounts into Swiss banks.

This caused an overload of work for the DNRED, headquartered at 48 Rue Quivogne; they were so overloaded with financial investigations that they were obliged to open an office closer to the Swiss border. And so, they did: An official named Renard—"fox" in French, a most apropos name—was dispatched for this pleasant task. His pointed features suited his name and his crafty quest in the right direction. He was the perfect man for the job. The only thing he was missing was a tail. But we shall see that he made up for it in other ways.

Off Renard went, spending several luxurious weeks "scouting," enjoying fine wines, heavenly culinary delights, and cozy sheets at the plush Imperial Hotel near Annecy Lake. Eventually, all this had to end, and the Fox had to bear down and get to work; he reluctantly reported to his superiors that, yes, *mon dieu*! Bonneville was most suitable for their operation. The officials listened, of course.

After Renard's suggestion was accepted, he was given complete control over all Customs posts on the French-Swiss border, *and* he could hire as many people as he saw suitable for the sub-rosa undertaking. Further, he was given absolute control over the local *gendarmerie*—something he cherished because it equipped him with immense power—and two-way radios with unique police frequencies. The Fox, a man who never passed a mirror he did not like, seemed to be the perfect person for the job. (During the Algerian war, the Fox had been an army interrogator and, it was said quietly, a specialist in torture with electrodes that never failed at prying open a can of secrets.)

Renard developed an under-the-radar low-key attitude that did nothing to hint at his broad, covert iniquitous authority. To ensure their cooperation, he became familiar with the directors of Customs posts and *gendarmes*. He went about soft-footed, like a fox, and carefully studied the border and all its intricacies.

During the tourist season, most crossings were made by *frontaliers* going daily to and from France to work in Switzerland. This arrangement suited the Swiss because it reduced the need for housing; it was a good way to export a problem. Twenty-five thousand frontaliers were working in Geneva.

Most of the *frontaliers* worked in the expanding financial sector handling French accounts. There were nearly 400,000 illegal French accounts in 1976 in Swiss banks. This accounted for almost 400 billion French francs, or about £40 billion or $60 billion. These accounts began to grow exponentially after the Fox began his work. Coincidentally delightful. He quickly saw that here there was a great opportunity. And there is little doubt that he used it to his advantage.

Then, one day, a boundless piece of luck struck the Fox right between his ears. The Fox discovered that a senior member of the Communist Party was working in one of the big three banks in Geneva. How wonderful.

This was a gift.

Renard set about to "work the system" for himself and would give his comrades a taste to keep them happy. With the stealth and cunning of a Fox, Renard quickly discovered that the Communist official's ideals did not preclude a diminished interest in material gain. Oh, no. So, they struck a deal. The Communist official asked himself why only the rich should benefit from the world's riches. They dove into a plan with enormous exhilaration and profound enthusiasm.

It was a grand coup for the Fox—like scoring a massive chicken coop, and only he had the key.

By 1982, the Fox had amassed sixteen thousand illegal accounts. He kept quiet and did nothing. After all, thirty years of experience taught him the importance of intelligence *before* interrogation. Like lawyers, Renard wanted to know the answer to his questions before he asked them.

One of the places he went to was in Amphion-les-Bains.

Since 1977 Monique Lacroix was one of the fortunate people living there—she was a *frontalier*.

Monique was tall, lithe, with the figure of an athlete, a toothpaste smile, and she kept it that way through exercise, mainly on the tennis court.

On a particular morning in November 1982, Monique rose at 6:30 a.m., prepared her two children for school, got on her scooter, and drove to the ferry landing. She was there for the 7:15 to Ouchy, a postcard-perfect port in Lausanne. After parking her scooter, she reached into her shoulder bag and showed her passport to the *douanièr* on the jetty. The crossing took less than half an hour, just enough time for Monique to finish reading that morning's newspaper.

In Ouchy, Monique had to pass through Passport Control and Swiss Customs. She handed her French passport to a police officer who checked for the correct stamp: *Police des Étranger's*. Because she was a *frontalier*, she was allowed to work but could not reside in Lausanne.

A few seconds later, she walked through the superbly manicured park and crossed the main road to the Metro station. Five minutes later, she arrived at the Place St. François city center. She crossed the square past the big-three Swiss banks, then the Cantonal of Vaud, the Lausanne Post Office, and the church of St. François. Her office was at the bottom of a hill toward the discreet side of the street.

The clock said 8 o'clock when Monique arrived at her desk.

Monique was superb at her job, and she was well paid. She was an intermediary between clients and professional specialists advising the company. She fostered and inspired confidence and had a straightforward manner and an air of sincerity. Regular salary increases indicated her employers much appreciated her. By November 1982, Monique Lacroix's salary was CHF 6,000 Swiss francs per month (about $1,900 in today's dollars). It was an excellent salary for a trust administrator with limited experience. And for a *frontalier*, it was exceptional, particularly with a bonus at the end of the year.

Today, as on most days, Monique spent the first one or two hours on correspondence. Certain items could be dealt with immediately. Those needing further consideration were divided into four categories: banking, investment, accounting, and legal. The legal problems were usually the most difficult; there were often no simple answers to their questions.

Monique's lunch appointment that November day—she had to meet a retired French industrialist—required discretion and secrecy, which she showed to all her VIP French clients. Meetings with French clients were the most challenging. Today she had to meet with that jittery, retired French industrialist who had arranged for most of his substantial assets to be placed outside France. The client was always nervous and so cautious that he took a wandering route to visit Switzerland: he traveled from his home to Nice and then by train to Italy. From Genoa, he boarded another train to Turin; after renting a car, he drove over the St. Bernard Pass to Montreux and checked into the Palace Hotel. At this point, he amended his itinerary because of his deep concern over the increased French surveillance. Monique agreed to meet him at the Hotel Bahyse in Blonay, a few kilometers up in the hills behind Montreux. She made sure she would not be late.

The main reason for this luncheon was to bolster the client's confidence and reassure him that their relationship was of absolute secrecy regarding handling his affairs; this was topmost. They discussed some of the problems in his will. She advised him as best she could, and if she had no answer, she would get back to him. Monique was honest, making him feel assured and confident in her. The industrialist and Monique had had this professional, discreet relationship for many years, and he had come to trust her. They discussed a few more issues, and she would tend to them and have answers at their next monthly meeting. Under no circumstances would she write to him from France.

She had this discretionary power from several years of meeting with the man and his trust in the company. Had he known she was a *frontalier*, he would have been highly anxious and panic-stricken about his risk and probably cut off the relationship. Monique knew this, but part of her skill set was knowing how to effectively deflect attempts to discuss anything but the business at hand. She had an easy-going, relaxed manner and could do this without offense.

***

When Monique Lacroix arrived home that evening in November 1982, André Chaluz received a call instructing him to be outside the *Palais de Justice* in Thonon-les-Bains, a spa town on the lake shore. It was ten kilometers away. Chaluz was to accompany a customs unit on a mission; he detested this sort of work.

André was a *gendarme*, and the reason he was chosen tonight was his police uniform, a means of intimation put in place by Renard. The unmarked car arrived; he didn't know the driver and had not met the man in the back seat either. But he knew who he was—Renard, the man with the face of a fox.

Abruptly, Fox-face told Chaluz that there would be three stops tonight: "Just make sure," Renard said, "that you keep the peace. Otherwise, keep your mouth shut."

Chaluz agreed with Renard, of course.

Chaluz's friends knew Renard wanted to be referred to as *Monsieur le Director*. Behind his back, they called him the Fox, but God forbid he should hear someone call him that. Also, they knew

Chaluz was an unlikely accomplice for the *douanièrs* for this night's mission. They also knew he would be better suited to be a local *gendarme*. His sense of decency was more suited to a small-town cop. Chaluz always had time for people. And as far as they knew, only one thing annoyed André Chaluz: the *douanièrs*. But there he was, obeying orders and going on the mission. Chaluz was honorable and abhorred how the *douanièrs* conducted themselves, apparently doing anything that suited them and their goals. He was not proud that his uniform was the only reason he was asked to join them tonight; he felt like a puppet (*marionette*)—the Fox needed him for intimation.

Now they were approaching Amphion.

The car stopped, and they walked up a road to a specific house. Renard told Chaluz that his uniform would be immediately recognized, seemingly to give him a sense of tedious importance on this mission.

The Fox rang the doorbell.

The door was opened by the owner, Monsieur Lacroix, Monique's jobless husband, who saw the men, particularly Chaluz and his uniform, and invited them in.

Renard, overly courteous and unctuous, presented his business card and apologized for appearing at this late hour. He said he would appreciate it if he could see Monique Lacroix.

Monique was upstairs with the children preparing them for bed and homework.

When she came down, she noted the anxiety on her husband's face.

Renard noted Monique's beauty; she was tall and slim, late twenties, had a figure of a sportswoman, and focused hard to get his mind back to the business at hand.

Monique appeared unmoved and calm. She asked Renard what she could do for him.

Renard reached into a careworn leather briefcase, took a sheet of paper, and stared at it silently for five seconds. It was a copy of a statement from Monique's bank, *Caisse d'Epargne de Genève*. He handed it to Monique.

Her smile vanished.

Renard asked her if she recognized the statement. She told him it was confidential and asked him how he got it. Renard wanted to know if it was her bank statement.

One side of the Fox's mouth curved slightly, indicating one of the few times he tried to smile. For a moment, he could not hide his cunning.

Monique told him she was a *frontalier*, something she was certain Renard was familiar with. Because of that status, Monique said she was exempt from most French restrictions against having a Swiss bank account.

Chaluz's heart stopped, and he lit up into a smile. Perhaps foxy Renard was about to make himself look like a complete fool. Chaluz was hoping so.

Renard returned Monique's smile.

He took the matter further, stating that permission to keep a Swiss bank account depends on the balance not exceeding the equivalent of two months' salary. However, she did not ask how he knew of her arrangement, which was uncommon. The permitted amount was government controlled and determined in November 1982 to be about CHF 800—Monique's unusual stipulation related to her salary, not to an absolute sum. Chaluz, for the first time tonight, was starting to worry about Monique Lacroix.

Renard glanced down at the sheet of paper and read it over again for a few moments trying to appear that he was refreshing his memory, telling her that her balance was closer to three months' salary. Yet only two months have been authorized.

Monique seemed to have a eureka moment: Since her salary was paid via direct deposit, there had been an overlap of some kind.

"I can fix that straightaway."

Convinced the problem was fixed, Monique glanced at the Fox for his approval.

"Okay?" she asked.

Renard slowly closed the file, slipped it back into his briefcase, and snapped the clasp shut without looking down.

Then he said he had to report the matter to the *Procureur* in Thonon, and proceedings would have to be taken against her.

Monique showed her worry. She was confused; at first, the Fox indicated that the matter was trivial and now—*proceedings.*

He assured her that the matter had evolved into a serious issue.

The Fox waited, and the room filled with their breathing.

Monique appeared troubled, shaking her foot and pressing her slipper back.

Renard told Monique about the probable outcome "based on other cases": She could go to prison for three months and be fined a year's salary.

Stunned, Monique said that was equal to CHF 22,000 and did not have that kind of money.

Tears in her eyes added to Monique's demeanor.

She begged Renard to understand her predicament and how she and her husband struggled to pay their bills. They had two children; her husband was without work. She wanted to slap Renard's foxy nose and throw him out the door—*bastard!*

Renard told her that if her fine were not paid by the end of her sentence, she would have to stay in prison for a further period determined by the court, possibly two years, and her house and belongings would be confiscated.

He watched as she struggled to contain her panic.

She took a deep breath, and her chest expanded.

Renard's demeanor angered Chaluz, and he sensed that he was enjoying himself with Monique—the cat, the mouse thing again.

The next day Lausanne was suitable for Monique's mood, wet and windy with big, gray, bulbous clouds. At work, she could not concentrate on the tasks she had. And to make matters worse, she was behind in producing valuations for some clients' investment portfolios. She called Banque Léman and spoke with Jacques Michel. Squash was out of the question today.

At lunch, she met him at a small harbor café. What the discussion was, what she told him, could only be speculation, but with certainty, one could assume that Renard's surprise visit was the focus at that moment.

However, as they often did, Jamie Baruch and his Englishman friend played alone and speculated on the relationship between Monique and Jacques Michel. Monique knew that her height, slim figure, toothpaste smile, and blonde hair were guaranteed to gather impure thoughts and admiring glances. And she seemed to enjoy flirting with Michel on the squash court. The Englishman and Baruch were aware that Michel had recently separated from his wife; neither knew there was a Monsieur Lacroix.

That same afternoon Monique's husband drove to Thonon and met with his lawyer about the previous evening's interview. It was absurd, the lawyer said. Monique had not committed a crime. The lawyer knew of Renard the Fox through other clients—he was bad news. The lawyer also believed that prosecuting Monique was not uppermost in his mind. The Fox was after something else, another prey, something much more valuable. Renard, the lawyer said with certainty, was after something that would lead to money—because *douaniers* were rumored to get a 10 percent cut of whatever they confiscated. So the Fox was looking for a big day and he had his teeth set on Monique. The lawyer told Monsieur Lacroix that the previous evening was contrived to create grounds for negotiation— the bargaining, he said, was yet to come. This was often the *modus operandi* for the Fox and his cubs.

Four evenings later, the Lacroix's doorbell chimed, and they did not have to guess who was waiting on their doorstep.

There was Renard and his fox grin bearing some contrived news.

In his best pompous splendor, he announced that he had good news.

Monique's eyes widened.

Big grins showed up.

The room filled with joy.

Renard said Monique's case had been considered with his patron, and they decided they could turn a blind eye to Monique's "transgression."

Joy abounded.

But only for a moment.

Renard added, "Of course, this would involve a favor on your part—something you could do for us with certainty would not take much of your time."

"Yes."

"You would have to provide certain information," he paused.

Monique's smile took flight.

Chaluz was not unmoved by this obvious nonsense rolling off Fox's wily tongue. He raised his shaggy eyebrows, not caring if anyone saw his look of surprise.

He could not guess what the *information* could be but naturally hoped Monique Lacroix could provide answers to his questions.

"If it is useful information," he stated, "it could end the whole matter."

This whole matter—Renard's late-night call, the gendarme's uniform, the simple extortion proposition, and Monique the perfect target—was, in theory, a perfect scam involving a French official and his government. Victims were almost always willing to cooperate instead of falling to his threat.

Finally, his grandiloquence ended abruptly.

Sans his half smile, the Fox again produced his business card and asked Monique to call him within seven days.

Then, as quickly as he came in, the Fox stood to leave Monique with a jobless husband, a child, and her profound panic.

The Fox figured he was about to score a big win.

He told Monique to use discretion, not to talk to anyone, and that the *douanièrs* never reveal their sources. He emphasized, for example, not to divulge how he knew of Monique's bank account—of course not—and the exact days when the balance was over the permitted limit.

They left the three of them. Only the *gendarme* Chaluz wished them a good evening and a tip of his cap.

Later, a few miles away at a café in Ouchy, Michel leaned over his delicious rabbit stew, took a sip of red wine, and told Monique that there was a good chance that he might soon have information—perhaps tomorrow—that would make Renard a very happy official; however, he could not promise this. "So don't get your hopes up."

The information exchanged hands in the next three days; soon after, the telephone rang in Renard's office in Bonneville; he was unavailable. Because the caller insisted on speaking only with Renard, he was given a phone number to reach him that evening.

No action was ever taken against Monique Lacroix—at least none that could be found in public records or elsewhere.

But Monique Lacroix no longer worked in Switzerland after her last confrontation with the Fox in December 1982.

13

Golden Goose

In 1982, Robin Mackness was forty-four years old. He was educated at Bedform School and Fitzwilliam College, Cambridge, where he studied law. He rowed for the Royal Air Force. Then he went on to make and lose three fortunes. He had been deeply involved in the world of investment and entrepreneurial finance. In Great Britain, he introduced Slumberdown, a quilt, "a better sleep for everybody." He had lived in Oxfordshire with his wife Liz and two children, eleven and eight.

Robin Mackness, in 1982, met someone with knowledge that made sense of the massacre at Oradour.

After five years of investigating, Mackness felt sure he had discovered the real reason for Diekmann's massacre at Oradour that would put all the other theories to rest. But the problem was, his discovery put him in prison for twenty-one months and made a shambles of his life.

Thirty-three years later, he died at the age of eighty-eight. Robin had also been a prolific writer to that point in his life.

As you might have guessed, this is not one but two stories of human slaughter, high finance, and betrayal in which the secret of a wartime tragedy, the massacre at Oradour, is revealed through a contemporary drama. A disturbing account that sets forth a simple explanation for one of the most cold-blooded slaughters of World War II outside the Holocaust.

Robin Mackness was not a best-selling author, but he reached out to one—a fellow Englishman—for help constructing his story about Oradour and something mysterious he had come across after years of research.

John Fowles, an Englishman and an internationally renowned bestselling English novelist, was the author of several major sellers: *The Magus, The French Lieutenant's Woman, The Collector*, and *A Life in Two Worlds*.

Among many others, Fowles received a letter on a certain day— not unusual because authors receive letters or text messages all the time seeking advice. The subject of this letter, however, grabbed his attention. It was neatly handwritten and came from a man in a French prison—a notion that furthered his curiosity—who was in command of his English. The neat handwriting told Fowles that the writer was an educated man. By coincidence, Fowles and the letter writer attended the same school, Cambridge, albeit at different times, where the letter writer had been a distinguished oarsman. The writer wanted it known that he had become a Freeman of the City of London, probably to establish his bona fides. Further letters to Fowles told him that the writer, Robin Mackness, was in prison for breaking international regulations—having been arrested for trying to move gold and hinting that there was an extraordinary story behind this theft and not a simple matter of robbery. Through his letters, Robin said that he could not divulge the matter because prison authorities reviewed all messages from the prisoners.

Then, silence.

By 1985 the letter writer, Robin Mackness, had served his time and was out of jail and living in England. He was, as Fowles had imagined, an urbane man, and he visited Fowles at his home in England and told the full story taking up where his last letter fell off.

About the meeting, Fowles said, "All novelists adore intriguing narratives, and I am no exception. At the beginning, there had been a hint that I might like to think of all this as grist for my own mill. I had declined that idea, but I had at the ready the names of two skilled friends, who might be prepared to 'ghost' the story, as I was not." Robin Mackness said that he didn't mind the rejection because he decided to try writing it since the last time they spoke.

Fowles was pleased. His guilt vanished, and the burden of helping a newbie writer fell from his shoulders. Besides, he and Mackness were opposites. Fowles knew nothing about Mackness's world of finance management and entrepreneurial hills and valleys. But, at the same time, Fowles felt a pang of envy at the sound of what amounted to a marvelous story—and the source was right there sitting before him, flat against his face.

Nevertheless, Mackness received an abbreviated and free lesson on how to write and get published—this coming from a man who, if not at that moment, would have bestselling books, and one, *The Magus*, made into a film (decimated by the critics). Mackness got more than he bargained for. Yes, Robin knew everything about international finance but confessedly very little about writing and publishing. If one has not been involved in writing, consulting with and getting guidance from someone who knows the writing business's chicanes would be wise. What made Fowles's ears pop was that Robin had his heart set on writing a fictional treatment rather than a straightforward account of the facts.

A few months after their enlightening meeting, Fowles received a first-draft treatment of Robin's story. Fortunately for both, the first draft—part fiction, part nonfiction—answered the problem for both.

To the reader, writing fiction might seem a simple matter. Still, the truth is, according to Fowles and most writers, that "in fact, writing is diabolically full of pitfalls and traps—and Robin had stumbled into many." Fowles sent his notes of the first draft to

Robin and pointed out in a nit-picking "schoolmasterish" way the wrongs, rights, and don'ts of the draft.

Robin took Fowles's advice, sat down, and rewrote the whole story of what happened and why—how his innocent and trusting attempt at gold-carrying for a friend had uncovered the incomprehensible truth involving an unfathomable savagery, a Nazi massacre at Oradour-sur-Glane, France, on 10 June 1944. If there were people who posited a defense for the Nazis' actions that day, weak, strong, or indifferent, a mention of Oradour would shut them up. Coincidentally, Fowles had been living not far from Oradour after it happened.

Robin took all the checkable details he had amassed to a most qualified historian of the period, Professor M. R. D. Foot, British military historian and British Army intelligence officer; Foot had also spent time working as an operative during World War II.

"Meanwhile," said John Fowles, "ordinary readers, at least outside France, where all such delving into a tragic past must be painful, have an intensely gripping story ahead of them. In Michael Foot's words, it provides an awesomely simple explanation of an infamous puzzle, hitherto almost obscure."

He also suggested that it is required to be read in one sitting. "I should be very surprised if anyone who begins fails to follow that suggestion."

And so, Mackness's story, like many stories, began with a question over a beer.

***

Sitting on the sidelines of a squash court, Jamie Baruch wanted to know if Robin Mackness knew that one of the portfolios Robin managed for the bank belonged to a Frenchman. Mackness shook his head. He sipped his beer, savored it, and took a moment to ponder. The question sounded incidental to other matters on his mind.

Besides, what he heard so far was starting to smell of risk, chance, the *gendarmes*, and on and on. More than anything, it was Jamie's tone and, because he had known him a while, how he spoke. At this point, Robin Mackness, the lawyer, had no idea what he might be getting involved in. Jamie clarified his remarks, stating that the French are not allowed to have bank accounts in Switzerland. Mackness knew this but told Jamie he did not think there was a need to worry about anyone else's laws.

The conversation had been going back and forth like this for a minute or so after a squash game with Monique Lacroix and Jacques Michel. Monique left right after the match with Jacques, who drove her to Ouchy.

Mackness felt something unusual in the air but could not figure out what it was or how it could involve him. He allowed him to go on.

Jamie said that a client wanted to increase the size of his account and wondered if Robin would be willing to help.

The client wanted to transfer some gold, Jamie told Robin.

Mackness's ears perked up when he heard *gold*.

The client lived in Toulouse, and, as Robin knew, the French were known to be great hoarders of gold; they never trusted banks. Also, they went to great lengths to hide their gold, from pendants to gold bars—as was evident when the Germans occupied the country during WWII.

Mackness was getting a bit impatient.

He asked what Jamie wanted from him.

Jamie said that someone—he did not say who—could get the gold from Evian into Switzerland. "But—"

"But you need someone to get it to Evian?"

"Of course."

"Have you thought about courier services? They're popular these days. And pigeons are really cheap. A little bird feed, and—"

"Yes, there are dozens of pigeons. The client's too jittery for an avian journey. He is looking for *absolute* secrecy and someone he can trust with his life."

"Has he thought about driving it there himself?"

"He assures us that it will be worth our while."

"You mean *my* while."

Robin was starting to get a good idea of where this transporting gold business was going—the man with the gold wanted the bank to take all the risk for him because he was too skittish to take it upon himself.

Robin was still non-committed. A good poker player he was.

Jamie said, "The client would not trust another Frenchman in a million years. And you, with your British accent . . ."

"Just get it from Toulouse to Evian, that simple." It was not a question; it was an accurate observation.

"Can you see that it's a domestic operation within the borders of France? So, you would be avoiding any contact with the French control authorities. Very discreet."

Robin had the greatest trust in Jamie. Their eighteen-month professional relationship had turned personal. And there wasn't the slightest impropriety on Jamie's part or Robin's.

Mackness was intrigued; it would be a bit of an adventure. "There's nothing illegal about it?" asked Robin.

"You won't have to cross a single frontier—you would remain within the French border—so no one will be checking you or your car."

Robin said he would give it some thought, but at this point, he thought he knew what he would do.

A few days later, Robin asked Jamie about the client, who he was, how long he had been with the bank, etc.

Jamie said, "Jacques Michel had the account before he handed the portfolio over to us."

At some point, the assets—gold bars—had been transferred bar by bar into Switzerland in one-kilo bars. There wasn't much more to tell Robin.

"How big?" asked Robin.

"About the size of a cigarette pack."

"And?"

"And what?"

"And for my effort? If I go?"

"Twenty kilos you would collect would go into our account."

Robin tried to appear casual but had to ask: "How much is in the account right now?"

"Five-hundred-thousand American dollars' worth."

A million dollars in total.

The surprise in Robin's mind superseded the delight on his wary face.

And what was more surprising was what Jamie said next: "The Frenchman is a goose with many golden eggs."

***

Late one evening, Robin Mackness thought much about Jamie's proposition and what to do about his potential "gold courier" offer. He wanted to get to the end of his decision because the initial offer of carrying the gold was two weeks ago. At first, the offer sounded adventurous and possibly highly profitable—all that gold and more from the "golden goose" would make many people extremely happy and would further Robin's career. While it sounded exciting, it also seemed to be an odd mission for a man with his background—a lawyer and financier. Not James Bond. But Jamie had assured him that he was not being asked to do anything illegal—he would not be crossing any border. Thus, his car would not be inspected because he would end his task at the holiday resort town of Evian. For Robin, the real risk was delaying his decision; the longer he procrastinated, the more momentum he would lose. He ran the numbers through his head with gold shining in the background. Twenty kilos of gold bars added to half a million in the account would stack up to a total of one million dollars. Pulling this together added up to saying *yes* to a simple drive across France in his BMW. Or was it? It would also prompt Jamie to put in a good word for Robin to join the board at Bank Léman, which was far more important than driving a load of gold across France—or so he thought.

On the phone, Jamie was delighted to hear Robin's decision. In the next few days, he would give Robin the client's telephone number in Toulouse. Robin would make his arrangements and tell Jamie when he expected to arrive in Evian.

Robin devised a plan: drive to Toulouse, spend the night, meet the client, rent a car, drive back to Lyons, pick up his BMW, and go on to Evian. But then, after Robin pulled out the maps and timetables and calculated the route and mileage, a five-hundred-kilometer drive to Toulouse and back in December with possible weather challenges suddenly seemed unappealing.

The initial transfer, Jamie told Robin, would be twenty kilos of one-kilo bars, each one about the size of a bar of soap. A kilo at that time had a value of £10,000—a total consignment of £200,000. Such an amount of gold would be impossible to carry aboard a commercial flight; metal detectors would light up like a pinball machine.

***

When Mackness got the call, it came from Jamie's secretary. This was off-putting. Jamie's secretary? This was supposed to be a discreet operation, and now the hidden circle had widened to include Jamie's secretary. The plan was already starting to wobble, and Robin began to feel uncomfortable again.

On Monday the 13th Robin drove to Lyons. He left behind his address book and calendar. The French police were known for scrutinizing address books and people's diaries, which often could lead to unpleasant, time-consuming situations. He told no one, including his wife, that he was headed toward Lyons. This included his colleagues at the office. His wife was to call the next day and say he would not be in until Wednesday.

At Satolas Airport in Lyons, he parked his car—a silver BMW 735—then took a plane to Toulouse, rented a car, arranging to drop it off in Lyons the following day.

Jamie's secretary had given Robin a number to call upon arrival that night after he checked in.

A man answered Robin's call.

"Is this Mister Raoul?" asked Robin.

"Who is calling?" questioned a voice defensively.

"This is Mister Nibor," said Mackness using the code word.

"Raoul here." Tension in his voice.

They agreed to meet on Tuesday the 14th of December at half-past seven at the Sofitel Hotel cafeteria at the Toulouse Airport.

Mackness arrived on time.

The man sitting slumped at the table in the airport lounge was around sixty, timorous, nervous, and unremarkable except for ears that appeared stolen from a baby rabbit. Robin would never have spotted him, except he was the only highly anxious sixty-year-old man slumped over the table.

His name was Raoul Denis.

The golden goose.

Inconspicuous, except for furtive glances over his shoulders through large tortoise-framed glasses. His hands rested on the table, repeatedly folding an empty sugar packet.

They introduced themselves.

Before Robin sat, they shook hands, and then Robin knew how nervous Raoul really was: his palm was sweaty. Robin was starting to feel like the matter was evolving into a top-secret intelligence operation. He took a few glances around the room.

The waitress quietly placed a large carafe of coffee between them and disappeared, and Raoul said to Robin, "You are not French, are you?"

"The accent."

"Yes."

"British. Born and raised."

"*Très bien*. I have to ask you, sir," Raoul said, "before we go any further: you surely know that this is a most confidential, discreet matter, correct?"

"Why?" asked Robin, knowing the answer but wanting to hear Raoul say it.

"Because it involves a lot of money, *énorme*, large quantities of gold, and if things go—how do you say *erreur*—"

"Wrong."

"*Oui*. It could affect my family. *Est-ce que tu comprends?*"

"I do. I understand. If so, it could impact my family and me too. And also, because what you have, what we're dealing with here, involves 'black gold,' meaning gold that has not been declared. But as far as the Swiss are concerned, gold is gold—unless it has been stolen."

The remark was thrown out more as a question than a declarative notion. Robin thought that the little man with the big ears and eyeglasses could not possibly be dealing in stolen gold. He would be too timid for work that led to the precipice of criminality.

Robin said, "My point is if we are to do business, then I must know the whole story. Beginning to end. Because if I am going to risk going to prison . . ."

Robin did not need to finish the thought.

Raoul took that notion in, inhaled deeply, and said, reaching for the carafe, "It's not the French I fear, Monsieur."

Surprised, Mackness pressed back in his chair.

What else could it be? It sounded menacing.

"Then who?"

"The *anciens résistants*," Raoul said with his half-French, half-German accent, "members of the old *Résistance*—from the war."

"Again, if we are to proceed, I need all the facts," said Robin, disregarding Raoul's brief trip down memory lane.

Raoul rolled his eyes and looked up at the ceiling hoping for a rapid solution—his nerves were jingling.

He dropped sugar into his coffee. Robin was starting to get annoyed, not at Raoul but himself. This activity here looked like some childish fantasy being played out, something Jamie was having him do without a full explanation. But why would Jamie allow this if he knew it could jeopardize Robin? It was more than just transporting gold bars from point A to B, and so far, Raoul was holding his cards close to his vest. Further, Jamie had said this was to be discreet, but he gave his secretary the details. Now, Jamie was in the loop, and so was his secretary and this little, nervous man who kept searching the room for a threat.

Robin's mind now told him he could be an accessory after the fact.

Robin leaned in: "If I go any further, it's *after* I hear everything, all the facts. I must know what I could go to jail for if this falls apart."

Raoul's face went from concern to ice-cold panic, and he looked even more dejected. After all these years—1944 to 1982—he was being compelled to relate details of his involvement in a major massacre. For the first time. It was painful.

Robin stood up, prepared to leave the nervous man twisting the empty sugar packet.

Raoul said, "Please."

Both were now on equal footing.

Raoul certainly knew the risk he'd put himself in if Robin walked away. Robin would leave him exposed. Robin knew, too, that if he left, he could be identified as the man who had received some extremely sensitive information.

This could be dangerous, Robin.

Robin stared down at Raoul. For some reason, he pitied him; he had information and needed to share it with this man staring at him. He sat there, a trapped animal.

Then Raoul Denis knew he had no choice: He had to tell Robin Mackness what he needed to know.

He seemed less jumpy now for giving himself permission to release a burden imprisoned in his mind for too many years. Raoul the confessor. Robin the inquisitor. Those were the distinct roles on the table at this moment here in this lounge at the Toulouse Airport. That was their reality.

"*S'il vous plaît,*" said Raoul, seemingly more comfortable speaking in French. "*Asseyez-vous,*" and placing his fingers on Robin's sleeve.

Robin abided his wish.

Raoul said, "Are you familiar with southeastern France?"

"A bit, yes."

"Do you know Oradour-sur-Glane."

"Heard of it."

"You know something terrible happened there, no?"

Robin gave it a couple of seconds' thought. Nodded.

Raoul said, "The massacre. The massacre was on 10 June 1944. More than six hundred men, women, children, and babies were slaughtered within four hours, and every edifice was burned and razed by explosion and fire."

Robin looked at the little man with nervous fingers, wondering how he could have possibly been connected to one of the worst war crimes of WWII.

At the time, Raoul was probably twenty. Did he escape the massacre? Participate in it? Maybe relatives were killed there, his parents perhaps?

Now, a drape of silence fell over them; two men caught up in an escalating, gritty drama that could soon alter both their lives. Forever.

"I feel," Raoul said slowly, looking around the café, "that I am being pursued."

"And that's why you look over your shoulder?"

Raoul did not have to answer.

It was at this moment that Robin, without the least doubt, strongly felt that Raoul Denis was about to tell him something that was horribly true, wholly believable, exceedingly horrific, and something possibly he did not want to hear.

Raul said: "But I must take you back to Leipzig fifty years ago."

14

Zone Franche

DRIVING BACK TO LYONS, ROBIN THOUGHT ABOUT RAOUL'S ELAB-
orate long-ago tale. His life story was not commonplace in any way,
and he could not share most of the loose threads with anyone—
except Robin, who now felt deeply involved in more than just
transporting black gold. The kind of story one keeps hidden and
locked away from *everyone*. No doubt what he heard was improb-
able—Raoul's life in three parts: born and raised in Leipzig under
Nazi occupation, his parents killed at Auschwitz, sister murdered,
changing his name, the French *Résistance*, the ambush, the deaths
of the "hooligans"—and that gold Lammerding and Diekmann
stole and stowed in a roadside hole Raoul dug not far from Oradour, the site of the massacre on 10 June 1944. But why tell Robin
the triptych of his life? Had he never told anyone else?

"Because," said Raoul, "I'm getting old, and I would like my
family to benefit."

There in the airport lounge, he did not tell Robin he was dying
of cancer—he did not need false sympathy; he would do that
toward the end. And he did not tell Robin of the terrible burden he
carried with him, starting soon after the smoke had abated that day.
The guilt he held all these years. He could never release the guilt.

After the Liberation, Raoul did not mention how many trips he made for gold; or how many times he rented a small van; he was vague.

He did say he used some to start an engineering business near Toulouse. His two big customers were the French government and Aerospatiale, established in the Toulouse area. He was smart, because if he took out large numbers of bars, people would wonder how he had become so rich when he had no visible means for producing large amounts of money.

Raoul did not survive WWII by being stupid. No.

The one thing, more than the gold and the details Raoul exposed, that bothered Robin the most was: Why did Raoul say he had always been looking over his shoulder? That could be significant. Was that part of his guilt? What did that mean? Was there someone else hidden in his story today who knew Raoul's secret, who was keeping track of him? Maybe, Robin thought, he would never find out.

And maybe it would be better if he never did.

Robin Mackness questioned Monsieur Raoul about all the aspects of the story that came into his mind, and none of the answers sounded fallacious or dubious. He later checked numerous details, and they proved correct. Besides, how could such a detailed story be made up? And for what purpose? The whole narrative was so elaborate, too elaborate, particularly Raoul's days in the *Résistance* opposing the *Boche*, that could not have been lies. Robin was nearly convinced the gold story was genuine.

After they left the hotel lounge, they walked to Robin's rental and drove to Toulouse, following Raoul's directions. Robin parked near the large town square and walked into a café; they took a booth and ordered coffee. Raoul nodded to a man sitting in a booth nearby when it arrived. The man stood, walked toward Robin's booth, and casually dropped two dark brown careworn leather satchels without saying anything. Raoul reached down and picked up one satchel; it was unusually heavy. Robin took the other satchel; a few minutes later Robin and Raoul left the café.

At the rental car, they hefted the satchels into the empty trunk.

If Robin thought Monsieur Raoul Denis was nervous at the airport lounge, he could see Raoul's hands trembling now.

Raoul opened one of the satchels, glanced around, and handed Mackness one of the gold bars; it was heavier than he had imagined, but undoubtedly the dollar number was higher than its weight. The bar in Robin's hand was worth £10,000. This bar was matte colored and the size of a soap bar, not the shiny gold you see on jewelry. Stamped below DR was *Deutsche Reichsbank* and the assay number.

After they got back in the car and drove off, Raoul stated that this was the first of several "runs"—a word he used to denote numerous future trips bearing gold ingots. To Mackness, this seemed to indicate that Raoul's trust was starting to build. He wanted Robin's assurance that he would repeat this once the twenty bars in the suitcases were delivered in Lausanne. The balance was to be in Switzerland as soon as possible. Robin assured him he could help Raoul Denis with the rest of the gold.

Robin stopped the car.

Before Raoul got out, he scribbled a phone number on a scrap of paper and handed it to Robin.

"Call me when you get there," he said. "But be *certain* you call from France, *not* Switzerland. The phones are probably tapped."

Robin promised he would call, but it was a promise he would not keep.

***

The drive back is uneventful at the outset, a clear winter's day painted with snow-capped Alps on the horizon. Robin had been delayed a few hours listening to Raoul's dreadful tale from years ago, but he was sure he would still make the rendezvous on time in Evian.

Then, suddenly, the weather turns; it is pouring rain.

Earlier, he had stuffed the two bulky satchels under the front seats of the BMW—they were not completely hidden. Then, before driving off, Robin Mackness stops before reaching for the ignition; he has to have another peek.

He unsnaps one satchel open, the one from under the passenger seat, takes up one of the bars, one with the DR mark glowing with extraordinary power; these gold bars are all the same size. *Similar to a Hersey's chocolate bar but a little thicker,* Robin imagines.

Then he thinks that he could be holding a problem, a clump of shit in his hand—or *multiple problems, Robin!*

Gold is beautiful; gold is forever, and gold buys much security and power. But it could be highly menacing.

As dangerous as a scorpion in one's hands.

Robin, listen, *people die for gold.*

DIE FOR GOLD!

The smile vanishes.

He places the bar back into the satchel, snaps the clasps shut, and presses it back under the seat.

He is still in no hurry, and there is no traffic. The rain has diminished to a misty drizzle, so visibility is poor as the wipers slash away. He looks at the clock on the instrument panel and thinks about the dinner party, the warm fire, and the friends visiting tonight.

But before he drives farther, a small car, a black Fiat or something similar, in the BMW's rearview mirror, speeds up to him. It is the only other car on the road. The car speeds past. Leaves a plume of spray and flashing blue police lights, veering right and forcing Robin's BMW onto the shoulder.

Robin slams the shift into third, braking hard, then second, and the vehicle stutters to a slippery halt.

A man in a black raincoat and an official's hat gets out of the rear of the Fiat.

Walking with authority.

Fast.

Yelling, "*Monsieur Baruch! Jamie Baruch?*"

This surprises Mackness.

He is befuddled.

How did anyone know he was here?

He lowers the window and looks at the man and the rainwater dripping from his thin nose.

He isn't big enough to trigger fear or a threat.

"Are you Monsieur Jamie Baruch?"

Odd, but he seems like he knows Jamie. His tone of voice.

"No."

Because now, the man opens his raincoat so Robin can see his Customs uniform—a *douanièr*. *Shit!* Then he pulls it back further, and Robins sees a Glock automatic in a shiny black leather holster.

Perhaps, Robin thinks, *Jamie is injured, or someone in his family—or my family!*

At the driver's window, the thin man in the black raincoat orders Robin to get out of the BMW, pulling out the door handle—*S'il vous plaît*.

"Do you wish to declare anything?"

What!

Robin feels like a fool.

Douaniers!

The black raincoat unbuttoned for quick access to the automatic, and Robin recognizing the uniform of a French Customs officer, a *douanièr*.

With excessive politeness, the official asks, "Monsieur, do you have anything to declare here?"

The words are rote, uttered by a robot because they have been spoken hundreds of times.

Robin shakes his head *no.*

The *douanièr* says, "You are in a *zone franche.*"

"Say what?"

Robin has no idea what the officer is talking about.

Instead of being slightly fearful and knowing this was not a stickup, Robin gets annoyed. Could this be, he wonders, a prank by Jamie? Absolutely not.

"Please, get out of the car."

Robin obeys, his face pelted by icy rain.

Then the official starts trying out his English, telling Robin Mackness that they are standing in a *zone franche,* an area within twenty-five kilometers of a port of exit from France.

Entering the zone means an *intention* to leave France.

"A *zone franche,*" the officer repeats as if everyone knows what that is.

How absurd, Robin thinks. *Intention? How the hell did this skinny peckerhead know my intent?*

"Sir," Robin says politely, slowly, "we are *nowhere* near the border. Certainly, *you* must know that?"

"Sir, I beg your forgiveness—you are within twenty-five kilometers of a point of exit."

Confusion, befuddlement.

Robin has no idea what this *douanièr* is throwing at him.

"Where? What?" It was a scene from a *Pink Panther* movie.

And again, "Would you like to declare anything?"

"*Declare anything?*"

Now a bolt of lightning slams Robin. It gores him.

An icicle slithers down his spine.

Anger skids into blind rage.

The *douanièr* repeating the question, but with a little less courtesy—"Again, do you wish to declare anything?"

Robin says, "Sir, we are nowhere near a port of exit."

Now Robin is further confused.

"Monsieur—Satolas Airport at Lyons," says the *douanièr*, pointing in the direction Robin was going.

Then, with steel in his voice, Robin says, "How can I be leaving? It's in a completely wrong direction." He points and says, "I am going *away* from the airport. I am certain there is a complete misunderstanding."

The *douanièr* ignores Robin's words, again asking, "Would you like to declare anything?" He enunciates each word.

Robin now knows exactly what these *douanièrs* are after.

Oh boy, does he!

Because it is stuffed under the driver's and passenger's seats.

The satchels loaded with gold ingots.

Black gold.

A second later, a vomitous thought sparks his brain with dazzling pain.

He has been *denounced*.

Some bastard denounced Robin Mackness.

Now he is furious.

Not at the *douanièr*, not for being stopped, not for standing in the cold rain getting soaked, and not at Jamie Baruch, not Raoul.

Robin Mackness is supremely enraged at himself.

For taking on this mission that he knew could lead to a crime.

Well, Robin, start thinking about going to jail.

He tries to defend himself, that surely this was a technicality or some *ha ha ha* moment, a trick, and—

The *douanièr* ignores him.

"Open the boot," he orders.

Three of them start scrabbling around inside the trunk. One is prepared and knows how to unlock the spare tire. Of course, they find nothing.

"Now," the *douanièr* demands, "the back seat."

Two of them are deft at lifting the seat cushion. Nothing.

Robin thinking, *they are getting warmer.*

He takes a deep breath. He'll be okay if he can suck more air into his lungs.

He can't let this play out, no, not toward the inevitable.

But what to do?

At that moment, Robin remembers Raoul's scrap of paper.

The phone number.

And how it could implicate Raoul and this whole operation.

A bit too late you are, no?

Cursing himself for not memorizing it.

He manages to reach for it and toss it out the window, simultaneously shivering when he thinks what would happen if the *douanièrs* got hold of that telephone number.

Then Robin blinks, clearing rainwater from his eyes, and when he opens them, he shivers with panic. With certainty, he has to get away immediately.

The *douanièrs* were gleeful, so proud of themselves, and glancing down. Almost ignoring Robin as if he did not matter now.

Because one of them, the chubby one, is holding an ingot in the palm of his hand, gloating, while the others are reveling.

Robin was not sure he could do it.

The front passenger doors are open, and from the driver's side, squatting at the door, Robin watches the small-framed officer trying to open the glove box, but the latch is stuck, and Robin Mackness, the lawyer, is thinking, *Oh, fuck it, what do I have to lose, because one way or another these customs cops are going to nail me.* So he reaches over the shifter pretending to go for the glovebox and help the *douanièr* and then slams his butt down onto the driver's seat and starts the engine and slips the gear shifter into Drive, feet on the clutch and the accelerator, a surge of power and the burning stink of squealing rubber, accelerating forward thumping the doors closed and the customs cop's kepi flipping to the floor, and the last thing Robin Mackness the lawyer sees is the cop lurching away trying to avoid getting cut in half, his shoulder slamming the door jam and the cop letting out a scream. Nearly dragged off in a cloud of rain and pebbles.

He swerved around the *douanièr's* car.

And there was a lot of scurrying and scrambling in the rear-view mirrors. Without the slightest doubt, Robin heard three shots from an autoloader coming from the direction of two cops at the nose of the Fiat, puffs of gun smoke. Robin is certain one of the cops was a marksman because a 9 mm round slammed into the trunk lid, and there they were, gloating, retaking aim because they were sure they would find what they came for.

This isn't good for Robin. And although he got the jump on them, they were tumbling into the Fiat and screaming off the shoulder, going with inadequate speed and torque to overtake the fast BMW.

A BMW Seven series is a fast car for its size and weight. It would be impossible for the nut bunnies in the Fiat to catch Robin in a straight line. Not enough torque, horsepower, stuff like that.

The Fiat, now with the four *douanièrs,* diminishing, shrieking to try to catch Mackness.

He takes the first exit on the autoroute and chucks a handful of coins at the toll bucket. Then he reaches down to the floor on the passenger side, picks up the kepi, and flings it out into the rain.

At the village he comes to a *gendarme* stand, standing in a doorway munching on a jambon. He suddenly appears shocked. A radio alert must have been sent out.

The first idea that slams Robin here is to make a dash to the German border, where he heard the *Polizei* might be laxer with people carrying hundreds of thousands of dollars in gold ingots.

A few kilometers down the road, Robin sees an insurmountable challenge.

The *douanièr's* radio alert must have been picked up all over the local area. There, in the road, several people were trying to flag him down. He could have rammed through the crowd, probably killing some. He slowed and took a curve to escape the human blockade. Ahead, several police cars. Uniformed *douaniers* are waiting, pistols and automatic weapons pointing, and they did not take the time for aim with precision.

They started firing and Robin hears the bullets slamming into the BMW.

He decided that was it, he had had enough and came to a tire-screeching halt and was immediately confronted by a uniformed *douanier* pointing a pistol barrel at his head.

Behind the wall of guns, a voice says, "Do not move, or we will shoot you!"

That command was plain enough and understood in any language.

Robin froze.

***

For the next couple of hours, he lived in a cloud of confusion, often looking at his watch, figuring out *how much time do I have left, and I could still make the deadline in Evian.* Then, he thought, *you must be crazy, you're not going to meet the deadline of six o'clock and then the contact will vanish.*

Two *gendarmes* walked quickly to the car after ordering Robin to get out.

"*Je n'ai pas d'arme à feu,*" says Robin. I do not have a gun.

They came up to the driver's door and ordered Robin out of the car with the muzzle of a machine pistol. They told him to turn about and handcuffed him. Now, the area was turning into a circus. More police cars arrived. They continued to ask about Monsieur Baruch. *Where is Mister Jamie Baruch?* While asking him this, one of them went through his pockets, lifted his wallet, and examined each item he found. Evidently, the main purpose of their pursuit was Jamie. Their puzzlement matched Robin's. It was evident that, in situations such as this, the *douaniers* were serious, because they had fired their weapons at Robin's car. Were they shooting to kill? Or just having a fun time out here in the rain?

Robin felt like a fool.

Why did he take this on? This stupidity? He should have swallowed the paper with the phone number. That's what James Bond would have done, he says to himself, almost laughing. He should have done this; he should have done that. And while this crazy, misguided thinking was banging around in his head, about a dozen uniformed *douaniers* circled Robin and the BMW, yapping at each other. Robin could not get exactly what they were saying. Others lit up Gauloises, the stinkiest cigarettes in the world. Robin thought this was probably the most excitement since the war. Inefficient by British standards, these *douaniers* were turning unprofessional, which pleased him: it diverted from him only for a bit. In the meantime, the drizzle turned to a downpour, and this crowd of yappers and talkers were like fools who had no sense to keep themselves dry. It became apparent to Robin that the *douaniers* were waiting for word to reach them concerning what to do with this guy.

An hour went by.

About two or three times, one shouted out that he would shoot Robin and pointed a pistol at him. *But why?* Robin still had no idea what they were after beyond the ingots they found and the absence of Jamie Baruch. Try as they did, their efforts were laughable, and even the sight of their guns did not affect Robin Mackness.

They threw him face down into the back of one of the cars and drove off.

The front seat passenger turned and, it seemed, teasingly said, "*Je vais vous tirer desus.*" I am going to shoot you. And Robin replied in the King's English, straight at this face, "Go fuck yourself." Robin's own words surprised him. The cop had no idea what he said.

Thirty minutes later, they pulled into the garage belonging to the *douaniers*.

Robin Mackness was ordered out and led up a small flight of stairs to a room resembling an office. Along the way, someone, a man, again threatened to shoot him.

Here, in the room, the cuffs are removed by one of them with alcohol on his breath, and he is ordered to strip down naked, and every inch of his clothes turned, inspected, and scrutinized; they find nothing.

More *douaniers* arrive, like curious bystanders at an accident, staring at the man with the British accent who had two satchels of gold.

Non-stop, and almost simultaneously, they start pummeling him with questions, all in French.

They're so stupid, thinks Robin; *they know I don't speak fluent French, but they persist, these crazy monkeys.*

And what is laughable is none of them wait for answers in French or English.

In his mind he says *fucking idiots*!

This proceeding is just the warm-up to a big game, certainly.

Meanwhile, Robin Mackness, the financier, the lawyer, is standing in the crowded room naked for twenty minutes. Then he is ordered to dress, the cuffs go back on, and off they go into another *douanièr* car.

A few minutes later, the car stops.

He expects to be taken to an official police station, but no.

They hurry toward an under-furnished apartment in a duplex.

Here the same routine as before: cuffs off, clothes off.

Naked.

The serious game starts here.

Two groups of *douaniers* are divided into good cop, bad cop.

This slightly renews Robin's respect, the professionalism of it. He would rather this and the pressure of it than deal with a bunch of amateur donkey-brained bastards.

The news of his arrival had spread quickly, and now the room is stuffed with a dozen of them, all gawking, jabbering, wondering, and questioning aloud. You would think he was a newly arrived alien from Uranus or Jupiter.

But then, he looks around and feels he is in the *good cop* group—just from the vibe. Suddenly, he remembers the skinny guy he nearly sliced in half with the car. It was his 9 mm round that holed the BMW, and now, oddly, he was behaving sort of nice because he was in trouble for having failed to shoot Robin or at least not containing him back on the autoroute. The other pleasant *douanièr* part of the "good cops" remains silent and formal and respectful, but the others, the "bad cops," call Robin by the familiar *tu*. Robin switches to being nice, seeming to be comfortable here sitting naked with handcuffs. Underneath this façade, this charade, everyone has switched to being oily, vanilla smooth, and sweet because they know that Monsieur Robin Mackness is a hard walnut to crack.

Then, the sequence starts again.

Someone from the back of the room asks, "Monsieur Mackness, tell us where is the gold and we can make this easy."

Brimming with innocence, Robin replies, "Haven't the faintest." But they are not too sure what that English phrase means.

"You are," one replies, "as you say in English, '*bullshitting*' us, no?"

"I only bullshit at poker, sir," Robin adds the "sir" to show how cordial and pleasant he actually is.

"You had twenty kilos of gold in your car, you were trying to leave the country, and now you are bullshitting us. This is not good."

"I don't know why you are asking me these questions. *Aucun.*"

From the back of the crowd, someone laughs when he hears the word *aucun*—none.

Robin opens up: he relates that he had no intention of leaving their country, their lovely French Port, or whatever *souffle* or *crepe* they were cooking back on the road. Furthermore, he tells them, "I was driving in the *opposite* direction from your cherished and revered port of exit."

"Okay," one of them says, "let us move ahead: Where did the gold ingots come from?" This one spoke good English.

Robin shakes his head. "*Je ne sais pas.*"

"Oh, *monsieur*, you speak French!"

Robin smiles, says, "Not at all. Maybe that is what the problem is we have here—my lack of speaking French, you're lack of understanding one bloody word of my king's English? And your jumbled idea of what I did and did not do!"

"I doubt that."

"Nonetheless, I have no clear concept of what it is you are after here."

"Monsieur, I swear to you that you will have clarity when the serious people get here." And then his hand forms a pistol, points it to his temple and fires a shot with his skinny fingers.

Robin rolls his eyes—"*S'il vous plait.*"

A female *douanièr* in a crisp uniform and perfect razor-cut blonde hair pushes across the room, splitting the crowd; she has a high-rank insignia on her epaulets—a Major of Police, Robin is not sure. Deference is shown, and they almost bow. She is serious, this Major of Police, and young and pretty with perfect teeth: maybe twenty-eight and good with the guns they have in their inventory. But she is not here to intercede, no. To merely make her presence felt and then leave—her aura says much. She knows what's going on but turns another eye. Smells of lavender soap and something else—perhaps sandalwood overtakes the room. Her chin comes down a notch, and she stares at the naked prisoner.

Studying Robin's nakedness like she would at roadkill, saying confidently: "They can be very serious. *Dangereux.*"

Robin shrugs his shoulders.

So?

Now things are at their most perplexing point—for Robin and every one of the *douanièrs* dawdling and quietly gaping with their hands in their pockets, picking their noses, and smoking. They have no idea, it is clear, where all this hot air is going. Where it came from. Because they have not pulled one speck of intel info from Robin Mackness—now knowingly seriously late for tonight's dinner party, the fire, friends, the good wine.

The lack of formality rises; the lack of proprietorship diminishes.

Robin is nervous. Before, it was a cat-and-mouse game. Now the pussy cats have turned into lions, and the mouse's tail is between his hind legs.

These people, these customs cops, are evolving into terrorists, getting their nerves up and knives ready to cut Robin's head off.

"*Je vois que vous avez les choses en contrôle,*" she says, turns and leaves the room.

Robin feels the matter is going from an arrest to a kidnapping.

Again, the routine starts.

The handcuffs and clothes are ordered back on.

They get back into the car and go to another similar location. This happens three more times.

Finally, the car climbs a small driveway with tiny weeds sprouting up and drives into a garage in a private house.

Again, he is stripped and cuffed. Now they are in an unfurnished living room, and they go back to the routine.

He stands naked before an older man he has not seen before. The man is about fifty and wears plain clothes.

With his pointed ears and slitted and wily eyes, Robin laughingly thinks to himself that the man reminds him of an elderly fox sans a fluffy tail. Where is your tail, Mister Whomever You Are? He wants to say this to fox face to provoke a laugh, lighten the mood, etcetera, but he holds back. Indeed, a choice filled with wisdom.

Robin almost tumbles off his chair when the man tells him his name.

"My name is Renard."

Robin tells him: "Monsieur Renard. As you might know, I am a lawyer. And I wish to see a lawyer to—"

"Listen to me," Renard says quietly. "This is not London, New York City, or any other country or city—here, you are *not* entitled to a lawyer. It is not included in the tourist package. This is our way here. *Comprendre?*"

"I believe I do. But I . . ."

"Bon."

"*Bon? Bon* for you, not *bon* for me."

"The next one will not have as much niceness as you have experienced."

"I have no idea what the hell that means."

"You will. He is not a friend of mine—only a colleague. I disapprove of his methods. They are medieval. The best I can do is to apologize for his actions."

Robin shifts gears again: "I am a lawyer. You cannot just arrest people and not charge them with something. Habeas corpus—are you familiar with that?"

"I do not need to be."

Renard, saying: "Let us talk about gold, Robin Mackness. Most of it is not marked, that is the French gold that the SS 'appropriated' in their *ratissages*. The French hoard their gold, you know that; they do not trust the banks, and who can blame them? Some of the other ingots we found, the ingots in your possession, are Nazi gold ingots from the *Deutsch Reichsbank* in Berlin and clearly marked, I might say. From the war, of course. This is indisputable. And," big pause here, "we believe there is much more." He concludes this sentence with a toothy grin.

"There is always more," says Robin, grinning.

"I mean, Monsieur, in *this* case."

"In *any* case, for God's sake."

Renard reaches for a pack of Rothman's cigarettes and lights one with a battered Zippo bearing a dime-sized French Customs logo. A spiral of smoke bothers his eyes, and he fans it away until it vanishes.

"There is a big problem," Renard says, "A very big one," taking his first puff and stinking up the room. Although he only suspected it, this sets the tone for Robin's next twenty months.

"The gold you had in your possession marked DR is, technically, war booty—that means it belongs to the French Ministry of the Interior. The rest *without* any markings belongs to the French Ministry of Finance."

"That means you, *douanièrs*."

"Very bright of you. How did you guess?"

"Corruption stinks like dog shit. As such, I do not grasp what this insufferable nonsense has to do with a Brit sitting in front of you, handcuffed and naked. By the way, I am getting a bit chilly."

"But it does involve *you*, Monsieur. It does."

In a second or two, Robin will clearly understand why the Customs men were gloating over the gold ingot back when he accelerated from them.

Renard saying, "We have amongst us *douanièrs* an incentive plan—like most companies. Everything we confiscate, we get a percentage—but only for alert officers intercepting something of value, of course."

"You mean, of course, starting back with Monique Lacroix? No need to respond. However, I am still unclear on how your incentive plan works for *me*."

"But it does work for *you*." Renard is refreshingly honest at this point.

Saying, "For us to get a bigger cut, we cannot declare the Nazi gold to the Ministry of Interior, oh, no, no. And you can tell this story to anyone, what I am confessing to you. No one will believe what you tell them. Nothing. As long as you are in France, if you want to leave, you should forget Nazi gold stories." And then he added a grin, a small but discernible foxy grin.

Renard was right.

The *douaniers* could bully him, tell him anything they wished, and distort the truth. Ultimately, they could fix it so Robin Mackness would never be believed and would wait until the cows came home before he got released from jail—which it seemed sure he was heading to.

"Monsieur, it is best for you to forget this matter."

Robin, trying his best smile, saying: "Some of those gold bars, as you know, are quite clearly stamped DR. You will have a hard time explaining those beauties."

"I saw them. I know."

Renard shrugs: "Tomorrow morning, our records will show the serial numbers on twenty gold ingots we found under the seats of your BMW." Those marked DR will be set aside—they will never be seen. But of course, they will remain with us, kept safely." He inhales and bats the smoke away, saying, "And not a single ingot will be DR stamped. *Pas un seul.*" Not a single one. "We will have all twenty, even though the DR's will vanish. We will still have all when you add the plain ingots and the DRs up. Do you understand all this? No matter. *Ce n'est pas une question qui vous préoccupe.*"

Robin thinking there will be no Nazi gold, and the mystery of the Oradour-sur-Glane massacre on 10 June 1944 will not be revealed; it will remain unknown. A true revelation will not be allowed.

And this is how it happened.

Ingots stamped with DR would vanish, leaving overnight no trace. Subsequent inventories would be void of identification. The DR ingots would dissolve into an incentive plan.

Imagine that.

There would be no *Reichsbank* gold whatsoever.

Lammerding's and Diekmann's efforts were all for naught. No "extension of pensions." Diekmann had his head blown off for nothing. The hooligans died for naught and should have kept their mouths shut, and their hands stuffed in their pants or scratching their noses.

Raoul, the only one who knew where the gold was, would remain mum about the gold, naturally. Yes, he told Robin his life story, including the matter of the ambush and burying the gold. But Raoul certainly did not reveal the *precise* location. He might as well have said it was somewhere here in France.

Before Renard took another puff, Robin's mind saw a scrap of paper from Raoul plastered in a puddle in the rain on the autoroute, but he could not see the phone number.

How would he ever get in touch with Raoul? To explain *this*. To have Raoul believe his story and think he was a liar who said he would call but then stole from him? Was that the plan of a man that Raoul trusted?

How could he hate himself anymore?

Robin Mackness wanted to cry.

Because he was sure he could not keep his promise and call Raoul.

15

The Fox

THE TALL MAN SAID SOFTLY, "MONSIEUR MACKNESS, YOU ARE now a prisoner of the *douanièrs*, and if you should stand trial, your fate will continue to be in our hands and our hands only. *Est-ce que tu comprends?*"

He was calm and professional.

This was 15 December 1982, Robin Mackness's first night in the Varces Prison, formally known as *Grenoble-Varces Penitentiary Centre*. The prison was commissioned in 1972, has 204 cells, accommodations for 332 prisoners, and is currently (as of January 2022) at 156 percent capacity; it houses female and male prisoners. Like all prisons, it is an unpleasant edifice. People who get in immediately look forward to getting out. Robin was no exception.

The tall man was a *douanièr* official. He did not wear a uniform and sat opposite Robin breathing calmly, sure of himself, wearing a bespoke business suit and a silk tie that had to have cost $150. His elbows were on his knees, and he was leaning forward a bit, nonchalant. Standing at the door, a "thug," as Robin said to himself, wearing the uniform of a Customs lieutenant with a holstered automatic at his hip. He tried to appear menacing, but Robin disbelieved his act.

The tall one started to speak again, but Robin held up his hand and stopped him.

"Is there a law in this country that prevents a prisoner from having a lawyer?"

"The Law does as *we* say. *We* are the Law. This is not London, okay? *We* can, if *we* want, lock you away forever—without justification. Please be clear on this. *We* release you when *we* feel like it. Everything here is *we*, not you. Further, I wish to tell you that *we* do not wish to punish you. A trial is not in our plans. We don't want that. A trial would be expensive and waste everyone's time, and we know how it will end. Besides, it would be bad publicity for us to have picked up the director of a Swiss company in a *zone franche*. It would appear that we are persecuting you, and if you know French history, the French hate persecution. We do not need that."

Most people—including the French at that time—did not understand what a *zone franche* meant. By definition: "A 'free zone' is a geographical area of a territory that offers tax advantages. For example, VAT exemptions, income tax exemptions, or customs duty exemptions (import or export taxes). The objective: to attract investors and develop economic activity in a territory deemed a priority by the authorities." Internationally, free zones are often located in major ports or near borders. Essentially, it means that innocent foreign tourists returning were at risk—as an insect approaching a spider's web—and technically, might be expected to turn in their French francs to avoid the clutches of the spider's venom.

At this point, Robin could see why the *douaniers* kept their investigation as quiet as possible. *Suppressing* it would be a better word. As a lawyer, he had never experienced anything like this before. He was nearly speechless regarding what was happening, feeling enormously out of control.

"So," continued the tall man, "please cooperate. We need three things from you. If you give us those three things, you gather your belongings, walk out of this unpleasantness, and you take your BMW and go about your business."

"And dare I ask what those three little things are?" Robin trying to sound aloof.

"Of course: One, the name of your client and confirmation that he is a client of Banque Léman."

Now, he was getting closer to Raoul. Robin would not give that up. If he did, he would not be able to live with himself.

"Second, here is what you will say if anyone asks: 'Alert frontier guards stopped me at the border, *not* on the autoroute.'"

Robin smiled. "I suspect you are kidding me?"

The tall man shook his head, and the subtle smile vanished. And the thug at the door grunted softly.

Robin added: "This is laughable and out of the question. It is illegal by anyone's standards. And it lacks morality and practicality."

This oily figure sitting there started getting on Robin's wrong side. Before, he was neutral toward a man he had never met. But now, the walls were closing in, and Robin Mackness was at the point of disliking the man with the expensive tie, shirt, and shoes.

Robin saying: "Doing a deal with you is out of the question. I don't trust you, don't know who you are. You employ gorillas who threaten to shoot people for no reason but only to intimidate them into saying anything to suit themselves. From what I am learning, you and your organization are both corrupt and immoral and hunting to wet your own beaks. Clearly, and definitively, I do not know who the client is. Let me know how many times I should say this, and I will. This whole matter has been handled in mufti—*sub rosa* if you will, which stinks of corruption. Also, your goons did not stop me at the border, and I won't say they did. I will tell them precisely where they stopped me, that they searched me and my car, and then I tried to flee, and they shot at me. The bullet holes in my BMW are a testament to this. And, as far as acting as your informer, as we say in England, you have got to be bananas."

The tall one was puzzled by this "bananas" expression. Robin adding, "It is a colloquial expression we have meaning 'you must be crazy.'"

With silence in the air, a woman entered the room and presented Robin with a long legal document (about twelve legal-sized pages); she told him he had to sign it, but Robin said he would look it over first. Eventually, he refused. One of the *douaniers* told him, "it doesn't matter anyway because we have signed the document for you."

Then he was driven to Thonon-les-Bains to see the examining magistrate, Judge Gerard Menant, who was not there. Menant was replaced by a young-looking woman named Nicole Planchon, who did not appear old enough to have graduated from high school.

Mackness pointed to his shirt and cuffs, the blood: "Is this usual?" he asked. "Because I would like to voice a complaint." But Planchon advised him not to because the *douaniers* would have the first say against him and would also have the final say in what would happen to him. "I am going to put you in touch with a lawyer," she said, "before the proceedings begin." She added that the lawyer would probably see him the next day. "Meanwhile, you must be remanded in custody, and I sincerely regret this."

Then the *douaniers* drove Robin fifty kilometers to Bonneville prison.

When they arrived, it was pouring.

It was late in the afternoon of 15 December 1982. Gloomy, dreary. A perfect day for being escorted into prison.

He expected to remain a few days and then be released.

Twenty-one months passed before he got his freedom back.

Theoretically, now, he was beyond the reach of control in Bonneville, but they still did their best to make his life unpleasant. Judge Menant prevented the British Counsel from seeing Robin for ten days, held his mail for a month, and refused access to his family for ten weeks. All this in the course of blatant harassment.

Three months later, his trial came up, and it was farcical. The trial judge ignored Robin's statement that he had made to Menant's deputy the day after his arrest; instead, he favored the one signed by all the *douanièrs* but not Robin. This was collusion of the first order—a conspiracy of unlimited imagination. The judge instructed Robin's lawyer to hurry up and cut short his comments. His sentence: eighteen months.

Meanwhile, Jamie Baruch was sentenced *in absentia* to two years for being the leader of the affair. Jointly, they were fined an astronomically ridiculous eight million francs, about eight hundred thousand pounds or one million dollars. By then, Robin knew he stood no chance of fairness—the entire matter was rigged.

In prison, officials were much more lenient than the *douanièrs*. The prison governor referred to Robin Mackness as his "political prisoner"—the "victim of an extreme left-wing government." And like almost everyone else, he despised the *douanièrs*. Once, before a visiting judge, he referred to them as *crapules*, scum of the earth. While the governor advised Robin not to file a complaint, he ensured that none of the *douanièrs* would be allowed near him. Nevertheless, despite the promise and living in fear, a guard announced that Robin had a visitor, which was a bit uplifting, even though he had no idea who the visitor was.

He was escorted past the usual meeting rooms, down a small passage to a little room at the end.

Then the guard opened the door, and there, standing before Robin, was Renard.

Robin Mackness refused to go in.

Renard lurched forward and grabbed Robin by the neck.

Robin lost his temper, and all the shock, pain, and anxiety swelled at the sight of the bastard Renard.

Robin clenched his fist and slammed it fast and hard into Renard's nose. He heard it crack.

Renard brought his hands to his face, and blood streamed through his fingers onto his white shirt.

Robin, despite knowing he would pay for this, was delighted to see Renard's blood, his pain.

Then Robin did the first thing that came to mind: he shouted out:

"KLAUS BARBIE IS IN THIS JAIL!"

He screamed it out several times. Giving away a state secret many wanted to be kept for a while. Barbie had been captured only days ago and was locked up here. The world was hungry for news about him and frustrated because they couldn't get to him.

At the time, Barbie was much in the news, and nobody knew where he was being held. He was a secret best kept for a while. Many guards came running. Returned to his cell, Robin waited for repercussions that never came.

On his eighteen-month sentence, Robin Mackness was eligible for release after nine.

He never told anyone where the gold was hidden or who might have it—truthfully, he had no idea.

The *Juge d'Application des Peiness* agreed to a mid-September 1983 release if Robin agreed with the *douaniers* regarding the eight-million-franc fine. Robin, of course, felt that no one expected him to pay that amount. The *douaniers* regional office at Chambéry accepted Robin's lawyer's offer of 1 percent—eighty thousand francs, or eight thousand pounds.

But terrible news arrived from Paris: they were not prepared to talk about the matter until the end of Robin's full sentence.

Robin Mackness would spend a second Christmas in prison.

***

When the cell door closed the first evening in Bonneville, it took a while to sink in and become real. Finally, Robin could not ignore that his whole life had been destroyed and ended in ruin and disgrace.

Now, Robin had nothing to do except ponder the details of the Nazi gold mystery.

First, he began to accept the nightmare he had unwittingly created, volunteering to transport gold for Raoul. In retrospect, it was absurd—a hackneyed plot from an old movie. His family was back in England and had started living off the benevolence of friends and family. Understandably, his Swiss partners asked him to resign from the bank. He wondered to what extent he had been the scapegoat in the matter—who was it, how did they design it? The "who" mattered most, then it did not matter at all. He cared. But then he didn't care at all. He was tricked into something with his eyes wide open.

In prison, Robin's one close friend was an Arab—probably, Robin thought, a terrorist, but he never asked—that was convinced it was Jamie Baruch who had denounced Robin. The Arab was also well-versed in Banque Léman. It was his opinion, too, that Banque Léman and Baruch's sentence *in absentia* was proof of his collusion. What better way for the *douaniers* to protect themselves than sentencing their source to a prison term he would never serve?

Spending quiet, endless hours in prison, Robin went through everything he had written, the notes he took from all the details of this dreadful journey. The more he read, the more he enlightened himself. And the more the puzzle started to come alive.

That is, most of it.

An intriguing thought popped up: in one way, there was a significant parallel between Raoul's tale and Robin's plight: it was a story of not one but two ambushes: Raoul's ambush with his *maquisards* and the *douaniers'* ambush of Robin on the rainy highway. But what did it matter if there was a parallel? Nothing counted now except here and now in jail and a ruined life. These thoughts sparked a sudden quest to learn as much as he could about what happened at Oradour-sur-Glane. The prison allowed him as many books as he wanted, as long as they were paperbacks—drugs could be hidden in hardbacks. He researched Oradour, took many notes, and the historic events of 10 June 1944 resolved into a terrible, inconceivable story.

On the afternoon of 10 June 1944, a beautiful sunny day, the Waffen-SS killed 642 men, women, children, and babies. What was most interesting to Robin was the absence in everything he read about Raoul's ambush on the evening of 9/10 June, less than two kilometers from Oradour. Robin only had Raoul's word.

That afternoon 10 June, a sunny Saturday, Oradour was crowded.

The population of 330 had grown to nearly 650. And today, Saturday, Oradour was one of the few villages in the area that had taken in refugees. Also, it was a day tobacco rations were distributed, and many farmers came into town to visit the local inns.

Once the SS troopers took up their strategic positions, single shots were fired into the air—signals. Over the main street, a white flare shot up into the sky, announcing the first stage of Diekmann's operation.

Now, Oradour was sealed off. It had collapsed into its own orbit.

Diekmann was in the Champ de Foire square and summoned the mayor. There had to be an identity check for everyone in the village. "The old and the infirmed, too?" the mayor asked. "Yes, everyone."

For the remainder of the day, two *miliciens* translators stayed close to Diekmann to interpret for him.

The villagers now understood that all this fuss was no more than an identity check.

On Kahn's orders, the troopers fanned out, smashing windows and crashing doors, searching all the houses, and turning everything upside down.

And so it began, the setting of houses afire, the shooting. The killing.

Diekmann was on edge; there wasn't enough time to question everyone about the gold. So, he became selective.

Diekmann went about his business: searching and asking questions about the cartons the gold was packed in. With his two French *miliciens* in tow, he walked to the first of the bars; he ordered the SS guards to move to the other side of the road. With the two *miliciens*, he entered the place and inspected the men's work; he was pleased. Only a few were not dead. Lying against a wall was an older man screaming in agony for his wife. This was too much for Diekmann; impatient, he drew his Luger and shot the man in the eye. Then, he went from wounded to wounded and, through the *miliciens*, asked them questions. If he did not get an answer, he shot the victims. Diekmann then went into the barn with his translators. An eyewitness said he was in there for ten minutes. We can assume safely that he went in to question those alive—about half of those in the barn were still alive, some screaming in agony, calling for help. As soon as Diekmann came out of the barn, he ordered the soldiers to carry on; they left, and when they returned, they were carrying combustible material; they tossed this among the bodies—both living and dying. Soon, all inside the barn were burning to death because the barn was soon ablaze. And so Diekmann went to the second barn.

The same procedure occurred at the barn opposite the doctor's abandoned car. Diekmann here was visibly angry, according to eyewitnesses.

The last barn was the Laudry, a distance from the others. Diekmann was furious because the soldiers had misinterpreted their order; seven people had escaped, and four survived.

At the sound of Kahn's first pistol shot, the first signal, the soldiers then shot all the survivors in the legs. This was senseless cruelty. Why shoot them in the legs and then burn them seconds later? This is one of the mysteries of Oradour. The soldiers thought it would prevent them from escaping.

So far, none of the men assembled in Champ de Foire could relate reliably what had happened and what Diekmann had done.

As the burning and destruction raged, Diekmann became belligerent; it was three o'clock, and he knew he had to report to Lammerding in Limoges at seven. His wristwatch was his guide. And he seemed on the verge of panic.

He had four hours to find something—the gold, of course.

He never did.

In Mackness's mind, his research provoked a much larger question:

Why was Oradour selected for this massacre?

It was a remote town far from the war up north on the beaches and roads around Normandy. Oradour might have been the moon with its eyes closed at this time.

The Germans had not been there *en masse* before 10 June. Occasionally, SS officers and men who craved French cuisine and wine made visits but in the same unofficial spirit as any tourist. Some of them became friends with the villagers.

No one knew why *SS-Sturmbannführer* Diekmann ordered the annihilation of 642 people.

There was plenty of speculation:

One: Because of their close friendship, Diekmann was outraged over the killing of *SS-Obersturmbannführer* Otto Kämpfe. Thus, the motive was deep-seated and personal, and revenge led to unprecedented slaughter and destruction.

Two: Diekmann, like many young men his age, grew up in the atmosphere of Naziism from their first days in kindergarten and then through their schooling. They were imbued with this fascination of Hitler as a savior, a leader the nation had been yearning for since WWI ended in humiliation.

Three: Because of the severe beating the division had taken in Russia, the men of *Das Reich* thirsted for revenge, and the French were the target for venting the brutality the Germans suffered at the hands of the Russians on the Eastern Front.

Four: It was just the SS way, a time to let loose their anger at the impending loss of WWII. This was absurd thinking. Though ruthless and brutal, the SS seldom slaughtered and killed without an organized action plan. Oradour was not preplanned—it was spontaneous. After Diekmann came up on the ambushed half-track, it was set in his mind that Oradour was where the gold was hidden. He'd tear the place apart at any cost to get it back—to satisfy himself and Lammerding.

Five: And perhaps the most absurd theory of all: someone falsely stated that Oradour was the home of terrorists and said so *only* as an act of revenge and would indeed send a detachment to decimate the town.

Six: unknown to all, Diekmann was there to find the six hundred pounds of gold ingots, French and German, that he and Lammerding intended for themselves.

Nothing would get in his way, not killing, torturing, pillaging, or, most important, his conscience.

That was the reason.

Gold.

Gold ingots.

Since he did not find any gold ingots or the customized crates they were packed in, he was incensed and knew he had to cover up his rage or be found guilty of a massive crime that even the SS could not bear.

That no one knew this reason besides Kämpfe, Diekmann, and Lammerding has been the cause for questions and years of speculation.

One or two other Waffen-SS men might have known the why for Diekmann's butchery. But none has come forward.

And there had to be several who knew the reason was gold, but they never came forward. And probably, never will.

Toward the end of his search for the gold bars in the village that day, Diekmann had assumed that the chances of finding the gold were slim; he had not found what he was looking for, and there was no one left to interrogate; they were either dead or dying.

Remember what his troops said of their handsome, blonde knight?

Diekmann had a terrible temper.

His boyish features hid his ferocity. Now his rage swelled unhindered. With the time he had left, he probably assumed that there was only one thing to do: tear apart the whole village and set it aflame. Doing so would, he believed, hide his true reason for wiping out the village. At the same time, the two *milicien* translators accompanying him had no other purpose—they had to have known why Diekmann was there through their translations.

Diekmann grabbed his pistol again.

Cocked a round into the pipe.

He ended their translation collaboration not with a handshake but with two 9 mm bullets, one for each in the head, and then had their bodies flung into the blazing Laudry barn. Off he went searching desperately for the "prohibited merchandise." Getting his shiny boots scuffed in the process.

There is probably a good chance that Diekmann now clearly understood that he was both a failure and could be defined as a war criminal; he was not going to find the gold, not anymore, especially with the time he had before he had to join up with Lammerding. And despite feeling that perhaps he went beyond his duty as an SS officer, some could describe his action at Oradour as criminal. Imagine, if you will: one moment, you have $5 million in gold ingots within reach, and the next, you have zero.

His wristwatch was now the custodian of his life.

He now had to have dwelled on the consequences of facing a powerful SS general who held enormous power over his life and career. He now had to return empty-handed to Lammerding and his ire and the protection Lammerding had offered until now and report that he had not found the gold he had been responsible for transporting. To do so, with all this butchery and destruction building around him, Diekmann knew he was bound to heap much trouble upon himself. The *milicien* translators knew every detail through their translations—they knew the real reason for being in Oradour—the gold, French and German—but now they were dead.

Diekmann ordered Kahn to "take down the entire village"— blister it to the ground until it was dust. His fury had to have been colossal. The innocent Kahn. The pure as snow Kahn.

And so, Kahn obeyed Lord Diekmann, and Diekmann reminded Kahn that what they were looking for were fictitious concealed weapons, munitions, etcetera, and of course, other "prohibited merchandise," the phrase that he and Lammerding and Kämpfe coined weeks ago to camouflage the gold. Everyone under Diekmann knew never to question an order, so one would not question what was inside the cartons with the enigmatic markings.

Oradour was a village of stone and brick, sturdy edifices that took much effort to bring down through flames and grenades. Soon, hand grenades were lofted into the splendid blue sky, and flames took down the roofs and wooden window frames and wooden doors and furniture. As each building came down, frenetic searches went through the rubble—Diekmann, of course, probing through each pebble and stone, searching for the gold. No gold was discovered. Only one house was somehow spared, filled with precious items, including fine wines, which the SS consumed throughout the day.

So here stands fine-looking, blue-eyed Diekmann, Oradour under his shiny officer's leather boots, an *SS-Sturmbannführer* in

Hitler's most exclusive soldiers, commander of the 1.Battalion of the Panzer Grenadier Regiment *Der Führer*, which belonged to the 2.SS Panzer Division *Das Reich*, born 18 December 1914 in Magdeburg, Stadtkreis, Sachsen-Anhalt, Germany. Parents named him Adolf Otto Diekmann. Killed in action by a sharp blast of inopportune, serrated shrapnel skittering and whistling its way toward his skull on 29 June 1944, time unknown, aged twenty-nine, Caen, Department du Calvados, Basse, Normandie, France. In the service of *Vaterland und Führer*, his country, but at this moment, in the service of himself, Adolf Otto Diekmann. Diekmann was initially buried in a temporary grave at Banneville-la-Champagne War Cemetery. He shares a gravestone with a seventeen-year-old German Grenadier named Georg Bossel. Diekmann was then moved and interred at La Cambe German Military Cemetery, Department du Calvados, Basse-Normandie, France. Plot/Block 25, Row 4, Grave 121–122. That's where all this has come down to. This spot. This place is hallowed ground. The space we all stumble into. While it has never been sure whether he was called Adolf or Otto—many Germans used their middle name as their first—his gravestone is marked Adolf Diekmann. Other explanations of Diekmann should have been so simple. For what Diekmann had ordered Kahn to do, he was more than simply a "butcher" known only to himself. Butchers are simple people who cut and chop meat; they carve and cleave through experiences taught. Diekmann cut and chopped hundreds of lives that have asked hundreds of philosophers, "*What did I do here beneath my feet? Explain to me what lies here, the horror of it on my hands.*"

Not a simple question.

No simple answer.

Standing before the hell space, watching it burn off, smudging sky and cloud, Otto Diekmann, we must think at this juncture, has to be pondering what he has just done—the cause and effect. We wonder, don't we, what is going through the twenty-nine-year-old

SS officer's mind. Imagine that Diekmann has paused to consider now that he is a failure. At twenty-nine, he was a failure, and with the deaths of hundreds by his hands. Otto Diekmann had come here believing falsely that the gold was here—the gold he and Lammerding would take on to soothe their lives forever. But let us think that what swirls in this young man's mind is more than the gold ingots: the war, he knows, is certainly lost. Hitler's glory, the glory of the Third Reich, is here at Oradour, aflame, decimated. A *Höllenraum* (hells room) of ruin.

And so, dear Diekmann, the ruin of Oradour and the Reich is yours, the same.

It was now five o'clock in the afternoon, and the flames were subsiding.

Diekmann now has two hours left to return to Lammerding in Limoges and to relate that he had not found a twinkle of gold.

The extended pension had vanished.

What punishment would be waiting for you?

We can only imagine how infuriating and frustrating it was for Diekmann as he madly picked through the destruction and hot coals his men had been ordered to generate. A Waffen-SS officer, leaning, bending, seeking, sifting for six hundred kilos of gold that did not exist.

The cause of everything!

His men probably knew best to leave their *Sturmbannführer* alone, to stand afar, and that the loss of Kämpfe's life indeed, although not precisely, caused Diekmann's rage. Under the circumstances, it was best to follow their feudal vassal's silent example.

And so, the moment in history came and went.

Without pause, the destruction of Oradour continued until 7 p.m., then finished when the sun finally began its ebb, and the air took a chill.

The crackle of the flames had subsided, replaced by the grue-some screams of those left dying and the soon-to-be dead.

A cry that would go on forever.

16

Thonon-les-Bains

In February 1984, Robin Mackness was still in jail.

He was moved from Varces, the prison in Grenoble. The *douaniers* effected this because of a *contrainte par corps*, which allowed them to hold him because he could not afford the fine.

While there, he received an unusual letter postmarked Thonon-les-Bain.

The writer boasted that he knew much about Robin's arrest and was willing to relay this information to him—provided he swore never to reveal his name.

Robin gave the letter writer a pseudonym, André Chaluz, a former *gendarme*.

Ashamed of the French fiscal authorities and what lengths they went to intimidate people, particularly Robin, Chaluz quit the police service and France and immigrated to Canada.

He begged Robin not to reveal what Renard had done to Monique Lacroix the night they visited her at her home, that they used blackmail.

In Robin's mind, after what he had been through and how his life was ruined, he did not know how to comply with *Gendarme* Chaluz's urgent request regarding Monique.

But it never left his mind.

At that time, Robin's case began to diminish into farce and sadness.

In Paris, the *douaniers* rejected all pleas for clemency as long as Robin continued to refuse to give up his client's identity (Raoul). Paris responded that his release would be granted only upon payment of two hundred thousand francs, plus the client's name. This was out of the question. Robin was penniless. His wife and family had to move back to England and live off the benevolence of friends and family, plus his wife's social security. Robin saw himself remaining in prison for the rest of his life.

Luckily, his situation was taken up by an influential French female journalist who had decided that Robin was a hostage and had, internationally, done nothing wrong. He refused to name the journalist for fear of ruining her career. Her advice was good: she told Robin to decline any deal Chambéry proposed because by then he had become an embarrassment for the *douaniers*, and they were eager to get rid of him and move on.

A few days later, Robin Mackness was told he was free.

On Saturday, 22 September 1984, he ate lunch at a sidewalk café. He had been in prison since Wednesday, 15 December 1982.

During his prison time, Robin wrote 2,186 letters, received 2,146 replies, and kept a diary containing nearly half a million words.

While eating, he pondered the loose ends that had never subsided.

One aspect of Raoul's story about the gold bothered him: the mixture of unmarked ingots and those marked DR. He also tried to determine precisely how much gold Lammerding possessed in his office safe. But that was impossible.

On the afternoon of 3 February 1945, a bevy of American B-17 bombers destroyed the *Deutsche Reichsbank*. Any records of gold sent to Lammerding would never be found. All he ever saw, along with the *douaniers*, was five of the twenty bars they confiscated from him, which were assay-stamped DR. Remember, they were switched overnight, and he had no idea what had happened to them. This mystery will never be resolved.

In the summer of 1986, Robin met with a man with whom he had been in Varces prison. They started talking after the man noticed Robin was reading a book with the SS runes on the cover. He told Robin he knew a man Robin should meet.

A few days later, he met the man, and they talked for about two hours. The man had no idea that the search at Oradour had been for gold. He suspected Diekmann was looking for an important terrorist, arms, and ammunition—never gold. He specifically mentioned remembering Diekmann killing the two *Milice* translators and tossing them in the fire of the Laudry barn. Robin believed this man had changed his name and that he had been there, a witness to the Oradour crime.

The next day, Robin drove to Oradour, where he met another man. He was seventy, a Frenchman, wearing his medals, tricolor slash, and a new red beret. They walked silently to a small cemetery. There, he pointed to a simple grave meticulously cared for. The headstone said *Soldat Allemand*.

The man said they were looking down at the grave of Helmut Kämpfe and that he had put Kämpfe there with three others. He added that Kämpfe was a brave man, a true soldier for his country. The man admired bravery. He would know, of course.

This triggered the memory of the last meeting Robin had with Raoul. Several times Raoul had told Robin that frequently he would look over his shoulder, never giving a reason. At this last meeting, he did confide his secret.

He told Robin that if he had not stolen and buried the gold, everyone at Oradour would have lived.

Raoul had lived every day after the ambush feeling secure because he had so much gold. But if he had not ambushed Walter and left the gold in the half-track, there would not have been a massacre at Oradour.

After he came upon the destroyed convoy and the dead, Diekmann would have ordered the half-track and the bodies removed along with the gold. He would have been more concerned about the gold and would not have spent the time to destroy Oradour—there was no reason to attack Oradour. Except to find that gold.

Raoul lived with this his whole life—he, Raoul Denis—was responsible for Oradour, no one else. No one else but him. His greed got to him as it does to all of us. Robin could not convince Raoul that Diekmann killed those people, not Raoul. He tried to hold back Raoul's tears. Raoul had thousands of dollars in gold but died a guilty man.

Robin drove away from Kämpfe's grave through Thonon-les-Bains.

He drove slowly, thinking, thinking, and absorbing the sights; the surrounding area was more appealing now than his first ride handcuffed in the back seat of a police car and a boorish policeman in the passenger seat.

Moving gradually up the hill toward the railroad station, he spotted the neat gold and black sign hanging from the gutter: Thonon-les-Baine.

Then, just up the hill, there was the house.

He parked the car, stepped out, and walked unhurriedly to where the story began.

Monique Lacroix was still as attractive as Robin remembered her, legs long and perfect, the toothpaste smile, and as trim, as she was when flashing on that tennis court.

She held the door for him, and when he passed her, he took in her perfume: *Millesime Imperial Eau de Parfum*. The $755 Creed scent.

She appeared monied.

They stood hesitant, both with flourishing smiles.

Wordless.

Since yesterday, Monique knew Robin would visit.

They took coffee in the garden at the back of the house and watched a glorious hummingbird with a red iridescent head scurrying, feeding as they talked about many things. And about nothing.

The sun allowed the remainder of its descent, and the air started to cool.

There were many questions, but they no longer mattered.

They never mentioned gold.

They did not speak about the bank.

Neither spoke Jamie's name.

And they never mentioned the Fox.

But before Robin finished his second cup of coffee, he knew he had done the right thing—for himself. For Monique.

And he respected Chaluz's hope.

Robin had closed the circle.

The circle that went round and round in his mind.

The thought that was more important than all the gold he could ever bear.

Or the bitterness he would never feel again.

Bibliography

"Adolf Diekmann." Historica Wiki. https://historica.fandom.com/wiki/ Adolf_Diekmann.

Beck, Phillip. *Oradour, Village of the Dead.* London: Leo Cooper, 1979.

Bishop, Chris, and Jorge Rosado. *Wehrmacht Panzer Divisions 1939–1945.* London: Amber Books Ltd., 2022.

Farmer, Sarah. *Martyred Village, Commemorating the 1944 Massacre at Oradour-sur-Glane.* Berkeley: University of California Press, 1999.

Forman, Aaron. *Forman's Guide to Third Reich German Awards . . . and Their Values.* 3rd edition. San Jose, CA: R. James Bender Publishing, 2001.

Fouché, Jean-Jacques. *Massacre at Oradour, France, 1944: Coming to Grips with Terror.* DeKalb: Northern Illinois University Press, 2004.

"German military administration in occupied France during World War II." Wikipedia. https://en.wikipedia.org/wiki/German_military_ administration_in_occupied_France_during_World_War_II.

Glantz, Helmut, and David Heiber, eds. *Hitler and His Generals: Military Conferences: 1942–1945.* New York: Enigma Books.

Hamilton, Charles. *Leaders and Personalities of the Third Reich, Their Biographies, Portraits and Autographs, Volume 1.* San Jose, CA: R. James Bender Publishing, 1996.

———. *Leaders and Personalities of the Third Reich, Their Biographies, Portraits and Autographs, Volume 2.* San Jose, CA: R. James Bender Publishing, 1996.

Haskew, Michael E. *World War II Collectibles.* 2nd edition. Iola, WI: Krause Publications, 2007.

Hastings, Max. *Das Reich.* New York: Holt, Rinehart and Winston, 1981.

Hawes, Douglas W. *Oradour The Final Verdict: The Anatomy and Aftermath of a Massacre.* Bloomington, IN: Authorhouse, 2007.

Hébras, Robert. *Oradour-sur-Glane: The Tragedy Hour by Hour*. Saintes: Chemins, 2003.

"Heinz Lammerding." Wikipedia. https://en.wikipedia.org/wiki/Heinz _Lammerding.

Johnson, Aaron L. *Hitler's Military Headquarters, Organization, Structures, Security and Personnel*. San Jose, CA: R. James Bender Publishing, 1999.

Lawrence, Rick. "Adolf Otto Diekmann." Find a Grave. https://www .findagrave.com/memorial/94936710/adolf-otto-diekmann.

Loringhoven, Bernd Freytag von. *In the Bunker with Hitler*. London: Orion Publishing Group, 2005.

Lumsden, Robin. *SS Regalia*. Greenwich, UK: Brompton Books Inc., 1985.

Mackness, Robin. *Massacre at Oradour*. New York: Random House, 1988.

Nibblelink, Ron. *They Played for Keeps*. Independently Published, 2020.

Pauchou, Guy, and Pierre Masfrand. *Oradour-sur-Glane: A Vision of Horror*. Association Nationale Des Familles Des Martyre D'Oradour-sur-Glane, 2003.

"Oradour-sur-Glane." Wikipedia. https://en.wikipedia.org/wiki/ Oradour-sur-Glane.

"Oradour-sur-Glane." Holocaust Encyclopedia. https://encyclopedia .ushmm.org/content/en/article/oradour-sur-glane.

Perigord, D. *Patricide: Masacre at Oradour-sur-Glane*. Frederick, MD: America Star Books, 2014.

Porter, David. *German Tanks of WWII 1939–1945 Tanks-Self-Propelled Guns*. London: Amber Books, 2022.

Shirer, William L. *The Rise and Fall of the Third Reich: A History of Nazi Germany*. New York: Simon & Schuster, 1987.

Stone, David. *Hitler's Army: The Men, Machines and Organization 1939–1945*. Minneapolis: Zenith Press, 2009.

Taylor, Roger, James Bender, and Hugh Page Taylor. *Uniforms, Oranization and History of the Waffen-SS*. San Jose, CA: R. James Bender Publishing, 1969.

Weidinger, Otto. *Das Reich V, 1943–1945, SS Panzer Division Das Reich*. Winnipeg, MB: J.J. Fedorowicz Publishing, Inc., 2012.

Williams, Max. *The SS Leadership Corps*. Church Stretton: Ulric of England, 2004.

A Word about SS Ranks

Among military grades and titles, the most difficult to comprehend are Waffen-SS and SS ranks. Their ranks and insignia dated back to their early years when they were paramilitary organizations and wished to be recognized apart from the German army's uniforms and ranks.

I have represented all the original ranks of the Waffen-SS to lend authenticity and to inform the reader. The SS ranks are presented in their original German form with an anglicized version in English, such as *SS-Obersturmbannführer* (First Lieutenant or SS-Head Assault Leader), and *SS-Brigadeführer und General Major der Waffen-SS* (Brigade leader and major general of the Waffen-SS, or simply Brigadier General).

Glossary

Chantiers de la jeunesse: Set up by the Vichy government to run compulsory forest work camps for all twenty-year-olds, who were subjected to intense political indoctrination.

DNRED: *Direction Nationale du Renseignements et des Enquêtes Douanièrs*—investigation branch of French Customs.

douanièrs: French Customs officers. Their authority is more extensive than their counterparts because they are also in charge of fiscal controls.

frontaliers: French resident nationals who crossed the border from France to Switzerland each day, then returned home to France each night.

FTP: *Forcées françaises de l'intérieur.* A title that came from the Free French headquarters in London to all *Résistance* forces who carried arms in France under Gaullist command. In the war's last months, most spent time blockading German garrisons in French Ports.

maquis, maquisards: A French *Résistance* unit, regardless of politics or objectives. *Maquisards* covered the whole range of individual *résistants* from freedom fighters to those merely trying to avoid German attention.

milice, miliciens: A French paramilitary unit established by the Vichy government—it was later extended to the whole of France and recruited Frenchmen to combat the *Résistance*, and act as informers. Many joined just to avoid forced labor. Most were opportunistic bullies who took pleasure in their treachery. They all had detailed knowledge of local areas, and this caused them to be a menace.

ratissages **or** *rafles*: Raids upon villages by the German occupation forces. Usually conducted as reprisals against French towns or citizens. An arbitrary means of striking fear into the French population. Often done to discourage the *Résistance* and to squeeze out forced labor escapees.

résistants: Like *maquisards*, this is a generic word that describes all those who had opposed German Occupation.

SD (*Sicherheitsdienst***)**: The much-feared SS Security Service. They reported directly to Heinrich Himmler and numbered about six thousand agents throughout Europe. They were closely linked to the *GeheimeStatsPolizei* (Gestapo). Almost all Frenchmen referred to German police as Gestapo.

STO (*Service de travail obligatoire***)**: A forced-labor program that every Frenchman was conscripted into. Essentially, a slave-labor program.

2ND SS PANZER DIVISION—TANKS AND ARMOR

Panther V: In 1944, *Das Reich* had sixty-two. Unquestionably, this was one of the most outstanding battle tanks of WWII. It weighed forty-five tons, had a crew of five and a highly effective 75 mm gun. It remained at the forefront of German armored units until the end of WWII.

Panzer IV: *Das Reich* had sixty-four, and it was the most highly produced, fearsome German tank of WWI. It weighed twenty-three tons—half the weight of the Panther V, but much more maneuverable. It had a maximum road speed of 25 mph against the Panther's 34 mph. By the time of the Normandy invasion it had become obsolete but continued to be extensively used in battle.

Sturmgeschütz III: Self-propelled assault tank. One battalion of *Das Reich* was equipped with these. A turretless tank built on the chassis of the Panzer III to support infantry troops. It was referred to as the "poor man's tank" because it was a cheap substitute for the larger tanks. Because of attrition on the Eastern Front, German factories could not make them fast enough. It had a low silhouette that presented a difficult target for enemy tanks. Heavy armor and hitting power made it a formidable weapon.

Schwerer Panzerspähwagen: SPW (heavy armored reconnaissance vehicle): An armored half-track personnel carrier. It was produced in a multitude of variants. *Das Reich* possessed more than three hundred, some mounted with mortars, 75 mm antitank guns, or flamethrowers, others were armed with machine guns for use as infantry personnel carriers.

Das Reich had a total establishment of more than 3,000 vehicles, 359 of them armored, in addition to the tanks.

INDEX

Air Force Group Command 3 *(Luftwaffengruppenkommando 3)*, 23, 62

Allgemeine-SS, 28

Allies: arrival of, 55, 59, 61; Denis as guide for escaping foreigners and, 49–50; Dresden bombing by, 159–62; Himmler's negotiations with Bernadotte and, 8–9, 11; looming invasion of, 4; looting and, 133. *See also* Normandy Invasion

Alsace-Lorraine recruits to *Das Reich*, 20–21

Alsatians: conscripting, 33, 153; distrust of, 154; Kahn's speech to, 142; sentencing of, 154–55, 164

anti-Semitism, 48

armor, of 2nd SS Panzer Division, 243–44

Aufklärungsabteilung. See SS Panzer *Aufklärungsabteilung*

Bach-Zelewski, Erich von dem, 32, 111

Barbie, Klaus, 220

Barth, Heinz, 30; postwar depositions of, 141; sentence and death of, 154; Tull massacre and, 93; violence promised by, 116

Baruch, Jamie, 177; *douanièrs* seeking, 204–5; on forbidden foreign bank accounts, 185; Mackness meeting over gold bars with, 184–88; sentencing *in absentia* of, 219

Battle Group Lammerding *(Kampfgruppe Lammerding)*, 19

BBC, 52

Beaubreuil brothers, 125

Berman, Joseph, 123

Bernadotte, Folke, 8–9, 11

Binet, Mme., 120

Bissaud, Marcel, 123

Blaskowitz, Johannes Albrecht, 43

Bletchley codebreakers, 52
Bonneville, France: *frontaliers
  in,* 167; Mackness in prison
  in, 218–21, 231–32; new
  route and·population growth
  of, 167; Renard's post at, 169
book burnings, 47
Boos, Sergeant, 155, 164
Bordeaux war crimes trial,
  140–41, 151–55, 164
Bormann, Martin, 5, 15
Bossel, Georg, 137, 228
Boucheteil, Louise, 79
Braun, Eva, 5, 6; Fegelein, H.,
  and, 9, 13
Braun, Gretl: marriage of, 5;
  pregnancy of, 13
Braun, Werner von, 139
Braunhemden (Brownshirts), 32
Brehmer, Walter, 73
Brehmer Division, 73–74
bribery: gold bars for, 33,
  37, 40; Hitler and, 37–38;
  "legal," 37
British intelligence: "Edgar"
  and, 50; on *Das Reich's*
  movements, 52, 57. *See also*
  Allies
Brive, France, 73–74
Brooks, Anthony, 63–64, 69
Brownshirts *(Braunhemden),* 32
Buhle, Walther, 16–17
The Bunker (O'Donnell), 6, 14

Burgdorf, Wilhelm, 14
Busch, Joseph, 134–35

capital taxes, in France, 168
Central Intelligence Agency
  (CIA), 139, 153
Chaluz, André, 173–79, 231
Champs de Maar attack, 75–77
*Chantiers de la
  jeunesse:* definition of, 241;
  Tulle massacre and, 85–87
Chapou, Jean-Jacques, 74–78
Christukat, Werner, 152
CIA (Central Intelligence
  Agency), 139, 153
CJF *(Organisation des Chantiers
  de la Jeunesse Française),* 85
Close Combat Clasp in
  Gold, 39
Communist Party of Germany
  (KPD), 32
Comrades to the End
  (Weidinger), 128–30
cow dung, *Das Reich* slowed
  down by, 57–58, 71

D-Day. *See* Normandy Invasion
De Gaulle, Charles, 151
Denis, Raoul (Raphael
  Denovicz): as anti-Semitism
  target, 48; appearance of,
  189; corpses burned by, 101–
  2; explosion blasting, 98–99;

gold bars anxieties of, 190–92, 197; gold bars discovered and buried by, 99–102; gold bars retrieval story of, 196; as guide for escaping foreigners, 49–50; guilt of, 195, 233–34; in Leipzig, 48, 193, 195; in Le Lardin, 54; life story of, 195; Mackness failing, 213; Mackness meeting with, 189–97; Mackness' plight compared to, 221–22; *maquis* group led by, 54–55, 88–90; *maquis* training, 50–51; *Messages Personnels* broadcasts and, 52; *milicien* denouncing family of, 53; on Oradour-sur-Glane massacre, 192–93, 195; prayers of, 89–90; in *Résistance* movement, 49; sabotage targets of, 58; in Siorac, 53–54; STO and, 50; vengeance of, 53

Depierrefiche, M., 120

Desourteaux, Jean, 121, 122

Diekmann, Otto: Bordeaux trials of men under, 133, 152; burial of, 137, 228; burned corpses discovered by, 105; career rise of, 29; death of, 137, 138, 163, 228; Frayssinet-le-Gelat massacre and, 129, 158; Gerlach and, 108–9; gold bar anxieties of, 111–12, 138; gravestone of, 137, 228, *p4*; Kahn receiving orders from, 143–46, 227, 228; Kämpfe's disappearance and, 91–92, 95, 106, 224; Kämpfe's friendship with, 39; Lammerding arguing over missing gold bars with, 106–8; Lammerding blaming massacres on, 140; Lammerding's gold bar plan and, 42; Lammerding summoning, to Limoges, 103–6; in Limoges, 111–12; *milice* translators and, 222–23, 227, 233; names of, 29; at National Socialist Cadet School, 128; Oradour-sur-Glane arrival of, 115–17, 222–29; Oradour-sur-Glane as massacre target and, 113–14, 224–25; Oradour-sur-Glane massacre and, 112, 125–26, 128–31, 152; Oradour-sur-Glane massacre defense of, 136–37; Oradour-sur-Glane plan of, 98, 107, 112–13; pep talk of, 116; psychology of, 127, 228–29; Sd. Kfz 251 half-track transporting gold bars of, 46, 66–67; Stadler requesting court-martial of, 130–31, 135–36; temper of, 226; Tulle massacre and, 82; violence caused by, 129–30, 137, 157, 223–24; Weidinger meeting with, 112

DNRED: *Direction Nationale du Renseignements et des Enquêtes Douanièrs*, 241; capital taxes and, 168; forbidden foreign bank accounts and, 168–70; methods of, 168; operations of, 167–68; Renard's post at Bonneville for, 169. *See also douanièrs*

douanièrs, 171; Baruch sought by, 204–5; Chaluz and, 174; confiscations and cuts of, 177; definition of, 241; discretion of, 179; indirect taxes and, 167–68; Mackness escaping and captured by, 202–5; Mackness interrogated by, 206–9; Mackness offered deal from, 217–18; Mackness stopped in *zone franche* by, 198–202; Mackness strip searched by, 206; reputation of, 168

Dresden bombing, 159–62

drumhead court-martials, 12

DSt (German Student Union), 47

dueling scars, of Lammerding, 31, *p2*

Eagle's Nest, 5

Eberhard, Erich Julius, 111

"Edgar," British intelligence and, 50

Eisenhower, Dwight: inauguration of, 155; *résistants* supported by, 70–71; on treatment of captured *maquis*, 132–33

Espinasse, Jean, 84, 87, 149

Fegelein, Barbara, 13

Fegelein, Hans Otto Georg Hermann: attempted investigations against, 8; awards bestowed on, 6; Braun, E., and, 9, 13; character of, 5–6; childhood of, 6–7; execution of, 13–16; at *Führerhauptquartier* conference on *Das Reich*, 16–18; Himmler and, 7–8; Himmler and Bernadotte negotiation troubles of, 8–9, 11; Hitler abandoned by, 9; Högl arresting, 9–11; Knight's Cross of the Iron Cross of, 5, 6; lack of training of, 4–6; "Lady in Red" and, 10; marriage of, 5; Müller interrogating, 11–13; remains of, 15

Feiners, Sinn, 133

Foot, M. R. D., 184

foreign bank accounts, France forbidding, 168–70, 175, 185. *See also douanièrs*

Forest, Michel, 119

Fowles, John, 182–84

the Fox. *See* Renard

France: Alsace-Lorraine recruits to *Das Reich* in, 20–21; Bordeaux war crimes trial in, 133, 140–41, 151–55, 164; Brive, 73–74; capital taxes in, 168; foreign bank accounts forbidden by, 168–70, 185; Frayssinet-le-Gelat, 129, 158; *Führerdirective* No. 51 on fight in, 19–20; gold bars hoarded by, 39–40; Guéret, 94; indirect taxes in, 167–68; Lammerding's extradition attempted by, 139–41, 152–53; Le Lardin, 54; Limoges, 73, 94–95, 111–12; Lonzac, 73; Lyons, 189; Nieul, 95; Siorac, 53–54; Sperrle Orders on *résistants* and civilians in, 23–26, 129–30, 132, 157–58;

STO and, 50; Toulouse-Montauban, 18–19, 21; Weidinger's extradition by, 141–42. *See also* Bonneville; DNRED; *douanièrs; maquis, maquisards;* Oradour-sur-Glane; *Résistance* movement; Tulle

Francs-tireurs et partisans français. See FTP

Frayssinet-le-Gelat, France, 129, 158

free zone. *See zone franche*

frontaliers: in Bonneville, 167; definition of, 241; forbidden foreign bank accounts and, 170, 175; Lacroix as, 171–73; salaries of, 172

FTP *(Francs-tireurs et partisans français):* definition of, 241; Normandy Invasion anxieties of, 73; Tulle attack by, 74–78; Tulle massacre and, 81–87; white flag controversy and, 78–79

Führerdirective No. 51 (Hitler), 19–20

Führerhauptquartier (Führer Headquarters), 3–4, 16–18

Geneva Convention, on reprisals, 132

Gerlach, Karl: Diekmann and, 108–9; Knight's Cross of the Iron Cross of, 95; *maquis* ambush of, 95–98

German Student Union (*DSt*), 47

Germany. *See specific topics*

Gleiniger, Walter, 136

GMR *(Groupes Mobiles de Réserve)*, 76–77

gold bars: Baruch meeting with Mackness over, 184–88; for bribes, 33, 37, 40; Denis' anxieties over, 190–92, 197; Denis discovering and burying, 99–102; Denis' story of retrieving, 196; Diekmann and Lammerding arguing over, 106–8; Diekmann and Lammerding's plan for, 42; Diekmann's anxieties over, 111–12, 138; discovery of, 36–37; *douanièrs zone franche* stop of Mackness with, 198–202; France hoarding, 39–40; Lammerding's plan with Kämpfe for, 39–43, 45–46; Lammerding's risks with, 91; for "legal" bribery, 37; Mackness' anxieties over, 191–92; Mackness interrogated by *douanièrs* over, 206–9; missing DR,

232–33; Normandy Invasion threatening Lammerding's, 59–61; Oradour-sur-Glane as probable destination of, 107–8, 112–13, 127, 225; packing up, 66; as pension fund, 107; providence of, 37; from *ratissages*, 41–42, 210; Sd. Kfz 251 half-track transporting, 46, 66–67; size of, 187–88, 197, 198; special crates for, 46; transportation challenges of, 38, 185–88; value of, 128

Göring, Hermann, 12

Great Britain. *See* Allies; British intelligence

Groupes Mobiles de Réserve (GMR), 76–77

Guéret, France, 94

Günsche, Otto, 13, 15

half-track transporting gold bars, 46, 66–67

hangings, Tulle massacre and, 81–87

Hastings, Max, 161

Hébras, Robert, 117–18, 124, 137

Heydrich, Reinhard, 8

Himmler, Heinrich: Allies and Bernadotte's negotiations with, 8–9, 11; Fegelein, H., and, 7–8; Lammerding and, 34; "private army" of, 28; on SS supremacy, 87–88

Hitler, Adolf: bribery and, 37–38; Close Combat Clasp in Gold bestowed by, 39; distrust of, 38; Fegelein, H., abandoning, 9; Fegelein, H.'s, awards from, 6; Fegelein, H.'s, execution and, 13–15; *Führerdirective* No. 51 of, 19–20; at *Führerhauptquartier* conference on *Das Reich*, 3–4, 16–18; on Himmler and Bernadotte negotiations, 8–9, 11; Normandy Invasion and slumber of, 61–62

The Hitler Book, 15

Hoff, Otto, 85–86

Högl, Peter, 9–11

indirect taxes, in France, 167–68

Institute of Sex Research, 47

Jewish people: Brehmer Division assassinating, 74; genocide against, 12; harassment of, 32, 47–48; Minsk massacre of, 157; in Oradour-sur-Glane, 120; problems blamed on, 47–48

Junge, Traudl, 5, 13

Kahn, Otto: appearance of, 29–30; death sentence of, 142; Diekmann's orders for, 143–46, 227, 228; on explosives use, 146–47; Frayssinet-le-Gelat violence by, 129; Lammerding covering for, 140; Oradour-sur-Glane arrival of, 115–16; Oradour-sur-Glane massacre and, 142–49, 222–23; postwar depositions of, 141; speech to Alsatians by, 142; violence caused by, 157; war crimes and defense of, 145, 148; wounding and injuries of, 136, 142, 148

Kämpfe, Helmut, 29; Close Combat Clasp in Gold awarded to, 39; Diekmann's friendship with, 39; disappearance of, 91–95, 106, 224; grave of, 233; Knight's Cross of the Iron Cross of, 39; Lammerding's gold bar plan with, 39–43, 45–46; *maquis* and murder of, 114; Müller and, 93–94; Oradour-sur-Glane invasion cover plan of search for, 112–13; photograph of, *p2*; probable kidnapping and murder of, 94, 108, 131,

136–38; *ratissages* conducted by, 39, 41–42; Sd. Kfz 251 half-track transporting gold bars of, 46, 66–67; service and awards of, 38–39

Kampfgruppe Lammerding (Battle Group Lammerding), 19

Kaschula, Herbert, 15

Keitel, Wilhelm, 16–17, 163

Kertheuser, Bruno, 116

Knight's Cross of the Iron Cross: Close Combat Clasp in Gold compared to, 39; of Fegelein, H., 5, 6; of Gerlach, 95; of Kämpfe, 39; Lammerding and, 27, 33; *Das Reich* recipients of, 4; of Stadler, 135; of Weidinger, 26

Korten, Friedrich, 73

Kowatsch, Aurel, 131; Lammerding blaming massacres on, 140; Tulle massacre and, 84, 87; on wounded Germans in Tulle, 79–80

KPD (Communist Party of Germany), 32

Krag, Ernst, *p2*

Krause, Alfred, 15

Krebs, Hans, 14

Kurz, Hascha, 83

Laclède, Pierre, 50

Lacroix, Monique: appearance of, 174, 234; Chaluz, Renard and, 173–79; client meetings of, 172–73; as *frontalier*, 171–73; Mackness and, 234–35; Michel and, 177, 179, 185; salary of, 172, 175

"Lady in Red," Fegelein, H., and, 10

Lammerding, Heinz Bernard: age of, 22, 33; anti-terrorism measures memorandum of, 60, 72; Bach-Zelewski and, 32; Blaskowitz's pressure on, 43; capture of, 139; career background of, 27–28, 110–11; CIA protection and, 153; dark side of, 32; death of, 141; Diekmann and Kowatsch blamed for massacres by, 140; on Diekmann and Oradour-sur-Glane massacre, 152; Diekmann arguing over missing gold bars with, 106–8; Diekmann's court-martial agreed to by, 136; Diekmann summoned to Limoges by, 103–6; dueling scars of, 31, *p2*; engineering degree of, 110; execution orders signed by, 111; France extradition attempts on, 139–41, 152–53; gold bar risks taken by, 91; gold bars discovered by, 36–37; Himmler and, 34; Kahn covered for by, 140; Kämpfe and gold bar plan of, 39–43, 45–46; Kämpfe's disappearance and, 91–92; Knight's Cross of the Iron Cross awarded to, 27, 33; lack of focus of, 34–35; "legal" bribery and, 37; Normandy Invasion threatening gold bars of, 59–61; Oradour-sur-Glane massacre and, 140–41; pension concerns of, 35, 111; photographs of, *p1, p2*; *Das Reich* delayed by *Résistance* movement and, 56–58; *Das Reich* led by, 18–19, 31, 33; *Das Reich* ordered to Tulle and, 64–66; reprisals ordered by, 130; on *Résistance* delaying *Das Reich*, 109–10; rise to power of, 31–32; Rundstedt's orders for, 64, 93, 106–7, 109; Schneider on, 28; Sd. Kfz 251 half-track transporting gold bars of, 46, 66–67; Stadler's criticism of, 29;

Tulle massacre and, 82, 140; violence caused by, 129–30; war crimes and death sentences of, 139; woes of, 91–92; wounding of, 138; Wulf and, 92. *See also* gold bars

landmines, *Das Reich* slowed down by, 57–58, 71
Leblanc, Abel, 77
"legal" bribery, 37
Leipzig, Germany: book burnings in, 47; Denis and family in, 48, 193, 195; Jewish people harassed in, 48
Le Lardin, France, 54
Limoges, France, 73, 94–95, 103–6, 111–12
Lonzac, France, 73
Lorenze, Heinz, 9
Lorrainers, Abbé, 121
Luftwaffengruppenkommando 3 (Air Force Group Command 3), 23, 62
Lyons, France, 189

Mackness, Robin: Baruch meeting over gold bars with, 184–88; in Bonneville prison, 218–21, 231–32; career background of, 181; death of, 181; Denis failed by, 213; Denis meeting with, 189–97; Denis' plight compared to, 221–22; Denis's story of Oradour-sur-Glane massacre told to, 192–93, 195; *douanièrs* interrogating, 206–9; *douanièrs* in *zone franche* stopping, 198–202; *douanièrs* offering deal to, 217–18; *douanièrs* strip searching, 206; escape and capture of, 202–5; Fowles working with, 182–84; gold bars anxieties of, 191–92; Lacroix and, 234–35; letters written by, 232; in Lyons, 189; Oradour-sur-Glane studied by, 222; regret of, 221; Renard interrogating, 210–12; Renard's prison visit with, 219–20; resolution of, 235; trial of, 219; in Varces Prison, 215–18; *zone franche* stop of, 198–202

Macron, Emmanuel, 118
maquis, maquisards: definition of, 241; Denis in charge of group of, 54–55, 88–90; Denis trained by, 50–51; Eisenhower on treatment for captured, 132–33; Gerlach ambushed by, 95–98; Kämpfe's murder and, 114; *ratissages* against, 39; *Das*

Reich and, 23; Tulle attack by, 74–78; Tulle massacre and, 81–87; types of, 34; white flag controversy and, 78–79. *See also résistants*
Marinegruppenkommand (Naval Command), 62
Meier, August, 73
Messages Personnels broadcasts, BBC, 52
Michel, Jacques, 177, 179, 185
milice, miliciens, 76–77; definition of, 241–42; Denis' family denounced by, 53; Diekmann and translators of, 222–23, 227, 233
Milice Française, 76–77
Miller, Michael D., 5–6
Minsk massacre, 157
Misch, Rochus, 14–15
Mohnke, Wilhelm, 13–15
Müller, Heinrich, 11–13, 93–94

National Socialist Cadet School, Diekmann at, 128
Nation und Europa, 27
Naval Command *(Marinegrup-penkommand),* 62
Nazi Germany. *See specific topics*
Nieul, France, 95
Normandy Invasion, 50, 55, 92; FTP anxieties with, 73; Hitler sleeping during,

61–62; Lammerding's gold bars threatened by, 59–61; *Das Reich* and Rommel missing, 61–62; Rommel on, 162; size of, 70
Nuremberg Trials, 16

obedience, of *Das Reich*, 159
O'Donnell, James P., 6, 14, 16
Oradour-sur-Glane (Hébras), 137
Oradour-sur-Glane, France, 16, 31; aerial view of, *p3*; bodies stacked together in, *p4*; Bordeaux war crimes trial and, 151–55; Busch on massacre in, 134–35; Denis on massacre at, 192–93, 195; Diekmann and massacre at, 112, 125–26, 128–32, 152, 222–29; Diekmann's convoy arriving in, 115–17; Diekmann's defense for massacre at, 136–37; Diekmann's plan for, 98, 107, 112–13; Dresden bombings compared to massacre in, 159–62; history and architecture of, 118, 227; "identification check" rouse in, 117–18, 120, 222; Jewish people in, 120; Kahn and massacre at,

142–49, 222–23; Kämpfe kidnapping retaliation and, 108; Kämpfe search as cover plan for invasion of, 112–13; Lammerding and massacre at, 140–41; Mackness studying, 222; *maquis* ambush of Gerlach and, 96, 109; massacre in, 121–32, 222–29; as massacre target choice, 113–15, 224–25; massacre timeline, *p1*; post-massacre, *p3*; as probable destination of gold bars, 107–8, 112–13, 127, 225; refugees and population growth in, 222; reprisal claims for massacre at, 138, 142; tranquility disrupted in, 119–21; war crimes at, 116; Weidinger making light of massacre in, 27
Organisation des Chantiers de la Jeunesse Française (CJF), 85

Panther V, 243
Panzer IV, 243
pensions: gold bars as, 107; Lammerding's concerns over, 35, 111; war crimes threatening, 114
Pétain, Henri Philippe Benoni Omer, 74

Peyroux, Amélie, 125
Picaper, Jean-Paul, 26–27
Pieper, Henning, 6
Pohlen, Rainer, 152

ratissages/rafles, 142;
  definition of, 242; at
  Frayssinet-le-Gelat, 129;
  gold bars from, 41–42,
  210; against Résistance
  movement, 39
Rattenhuber, Johann
  "Jonny," 14
Das Reich. See 2nd SS Panzer
  Division Das Reich
Das Reich V, 1943–1945
  (Weidinger), 21–22, 26–27
Renard (The Fox): Chaluz,
  Lacroix and, 173–79;
  DNRED post of, 169;
  forbidden foreign bank
  accounts and, 170; Mackness
  interrogated by, 210–12;
  Mackness visited in prison
  by, 219–20; reputation
  of, 177; under-the-radar
  approach of, 169–70
reprisals: Geneva Convention
  on, 132; Lammerding
  ordering, 130; legality of,
  81, 137; Oradour-sur-Glane
  massacre and claims of,
  138, 142; Das Reich seeking,

225; Tulle massacre and
  claims of, 81–82, 87, 142; as
  whitewashing, 116. See also
  ratissages/rafles
Résistance movement,
  France: Brehmer Division
  attacks on, 74; Denis joining,
  49; methods of, 22; ratissages
  against, 39; Das Reich
  delayed by, 51–52, 55–58,
  109–10; Das Reich losses
  caused by, 21–22, 109; Das
  Reich operations against,
  34–35; Das Reich sabotaged
  en route to Tulle by, 62–64;
  sabotage campaigns of,
  34. See also FTP; maquis,
  maquisards
résistants: definition of, 242;
  Eisenhower supporting,
  70–71; German relations
  with, 23; Sperrle Orders
  against, 23–26, 129–30, 132,
  157–58. See also maquis,
  maquisards
Roce, Maurice, 87
Romani, harassment of, 32
Rommel, Erwin: Diekmann's
  court-martial endorsed by,
  136; on Normandy Invasion,
  162; Normandy Invasion and
  absence of, 61–62
Rouffranche, Mme., 125

Rundstedt, Gerd von: Kämpfe's
kidnapping and, 108;
Lammerding receiving
orders from, 64, 93, 106–7,
109; on making peace, 163;
Normandy Invasion and,
61–62

SA (Storm Detachment,
Sturmabteilung), 32, 47–48
Schmald, Walter: appearance
of, 148–49; execution of, 149;
on Kämpfe's disappearance,
95; Tulle massacre and,
83–84, 149
Schneid, Sadi, 80–83, 86
Schneider, Jost W., 28
school closures, in Tulle, 69
Schwerer Panzerspähwagen
(SPW): Müller's, 93–94;
overview of, 243–44
SD
(Sicherheitsdienst): definition
of, 242; in Limoges, 73,
94–95; Schmald and, 83; in
Tulle, 73–74; Tulle casualties
of, 78; white flag controversy
and, 78–79
Sd. Kfz 251 half-track
transporting gold bars, 46,
66–67
2nd SS Panzer Division *Das
Reich:* age of personnel

in, 22; Alsace-Lorraine
recruits to, 20–21; British
intelligence on movement
of, 52, 57; casualties of,
32–33, 136; cow dung and
landmines slowing down,
57–58, 71; diminishing
standards of, 28–29; on
Eisenhower supporting
résistants, 70–71; emotional
stress and bad news
from home for, 22–23;
Führerdirective No. 51 and,
19–20; *Führerhauptquartier*
conference on, 3–4, 16–18;
Knight's Cross of the Iron
Cross recipients in, 4;
Lammerding leading, 18–19,
31, 33; *maquisards* and, 23;
membership to, 33; non-
German nationalities in, 33;
Normandy Invasion missed
by, 61–62; obedience of, 159;
operations against *Résistance*
movement, 34–35; ordered
to Tulle, 64–66; reprisals
sought by, 225; *Résistance*
causing losses among, 21–22,
109; *Résistance* movement
delaying, 51–52, 55–58,
109–10; *Résistance* sabotage
en route to Tulle, 62–64;
ruthlessness of, 157–58;

Sperrle Orders spurring on, 157–58; tank repairs of, 56; tanks and armor of, 243–44; to Toulouse-Montauban, 18–19, 21; Trouillé threatened by, 80; Tulle arrival of, 79–80; war crime trials of, 163–64; Weidinger on losses of, 21–22; Weidinger's book on, 21–22, 26–27; zeal of, 115

Service de travail obligatoire. See STO

Shirer, William L., 5

Sicherheitsdienst. See SD

Siorac, France, 53–54

Social Democratic Party of Germany (SPD), 32

Speer, Albert, 5

Sperrle, Hugo, 23–26, 157–58

Sperrle Orders, 23–26, 129–30, 132, 157–58

SPW. *See Schwerer Panzerspähwagen*

SS-Junker School Bad Tölz, 70

SS Panzer *Aufklärungsabteilung,* 71–72

SS Panzer Division. *See* 2nd SS Panzer Division *Das Reich*

Stadler, Sylvester: age of, 135; on Diekmann and Oradour-sur-Glane massacre, 130–31;

Diekmann's court-martial requested by, 130–31, 135–36; Gerlach's orders from, 95, 97; Knight's Cross of the Iron Cross of, 135; Lammerding criticism of, 29; potential decency shown by, 135–36

Stalin, Joseph, 15, 155, 159

Sten guns, 51, 52

STO *(Service de travail obligatoire):* definition of, 242; Denis and, 50

Storm Detachment *(Sturmabteilung,* SA), 32, 47–48

Stückler, Albert, 66, 75, 82, *p2*

Sturmabteilung (Storm Detachment, SA), 32, 47–48

Sturmgeschütz III (assault gun vehicle), 95, 243

tanks: damaged, 58, 109; half-track transporting gold bars blending in with, 46; repairing, 55–57; *Résistance* movement sabotaging *Das Reich,* 63–64; of 2nd SS Panzer Division, 243–44; on secondary roads, 57; transportation methods of, 63. *See also* 2nd SS Panzer Division *Das Reich*

Their Honor Was Loyalty
(Schneider), 28
Toulouse-Montauban, France,
18–19, 21
Trouillé, Pierre, 75, 85; *Das
Reich* threatening, 80;
schools closed by, 69
Tulle, France, 16; *Champs
de Maar* attack in, 75–77;
Chantiers de la jeunesse and
massacre at, 85–87; Chapou
and FTP attack in, 74–78;
Dresden bombings compared
to massacre in, 159–62;
Germans mutilated in, 81;
history of, 72; Kowatsch
on wounded Germans
in, 79–80; Lammerding
and massacre at, 82, 140;
massacre in, 81–87, 158;
mercy in, 87; *Das Reich*
sabotaged en route to, 62–64;
Das Reich's arrival in, 79–80;
reprisal claims for massacre
at, 81–82, 87, 142; Schmald
and massacre at, 83–84, 149;
Schneid's proclamation in,
80–81; school closures in,
69; SD casualties in, 78; SD
unit in, 73–74; war crimes
at, 116; Weidinger in, 141;
Weidinger making light of
massacre at, 27; white flag

controversy in, 78–79; Wulf's
plan for, 72

United States. *See* Allies

Varces Prison, 215–18
violent raids. *See ratissages/rafles*

Walter, Bruno, 46, 67, 88, 104
war crimes: Bordeaux trial
on, 133, 140–41, 151–55,
164; Kahn's defense against,
145, 148; Lammerding's
death sentences for, 139;
at Oradour-sur-Glane
and Tulle, 116; pensions
threatened by, 114; *Das Reich*
trials for, 163–64
Warlimont, Walter, 16–17
Weidinger, Otto: apologia
writing of, 26–27;
appearance of, 26; death of,
142; Deikmann meeting
with, 112; on Diekman
and Oradour-sur-Glane
massacre, 112, 128–32;
France extradition of,
141–42; Knight's Cross
of the Iron Cross of, 26;
photograph of, *p2*; on *Das
Reich's* losses, 21–22; trial of,
142; in Tulle, 141

white flag controversy in Tulle, 78–79

Wulf, Heinrich, 75, 79; on German mutilation in Tulle, 81; Lammerding and, 92; military career of, 70; SS Panzer *Aufklärungsabteilung* and, 71–72; on Tulle massacre, 83, 87; Tulle plan of, 72

Yugoslavia massacre, 157

zeal, of SS, 115

zone franche (free zone): definition of, 216; Mackness stopped in, 198–202